CW00342915

TACKLED

TACKLED

The Class of 92 Star Who Never Got to Graduate

BEN THORNLEY
WITH DAN POOLE

First published by Pitch Publishing, 2018

Pitch Publishing
A2 Yeoman Gate
Yeoman Way
Worthing
Sussex
BN13 3QZ
www.pitchpublishing.co.uk
info@pitchpublishing.co.uk

© 2018, Ben Thornley & Dan Poole

Every effort has been made to trace the copyright.
Any oversight will be rectified in future editions at the
earliest opportunity by the publisher.

All rights reserved. No part of this book may be reproduced,
sold or utilised in any form or transmitted in any form or by
any means, electronic or mechanical, including photocopying,
recording or by any information storage and retrieval system,
without prior permission in writing from the Publisher.

A CIP catalogue record is available for this book
from the British Library.

ISBN 978-1-78531-447-6

Typesetting and origination by Pitch Publishing
Printed and bound by TJ International, Cornwall

Contents

DEDICATION

To my family, who have supported me from day one. I could not have achieved the highs and survived the lows if it wasn't for the continued love and support you showed me – and still do! And to Lesley, my better half, who is so supportive and tolerant. I appreciate, wholeheartedly, the sacrifices you have all made in order that I could pursue my dream of becoming a footballer, not to mention my life thereafter.

And a special mention for Sir Alex Ferguson, an incredible man who had a huge influence on my football career and showed me the value of desire and determination, whatever you're doing in life. Thank you, boss.

The line-up

Everyone who has contributed to the book

Michael Appleton
Manchester United team-mate, 1992–97*

David Beckham
Manchester United team-mate, 1991–98

Clayton Blackmore
Manchester United team-mate, 1993–94

Dave Bushell
England Schoolboys manager, 1990

Cliff Butler
Manchester United statistician, 1991–98

Nicky Butt
Manchester United team-mate, 1991–98

Chris Casper
Manchester United team-mate, 1991–98

John Chappell
Salford Boys under-11s coach, 1984–85

Jimmy Curran
Manchester United masseur, 1991–98

Paul Devine
Salford Boys team-mate, 1984–85, 1988–90

Dion Dublin
Manchester United team-mate, 1993–94

David Fevre
Manchester United physio, 1994–98

Ryan Giggs
Manchester United team-mate, 1991–98

Keith Gillespie
Manchester United team-mate, 1991–95

Harry Hackett
Salford Boys under-14s coach, 1988–89

Denis Irwin
Manchester United team-mate, 1994–98

Andrei Kanchelskis
Manchester United team-mate, 1994–95

Steve Kelly
Salford Boys under-15s coach, 1989–90

Jeff Kerfoot
School friend

Joe Lydiate
Salford Boys team-mate, 1988–90

Brian McClair
Manchester United team-mate, 1993–98

Jim McGregor
Manchester United physio, 1991–94

Colin McKee
Manchester United team-mate, 1991–94

Paul Moseley
Salford Boys under-14s coach, 1988–89

Gary Neville
Manchester United team-mate, 1991–98

Phil Neville
Manchester United team-mate, 1992–98

Jonathan Noble
Knee surgeon

Geoff Ogden
Primary school PE teacher, 1986–88

John O'Kane
Manchester United team-mate, 1991–98

Paul Parker
Manchester United team-mate, 1994–96

Mike Phelan
Manchester United team-mate, 1993–94

Kevin Pilkington
Manchester United team-mate, 1991–98

Tony Potter
Junior school PE teacher, 1982–86

THE LINE-UP

Mark Rawlinson
Manchester United team-mate, 1992–95

Bryan Robson
Manchester United team-mate, 1993–94

Anthony Rouse
School friend

Jim Ryan
Manchester United reserves manager, 1993–98

Robbie Savage
Manchester United team-mate, 1991–94

Paul Scholes
Manchester United team-mate, 1991–98

Andy Scott
Salford Boys team-mate, 1988–90

Hannah Scott (née Thornley)
Sister

Rob Swire
Manchester United physio, 1991–98

George Switzer
Salford Boys & Manchester United team-mate,
1984–85, 1988–90, 1991–92

Lesley Tanner
Partner

Elizabeth Thornley
Mum

Lucas Thornley
Son

Philip Thornley
Dad

Rod Thornley
Brother

Gary Walsh
Manchester United team-mate, 1993–95

*Dates relate to career overlap with Ben, not necessarily
total time spent in role.

Foreword

If I think of my early years, if I think about the Class of 92, I think of Ben. He was one of – if not *the* – most talented members of that team. He had everything. And while this may be hard to believe, he was quite good-looking too.

But then one huge, earth-shattering moment completely changed the direction of his life and he never matched the heights of his game pre-injury. I actually consider that one of the great losses of *my* career because of what I thought of him, the time that we spent together and the great friendship that we have. The low of seeing him get injured and fail to fulfil his potential was devastating; to my mind there is nothing worse in football.

I love Ben to bits. He's mad as hell, funny as hell, daft as hell, snappy as hell – all of those things. But I've never been able to get angry at him; whatever used to happen, on the pitch or off, I just used to laugh. There are not many people I can say that about because, to be fair, I'm a bit of a miserable bastard. As such, to be in the company of someone who constantly made me laugh was a joy.

Ben introduced me to alcohol: we used to drink two-litre bottles of Woodpecker together on a Saturday night after a game. There wasn't anything we didn't know about each other and he had – and has – a lovely family too. It was a wonderful time in my life and Ben was at the heart of it; the moments we had together were incredibly special.

As we grew up, his personal life mirrored his football life: after his injury he was on a downer and floated towards things that he would have never normally done. In fact, he ended up becoming someone who, at times, he himself probably didn't like. But that was purely down to the trauma that he suffered, an experience that I can't even begin to imagine. I lived through it with him but you can never step into someone else's heart, mind and soul.

I've seen less of him in my later years but whenever we meet up, we go straight back into it like we've never been away. He's that kind of individual. He's a fantastic person and I'm just delighted that our paths crossed at the age of 13.

Gary Neville

Prologue

It's very hard not to emphasise the tragedy of what happened to Ben because we felt it – we all did. But because everything came to a halt so young, everybody at Manchester United still has this image of what he could have been; he's never had to grow old and show himself to be incapable of fulfilling his potential. In the minds of everybody who saw him play in the Class of 92, he's still at the height of his powers.

What was most important to us was that we still had our son. No matter what he might have gone on to become, he was still our lad. He was, and is always going to be, Ben.

So yes, we lost out – but we also won.

Philip Thornley

1

Manchester United reserves vs Blackburn Rovers reserves Wednesday, 6 April 1994

Ben: I knew I was in trouble. I'd heard the noise. I could feel it. My first reaction was to reach for my knee and I fell to the floor holding it – holding it together, basically.

I'd moved infield to pick up the ball and was running towards goal but, as I approached the penalty area, I was aware of Blackburn's right-back coming towards me. Out of the corner of my eye I saw Clayton Blackmore galloping into the space I'd vacated on the left-hand side. There was no sense in taking on the Blackburn player so I passed to Clayton.

I didn't smack the ball. It was a side-foot, 15 yards, because I didn't need to hit it towards the touchline. The right-back had come infield so I wanted Clayton to have a diagonal run straight into the box. And I could see that gaps were going to open up so I wasn't going to stand there and watch – I wanted to get in there as well.

But their right-back was still coming towards me, even though the ball had gone. He had time to pull out; he didn't need to make a tackle. But he *wanted* to.

Gary Walsh: You get to know the sound of a normal tackle and this didn't sound like a normal tackle. It sounded like a crack. And I heard it even though I was 60-odd yards away in United's goal.

Ben: I knew he was coming. I could see him coming. But while my left foot, body and arms were moving, my right foot wasn't coming with me yet. I'd planted it on the floor, ready to push off. I couldn't get out of the way quickly enough.

Dion Dublin: It was like a clap of your hands: there was one sound and it was very clear. It wasn't a crescendo of sound, it was 'Bam!' Gone. That's it. It was horrible. Horrible.

Ben: My momentum and the impact of his boot were opposing forces. The rest of my body was starting to go one way – he made sure that my knee went back in the other direction.

Bryan Robson: I was more or less on the centre circle, just coming up behind Ben, when it happened. When he went down, everyone started pushing and shoving because it was such a bad tackle.

Chris Casper: It was a shocker. I was injured so I was in the stands at Gigg Lane – Bury's ground, where we played our reserve games. I watched Nicky Marker come in and clean Ben out. I'll never forget that noise. It was so loud that I thought it was Ben's shin pad breaking. It wasn't.

Philip Thornley: We heard the crack. We were sat in the stands behind Alex Ferguson, who shot up, turned round and said, 'Come with me.' He knew straight away. He took me down to the edge of the pitch.

Elizabeth Thornley: I stayed in the stand with Rod and Hannah because they were only little.

Rod Thornley: I remember being upset. I never really got upset when it came to Ben but I was that night.

Gary Neville: It didn't actually look like a really shocking tackle from where I was at right-back. Plus I was young, so I think that meant I didn't realise the severity of the injury at the time.

Colin McKee: I was right next to Ben when it happened. Straight away I signalled to the bench for the physio, Rob Swire, to come on.

Ben: Some people actually get up and try to carry on when they do their cruciate; I wasn't going anywhere. It fucking hurt.

Rob Swire: I ran on to the pitch to have a look and I could see that his knee was a mess because it was already starting to swell. If you sprain an ankle, say, it takes several hours to swell because normal joint fluid is produced slowly. But if a ligament tears, the blood vessels tear too and blood pumps out immediately. You also get a misshapen knee with a cruciate injury and Ben's was slightly out of line.

Dion Dublin: The pain he was in, the anguish – that's the word – the *anguish* on his face, was unbelievable.

Brian McClair: It quickly became apparent that he was in a bad way. Marker had come in at the kind of angle whereby it was going to be sore because the full force of his weight landed on Ben's leg – and you're always going to get hurt when your foot is planted.

Rob Swire: I tried to talk to Ben but he was in a lot of pain, so he wasn't communicating. I just stabilised the knee and called the stretcher on; I wasn't going to pull it around and examine it because you don't touch the serious ones.

Ben: I wasn't really aware of what was going on around me as I was stretchered off; all that was going through my mind was utter devastation.

Chris Casper: Nicky Marker knew that there was only one outcome from that tackle – and the one thing that was never going to happen was Nicky Marker getting hurt. He knew exactly what he was doing.

Clayton Blackmore: It was dangerous. It was cowardly.

Gary Neville: When you're an experienced defender, your team's losing and someone's taking the piss out of you, sometimes you might think, 'Fuck it, I'll just go in for one.' It's not an unnatural reaction for a defender who's losing to lose his head.

Ben: The referee only gave him a yellow card. I've never understood that. And when the ref gave his witness statement for the legal proceedings that came later, he maintained that it was a mistimed tackle despite seeing a video of it. Why? To save face? I'd like to sit him down in front of that video again now and say, 'What the fuck are you playing at?'

Clayton Blackmore: He definitely should have been sent off – and sent down.

Andy Scott: I played with Ben at Salford Boys, then I signed for Blackburn – and I played in this game. Nicky Marker was a tough, hard player and I think he did know what he was doing, but I don't think his intention was to do the damage he did.

Ben: I agree, I don't think he could have envisaged the extent of it. But when you make a tackle like that, there's always a chance you're going to hurt someone.

Mike Phelan: When it happens it's a shock. Then there's the reality of the fact that it's your team-mate and what's just happened is wrong. Then there's emotion. There's something that goes through your head … it's hard to describe. There's a sorrow about it. It's an emptiness. Then there's anger after that, fury, because you realise it's career-threatening.

Chris Casper: I was in the treatment room with Ben, waiting for the ambulance. It was quiet. I think he knew there was a serious problem.

Hannah Scott (née Thornley): It was like someone had died. I don't think dad talked for a couple of days afterwards.

Jim Ryan: I followed Ben in but I couldn't say anything to him because he was … he wasn't … well, I just didn't know what to say to the kid, you know? By that time we'd realised that it was bad. I didn't want to say something stupid like, 'You'll be OK.' I think I ruffled his hair.

Dion Dublin: I just wasn't interested in the game after that.

Jim Ryan: When I went back out to watch, people on the bench were asking me how he was and I told them it looked terrible. It's not something you can shrug off. I just hoped that everything was going to be alright. Ben was such a cheery, chirpy lad. He didn't deserve that.

Bryan Robson: I spent the last 20 minutes trying to get Marker back but I never got the chance.

Mike Phelan: The aftershock of treatment and stretchers leaves you wondering what's going on in the game, where the next tackle is coming from. You've got a sick feeling in your stomach and the match becomes challenging for different reasons. You want a result, you want to do it for Ben. You want to do it as payback – you don't want them to get away with it. All of these things go through your head. Something else too: thank God it's not me.

Rob Swire: It was, by a long way, the worst knee injury I saw in about 30 years as a physio. To the extent that I didn't expect Ben to play football again.

Ben: While I was lying there it suddenly dawned on me: this could be it.

2

Childhood
1975–86

Ben: My full name is Benjamin Lindsay Thornley. It's my dad's middle name too because it was originally his mum's maiden name. I was the firstborn so they gave it to me; my brother lucked out and got Neil. As you can imagine, I've had some grief for it over the years. And I've never forgiven my dad – of all the names that he could have possibly given me. I never tire of wanting to muller him for giving me such a wank middle name. I appreciate that there are exceptions to every rule but I wish I wasn't one of them.

Philip Thornley: When I was young, one of the most famous cricketers in the world was Lindsay Hassett, so it was defensible. My father used to say, 'Well he's a tough guy, what are you worried about?'

Ben: Anyway, I was born on 21 April 1975 at Fairfield Hospital in Bury – where, as it happens, Gary Neville was born on the same ward two months before me.

Gary Neville: He is so Salford, with that grain in his voice, that you'd never think for one second that he was born in Bury.

Philip Thornley: The chances of getting an ambulance in those days were very slight; if you could get there by your own means, you did. Liz had had some contractions during a rough night so I drove her in the next morning. We hadn't gone far when I knocked down a kid on his way to school; he ran straight into the road. He hit the bonnet but just got up and went back in his house. We followed him in to tell his mum and find out if he was alright – she said he was fine so we got straight back in the car. I thought, 'How auspicious is this?'

Ben: After I was born I wasn't well: my mum had a difficult birth and when I came out I had a lot of meconium on my lungs. I needed help breathing and was propped up in the corner of an incubator; they couldn't lie me down because they needed to drain all this fluid away.

Philip Thornley: We asked to see the paediatrician to find out Ben's prospects and he said, 'We don't know what's going to happen. He might well survive but he might not.' They couldn't guarantee that he wouldn't be brain damaged. It turned out he was fine, although it wasn't until the end of May that we got him back home.

Ben: For the first few years of my life we lived on Woodstock Close in a place called Heywood, which is a small town in Rochdale; my dad was the deputy head at Hopwood Primary School. I was quite an early walker, which nobody thought I would be because of the problems I'd had, but from nine months I was on my feet. Not long after, my mum and dad decided to buy me a yellow, plastic sit-on hippo – and that's when the real problems started.

Elizabeth Thornley: He was renowned in the district for that little yellow hippo.

Philip Thornley: When he was on it he'd reach such speeds that he'd ruin his shoes because he dragged them on the road behind him to slow himself down. There was an old lady called Mrs Phoenix who took a shine to him because she knew how poorly he'd been. She lived at the end of our cul-de-sac and once Ben could whizz up and down on the hippo, he'd regularly take himself over to her place.

Elizabeth Thornley: She was good for a biscuit was Mrs Phoenix.

Philip Thornley: But one day he went down her drive so fast that he sailed through her porch window. Straight through it. So that was a trip to hospital; he had a few cuts but fortunately it was the hippo's nose that took the brunt of it. We offered to pay for the door but Mrs Phoenix said it was fine because she was planning on getting a new one anyway.

Elizabeth Thornley: We seemed to have a lot of visits to A&E with Ben.

Philip Thornley: He had a Tonka digger with a metal scoop on the front; it wouldn't be allowed now. He was running down the entry at the side of the house when I called him in: 'Come on, bedtime now.' So he came running, holding this thing, and tripped. The scoop went straight into his chin and blood poured everywhere. I gathered him up and whipped him off to Bury General. He had to have stitches but, to be fair, he didn't flinch.

Elizabeth Thornley: He was about two and a half so this was around the same time as the hippo incident.

Philip Thornley: Another thing I remember about him: when he was three you could stand him in the middle of a car park and he'd tell you every single model that was in there. Where he learnt that we've no idea because we've no interest in cars.

Elizabeth Thornley: It was the same when we went anywhere in the car: he'd stand in between the two front seats (this was the old days) to look out the window and he knew all of them. It was uncanny. Quite frightening.

Philip Thornley: It was very weird. He was a weird child.

Rod Thornley: He went on to buy some stupid cars as well.

Ben: My brother, Rod, was born in 1977 and my sister, Hannah, was 1978. Me and my brother used to fight a bit and he was totally different to me because he was always on his computer.

Rod Thornley: Ben was crap on it, absolutely awful.

Ben: He was a bit older before he became interested in football but I'm glad he did because he turned out to be half decent and made a few quid out of it. I went to watch him at Stoke City in 2005 when he scored the goal that got Altrincham into the Conference. These days he's a masseur for the Manchester United first team.

Rod Thornley: Gary Neville got me in at Man United. I was a lifeguard when I went there in 2000; I sacrificed 30 hours a week doing that to do 15 hours at Carrington, just on the off-chance that something might come of it. Within a month of being there, head physio Rob Swire turned to me and said, 'Listen, we haven't got an officially qualified masseur at the club – could we train you up?' Within a year I was qualified and I've been there ever since. I was also a masseur with England until 2014.

Ben: Because Rod and I fought when we were growing up, he's closer to my sister now and so am I. Me and Rod get on well enough, we're just not the kind of brothers to phone each other every day and say, 'Alright our kid, how's it going?' He'd say, 'Well, I'm alright, what are you ringing me for? Do one.' My dad's the same. Whereas with my mum it's, 'Hiya, I'm just ringing to see how you are because I've not heard from you in four-and-a-half hours.'

Rod Thornley: We used to always play football together but then it got to a point where Ben buggered off and did his thing, I went off and did my thing and it's never come back together. We can go weeks and weeks without speaking to each other and it doesn't affect us.

We're there for each other but we're not close. We only ring each other if we need something.

Philip Thornley: You talk to Rod on the phone and he'll say, 'Yeah, yeah, OK, I've got to go now, I've got another call coming in, cheers.'

Rod Thornley: There's never another call coming in.

Elizabeth Thornley: We know that.

Ben: Whereas with me they're always *wishing* I had another call coming in.

Hannah Scott (née Thornley): I can ring Ben for a chat but I'd never ring Rod for a chat because he's aloof and doesn't really care.

Rod Thornley: It's not because I don't like you, I just don't like speaking to you on the phone.

Hannah Scott: Thanks.

Ben: Hannah was very academic as a kid and she speaks French and German. She has four kids; she did have two but then in 2011, she and her husband Trent decided to have one more and ended up with twins. She's a very keen musician and is in a band, like my dad. Even with four kids she has more hobbies than me and my brother put together.

Rod Thornley: Let's not lie: we had arguments all the time. I fell out with the pair of them, whereas Ben and Hannah got on really.

Hannah Scott: For the most part. But it could be Rod and Ben against me, me and Rod against Ben, or me and Ben against Rod. And when we fell out we *really* fell out. It got physical. Mum and dad weren't around for those ones. We'd hear mum coming home at 5.30pm, 30mph up the gravel drive. 'Quick, put the tables back!' We all used to pull together at that point. We were alright together, weren't we?

Rod Thornley: Yeah. Sort of.

Ben: In 1977 we moved to Snowdon Road in Eccles. My dad had been appointed as headteacher at the school that he stayed at for the rest of his working life: Cadishead Junior School. It's in that house that I've got my first memory of watching football: the 1982 World Cup, when I was seven. It's still, to this day, the best World Cup I've seen; absolutely brilliant, loved it. By that time I'd started to follow United a little bit and they'd signed Bryan Robson from West Brom the year before. After 27 seconds of the opening game against France he scored one of the fastest goals ever in a World Cup and we beat them 3-1; from then on he was my hero. And that was what properly got me into football.

Bryan Robson: It was a great time for me. It was my first World Cup game, I scored, we won and then that night I got a phone call from my father-in-law to tell me that my wife, Denise, had just given birth to Charlotte, our second daughter. Denise reckons it was the excitement of watching the game.

Ben: I watched it all with my gran, my mum's mum. Agnes loved football but, for whatever reason, hated Kevin Keegan with a passion because he'd played for Hamburg. Whenever he came on she'd boo and hiss at the telly.

At that age I constantly wanted a kickabout. The garden we had then wasn't that big but fortunately the street out front wasn't very busy. I used to mither my dad to death: 'Can you come and kick a ball with me?' Whenever I managed to convince him there was one thing he used to drill into me. He'd say, 'Which foot do you prefer?' I'd always say I preferred my right. 'Then I want you to kick the ball back to me with your left.'

Philip Thornley: I'd tell him: 'If you can't play with your left foot you're only half a player.'

Ben: I'd go in the space between our house and next door when the car wasn't there, sometimes because mum and dad had parked it somewhere else for me; they didn't mind me banging a ball up against their wall. It sounds boring but I knew the ball was coming back and that's how I learnt to use both feet. Gradually I started to alternate and it came naturally to me.

Later, when I was at United, youth-team manager Eric Harrison recreated that. In the afternoon he used to send us into the gym at United's training ground, The Cliff, and all the way along the walls there were circles. He used to say, 'Go and practise hitting those circles and when the ball comes back to you, go and fucking do it again. Do it again and do it again, with both feet, until you're absolutely sick to death of it. And when you are, I'll come and tell you that you've got another half hour to do before you can pack up.'

It was monotonous. But I tell you what, it drives me mad to this day that you get very, very good footballers who have only got one foot – and it's because they haven't done the very simple task of banging a ball against a target on a wall. I used to love watching David Ginola because he was brilliant with both. Other not so celebrated players too: Andy Sinton and Peter Beagrie, for example. As I was growing up it was something I made sure I never lost.

Ryan Giggs: Ben played like Ginola. He could manipulate the ball and then he could go on his left and cross it or he could go on his right and put it in the top corner – I could never do that because I was all left foot. He was just different so he was hard to mark. He was an intelligent player.

Ben: In 1983 we moved to Stafford Road, which is only half a mile from Snowdon Road but in quite an affluent, leafy suburb called Ellesmere Park. It is full of Victorian semi-detached houses; my parents stretched themselves to be able to afford that place.

Rod Thornley: At Stafford Road we nicked wheelie bins for goals, or we'd grab the workers' cones with the red-and-white barriers across the top.

Hannah Scott: I was ball girl. I was only ever ball girl. I certainly didn't want to play though, I just liked being with them.

Philip Thornley: We used to spend time with a ball, either kicking and shooting or throwing and catching, as far back as I can remember. And Elizabeth had a fantastic throwing arm – she could throw further than I could.

Hannah Scott: Those were the days when we used to have summers, we'd be out in the garden …

Philip Thornley: Oh don't start that again.

Ben: My dad was very successful. He did such a lot of extra-curricular stuff that he didn't have to do, all inter-school stuff of a Saturday morning. They'd have cross-country between September and Christmas and he'd be at every one early doors. He's from a tiny place called Peel Green, which is right next door to where the Trafford Centre is now; he was born in Eccles and Patricroft Hospital.

My mum was born Elizabeth Edwards at the same hospital. My dad's a bit older than her: he was born in 1945; she was born in 1951. They first met through my mum's older brother when she was 11 or 12, which sounds terrible but obviously it was years later that they actually became a couple.

Philip Thornley: There was nothing unseemly about it, thank you. We went for dinner on Liz's 16th birthday and we got married at Patricroft Methodist Church in 1973.

Ben: I played my first competitive football match for my junior school, Clarendon Road, when I was in my first year in 1982.

Philip Thornley: One day he came home and said, 'I'm playing for the school tomorrow.' I said, 'You're playing for the *school*? You're only seven!' We thought he was romancing but sure enough, he'd been selected.

Ben: It wasn't like at secondary school, where you have one team per year group: this was the whole of the school, whoever was any good. The PE teacher, Tony Potter, picked me to play with a group of ten- and 11-year-olds when I was seven.

Tony Potter: Clarendon Road School was a red building, two floors – turn-of-the-century sort of thing. Our staff room was on the top floor at one end, overlooking the playground.

It was during lunch break one day, wintertime, that I was looking out the window at the infants, five and six years old, playing football. I said to my colleague, 'Harry, come over here and have a look at this.'

This one boy was absolutely tremendous. I couldn't believe that someone that age could be that good. Most kids of five and six, they can't even kick a ball properly. But the skill that Ben had at that age … I invited him along to school-team practices with the juniors and he got in the team the following year.

Ben: In my first game we lost 4-3 against Westwood Park but I scored. I didn't feel out of my depth. I could already shift a bit because I used to race my gran's collie dog, Lassie, when she took her for walks. It was always fascinating to me that I could beat something with four legs; I mean, Lassie was getting on a bit but I didn't know that then. That was what spurred me on to run and run and run – and get quite quick.

Tony Potter: There was one game at Eccles recreation ground, where we played all our home matches, when Ben got the ball at the edge of our area, weaved his way through the other team, went the whole length of the field and scored. Afterwards I said, 'There were two or three times on that run when there were people in better positions than you.

'When you play at a higher level you'll be expected to release the ball at the right time, so you may as well get used to it now. Pass to someone even though they might make a mess of it.' I'm not sure he liked the sound of that.

Philip Thornley: We never suspected that Ben would be good at football. I mean, I played sport as a child but I wasn't very good.

Ben: My dad never ever pushed me. Yes, he supported me and recognised that I had talent but he never said, 'Right, you need to discard everything else in your life because you're going to do this.'

Elizabeth Thornley: My father died when I was 11 so there was no sporting influence there. And I don't think my brother has ever kicked a ball in his life. That said, I quite like football. I watched the World Cup – in 1966.

Philip Thornley: There is some football heritage in my family though. My father's father, Tom Thornley, was the manager of an oil yard on the Manchester Ship Canal in the early 1900s. My father said that any number of times, Tom would find United agents waiting outside the gate for him. He played for a team called Eccles United and apparently he was a very good centre-half. United wanted him but he'd say, 'What, and give up what I'm earning at the oil yard?'

Ben: I went to my first match at Old Trafford with a lad called Anthony Rouse. He's a pal of mine from school, who I've known since the age of three, and his parents were friends of the family. Anthony's dad, Rick, was a solicitor; he was a wealthy guy. He had a C-registered injection Capri that was deep blue with a grey-leather interior – that car was the bollocks. Rick had four season tickets and on the odd occasion that somebody in his family couldn't make it, Anthony would always ask me along.

Anthony Rouse: Me and Ben were keen as mustard so we always wanted to get to the match early. My dad, however, was a man of routine and would always leave our house in Ellesmere Park at 2.25pm, slotting into his seat in the stadium just as the referee blew his whistle. It was infuriating because we wanted to get a wriggle on.

Ben: The first game I watched at Old Trafford was on a Friday night against Tottenham Hotspur in December 1983. I was in the South Stand, which was and still is the best place to sit. United beat Spurs 4-2. The one thing that sticks in my mind is Alan Brazil, who presents on talkSPORT now, scoring a spectacular sliced scissor kick to make it level at 1-1. I don't even remember who scored for United.

Anthony Rouse: Ben was always immensely passionate when we were watching the game but well behaved within the bounds of that passion. He always minded his Ps and Qs, especially in front of adults.

Ben: My dad used to go and watch United too; he was never a season-ticket holder but he went to see them before the Munich disaster in 1958 and during the rebuilding process afterwards. Like any other teenager he'd get on the bus with his pocket money and cram his way into the Stretford End – not every week but when he could.

Philip Thornley: My father used to give me a shilling and that was 12 pence; it was nine pence to get into the ground and one-and-a-half pence on the bus there and back. The first big game I went to was versus Bilbao in the 1957 European Cup. United had to win by three clear goals to get through, having lost 5-3 in Spain. It was at Maine Road because Old Trafford didn't have floodlights at that stage. The place erupted when they got the third.

I saw people like Tommy Taylor, Roger Byrne and Duncan Edwards. We used to go and watch Youth Cup matches when Edwards was playing. Once, when we were in the Stretford End, we were in line with one ball he hit that smacked the bar and nearly bounced back to halfway. And my mate Ken, who I used to go to games with, came into school one day and said, 'I went to United yesterday – guess who I sat next to on the bus? Eddie Colman!' Eddie was one of the players who later died in Munich.

Ben: In 1984, my third year at Clarendon Road, Tony Potter made me captain. I was nine and there were kids of 11 that he overlooked to give it to me, which was mad.

Tony Potter: When he was in my class he was one of those who was automatically good at everything he turned his hand to. He had a good sense of humour too; he got my jokes, which went over the heads of most students. I was really pleased when I found out that he was no good at drawing and painting because at least it meant he had a weakness ...

I made him captain because it made him more team aware and he was someone who thought about the game. We had one or two decent players in that squad but Ben was the best I ever saw at that age.

Ben: It was in that same year that I first played for Salford Boys under-11s. The coach was John Chappell.

John Chappell: We would send a letter out to the schools and they would nominate players. Tony sent in Ben's name and he was a year younger at the time, aged nine. But he had a good build and was able to hold his own against the older boys. He was a natural and always turned up to training with a big smile on his face, though he was tenacious because he wanted to make his position his own.

Ben: For one game we went to play Bootle at a brand-new sports complex. It was the first time I properly met Giggsy and saw him in action. We played in the same team – along with my mate Paul Devine – and won 8-1. Ryan scored six of them.

Ryan Giggs: I missed my trial for Salford Boys – I couldn't get there because I missed the bus or whatever – so I was in the second team that day.

Paul Devine: Ben and I were very young to be playing at that sort of level. It was the first time I'd come across him but we were at the age where you instantly become mates. Even then you could see that he was very talented. I suppose we all were really, but there were some that stood out and Ben was one of them.

John Chappell: Ben played 21 out of 31 games that season (if you include substitute appearances), scoring four goals – including one in his first game, a 2-1 win away at Kirby. He would have played a second year at under-11 but the teachers held their strikes. But for that, he would have played and he'd have definitely captained the team.

Ben: By my final year at junior school in 1986 I was really looking forward to playing football but it never came about: there was no competitive sport played outside because teachers across the country were striking left, right and centre over pay. Fortunately the boys who played at my dad's school had heard that my school was doing well with me at the helm. They all played for a Sunday team called Cadishead Sports and they asked me to join them.

Initially my parents wouldn't let me because games were on a Sunday morning and they were churchgoers. However, when they realised that I had potential and wasn't going to be playing any competitive football at school, they let me go. To start with they let me skip church once a month to kick off at 11am – and sometimes they'd bunk off themselves to come and watch me. But then, lo and behold, kick-off moved to 2pm so I could do both.

Anthony Rouse: I played with Ben as a centre-half for the school and Cadishead. Undoubtedly he had talent above that of anyone else on the pitch but he underpinned it with a steely determination. I understood what his mindset was like beneath that determination because we were close friends, but there were other players who sometimes struggled with it.

Ben: As a captain, or somebody who people look up to, you need to encourage. I didn't. I destroyed at times.

The level I played football at was a lot higher than any of my team-mates at the time, so when others didn't live up to my expectations it frustrated me. Such was my drive and will to win,

I didn't realise the detrimental effect I was having on some of the lesser players. They looked up to me and were still giving their all, but I was too young and immature to care about that.

If I was playing in a team where my captain kept having a go at me all the time, I wouldn't want to play for nor with him. And the thing is, I'm not a nasty person; if I saw someone today who was struggling for whatever reason, I'd want to go and help them. I was wrong back then, which makes me sad. And it makes me apologetic.

Anthony Rouse: He was full on. If he hadn't been such a standout, players probably wouldn't have taken it.

Ryan Giggs: He used to go a bit psycho at referees as well.

Rod Thornley: We could never understand why he would get angry over such small things. If you want to see it in action now, sit down and play Mr & Mrs with him.

Hannah Scott: Or Pictionary.

Rod Thornley: You will see the most irrational anger you've ever seen in your life. He was on the couch on *Soccer AM* once – he must have been at Huddersfield at the time – and Tim Lovejoy and Helen Chamberlain were asking people to ring in. So while I was on my way to play for my team, Congleton, I phoned up and said, 'I can be lying in bed at night when Ben's in his bedroom and all I can hear is, "Shit! Fuck! Jesus Christ! Fuck!" And it's because he's playing darts on his own in his room.' The whole studio was in uproar. And it's true. What an absolute weirdo.

Elizabeth Thornley: We had doors with holes in at Stafford Road thanks to Ben.

Philip Thornley: They happened just after his injury.

Ben: A guy called Harold Bloor was in charge of Cadishead and he poured his heart and soul into the club. He did everything for us under-11s, taking us to football festivals in places like Rhyl and Prestatyn. But there wasn't any coaching as such. Training consisted of splitting us up into four teams of five and having a kickabout, nothing technical.

Harold was a great guy. He was a season-ticket holder at Man United and occasionally he would take a couple of the lads, back in the day when you could still pay at the turnstile. Sadly he passed away in 2014. I owe him a lot because Cadishead was where I started to really develop. Scouts in our area used to go and watch Sunday teams that had a reputation. Deans was one and that was who Ryan played for; another, called Barr Hill, was also well known. We played in the Salford league, which put us up against these teams, and we gave them a good run for their money.

Joe Lydiate: I first came across Ben when I played for Barr Hill. Back then we were one of the main teams going and while Cadishead were a good team, the person who made them was Ben.

Ben: At that point I was quick, I could use two feet and I could beat players. My team-mates could give me the ball and I'd be able to go past two or three and lay it off or create something. When I wasn't playing in a match I'd go to a field and run from side to side – no cones or anything, just moving the ball between my feet. And if anybody, anywhere, was playing on a pitch I'd stand there in the hope that somebody would ask me to join in. After a while people got to know me and they would knock on my door and say, 'Come on, we're going over the back fields.' I never refused. All I wanted to do was have a ball at my feet.

Anthony Rouse: It didn't matter who was playing, he'd go and play with them. There was no 'They're bigger than me' or 'I don't know them' – part of the fun for Ben was taking on different people.

My house backed on to a field used by a school called John Bradley, which had two full-size football pitches. Ben's house was a minute's walk away so we would spend hours and hours and hours playing there. But if it was just me and Ben it wasn't up to much, so we'd drag Rod down. If we played headers and volleys and Rod didn't tee Ben up to his satisfaction, that was it: the potty mouth would come out and he'd be running after Rod.

Ben: Apart from World Cups and FA Cup final day there was basically no football on the telly whatsoever, so I kept myself busy playing it rather than watching it. That didn't turn out to be such a bad thing in the end.

3

Surgery
1994

The room was silent. The game had finished and the other lads were coming in sporadically to see how I was. I was so devastated because I knew I was in a bad way.

The ambulance arrived and took me to Bury General; a short time later I was back in an ambulance to be transferred to Whalley Range, a Bupa hospital. What I find hard to remember is, at what stage did I get out of my kit? At what stage did I have a shower? That's all a bit of a blur.

At Whalley Range I was examined by Jonathan Noble, Manchester United's consultant orthopaedic surgeon. He'd been associated with the club for 12 years by that stage and he specialised in knee surgery. When he was called in he was in the middle of a dinner party at his house (though why he was having a dinner party on a Wednesday night, I've no idea). When he met me he said, 'I'll let you apologise to my wife.'

He had no difficulty making a diagnosis because, in his words, 'everything was buggered'. He decided to wait until the following morning to operate so that he could carry out the operation with his team – the people who did knee surgery with him week in, week out.

It all started at 6am. Dr Noble says that when he opened up my knee to assess the damage it was like putting a book on its spine and watching all the pages fan out; it had fallen apart, completely smashed to smithereens. He realised that it must have been one hell of an impact. This is what he was greeted by (and this is from my medical records by the way, not off the top of my head):

- A rupture of both cruciate ligaments
- A complete rupture of the medial collateral ligament
- A detachment of the medial meniscus
- A complete rupture of the medial capsule of the knee, from the mid-point posteriorly to the patellar ligament anteriorly
- A partial tear of the posteromedial hamstring attachment.

All of that from one tackle. That's a lot. And yet, ironically, Dr Noble tells me that it was one of the easiest major knee-repair operations he ever had to do. Because it was such a mess he could get in without a problem, then get around corners with stitches and whatever else because there wasn't anything in the way.

While he was in there he repaired everything, which was a bit controversial when it came to cruciates. The common thinking among medical professionals then, and even more so now, was that you shouldn't repair cruciate ligaments but *replace* them. But my case was a little different. Normally when cruciate ligaments tear, they explode. Dr Noble says it looks like spaghetti bolognese because 'there's a bit of blood and all these little bits of white string all over the place'. But it turns out that I've got good, chunky ligaments and both the anterior and posterior had been pulled off the bone intact, so he reattached them.

To do that he improvised, using a technique he normally used for hand surgery. He drilled holes through the bone, did a sort of criss-cross weave through the ligaments with needle and thread and then pulled them back on to the bone. Having done that he then repaired my medial cartilage and my meniscus – which went back very nicely, apparently – then my medial ligament and all the other soft-tissue structures on that side of the knee. All up, the operation took him an hour and 20 minutes, despite it being one of the three nastiest knee-ligament injuries he saw during his long and distinguished career.

After the operation he was sceptical that I'd play again because of the extent of the injury. But I was extremely fortunate to have a surgeon who was so good – and that's a vast understatement. He was exceptionally thorough with everything he did; he wasn't voted president of the British Association for Surgery of the Knee for nothing.

I remember waking up afterwards with a drip coming from my knee that, when they took it out, was extremely painful. I yelped. No, I screamed. I wasn't expecting it. My whole leg was in a cast, from my ankle all the way up to the top of my thigh. It was a strange, uncomfortable feeling and I hated it. I just wanted it off. Even the thought of it now ... Not happy times for me at all. A few years later in 1998, when I was at Huddersfield, I broke my foot. I thought, 'Please don't say I need a plaster cast.' Fortunately they gave me one of those Velcro-fastening boots, which was so much better.

Alex Ferguson phoned me to see how I was. He phoned my mum and dad as well (one time he phoned my dad when he was fixing the garage roof but he still took the call). The manager was also in regular contact with Jonathan Noble, who I got in touch with again for the book. He told me, 'I'd operated on a lot of Alex's players but here we were dealing with a young lad and he was obviously terribly worried about you, and needed to talk about it. I can remember one Sunday morning, for example, sitting in his car outside the hospital to discuss your progress. I admired and respected his interest in you; he was more like a concerned uncle than a manager. It just showed what I knew anyway, which is what a decent bloke he was – and is.'

Sadly, Sir Alex Ferguson wasn't able to get involved with the book in the end. I spoke to him when we played Arsenal at Old Trafford on 29 April; I was pitchside for MUTV doing my little pre-match bit to camera when I spotted him in front of the dugouts. We weren't live so I asked the camera crew to hang fire for a couple of minutes while I went over to where he was stood with Claire Robson, Bryan Robson's daughter who works in United's marketing department.

As I approached, Sir Alex turned to Claire and said, 'Here's the lad who would have played for England.' I briefly outlined what I wanted to talk to him about and he told me to come up to the directors' room after the game, which I duly did. He invited me in and said, 'Tell me.' I explained the format of the book and how honoured I would be if he was willing to contribute his thoughts, to which his exact words were, 'I can do that for you, son.'

He gave me the number of his secretary in his Wilmslow office so that we could set up a meeting. I left it a couple of days before calling, asked the lady I spoke to if she would pass on my message to Sir Alex and within ten minutes he called. He came up with a few dates off the top of his head that he thought he could do in late May and said he'd ring back later that afternoon with a definitive answer.

Next thing I knew, the news broke that he was in intensive care. I was both astonished and devastated to learn what had happened to him.

It was with great relief that I started to hear from different sources that he was improving, with close friends and family being allowed to visit. But when we tentatively made contact again to see if he was well enough to speak to us we were told that, under doctor's orders, he wouldn't be conducting any business until he was fully recuperated and had been on a family holiday. Sadly – in terms of the book – that made it too late for him to contribute.

It's a huge regret that Sir Alex hasn't been able to take part. However, the flipside is how happy I am that, at the time of writing, he's on the mend and will hopefully make a full recovery.

Back to 1994 and after surgery and a night in hospital I was in so much discomfort from the cast that the next morning I asked mum to bring me a knitting needle. She refused so when I got home I found one myself and scratched right down inside. It was such a relief. But when I went back to hospital after about ten days to have my plaster changed (they put me in a normal plaster cylinder, leaving my foot and ankle free) it transpired that I'd pulled out two stitches with the needle. I'd done it without realising because, even now, there are certain parts of my knee where I don't have any sensitivity at all. You could stick a pin in (which isn't an invitation) and I wouldn't know. Jonathan Noble definitely wasn't happy about those stitches coming out. Was he fuck.

When I got my plaster changed and saw what was inside, it looked like a chicken leg with a 9.5-inch scar. There was no muscle definition. Your muscles will start to waste even if you only lie in bed for three or four days and I'd noticed that the top of the cast had been getting looser. But actually seeing my leg was awful. It made me cry. I thought, 'What the fuck has he done to me?'

Before I left hospital I had my first bout of physio, where I was taught exercises for my quads and how to get about on crutches without going arse over tit. Then, a few days later, I was discharged. When I got home my mum and dad had put a bed downstairs in the dining room for me; most of the time I just lay there, wallowing in my own self-pity.

Hindsight is a wonderful thing but considering how long I was laid up for I probably should have done more – if it happened now I'd start learning a language or something. But it's difficult when you're an 18-year-old kid and all you can think about is getting to the stage where you can start rebuilding your leg and getting fit again.

For six weeks I was just a zombie and with being so sedentary, I started putting weight on. I'd been in great condition until that point; there hadn't been an ounce of fat on me and I was a healthy weight. Yet within the space of a couple of months I put on the best part of a stone, even though I tried to eat the right things. Then I'd look at myself in the mirror and get even more depressed.

Before the injury I was so skinny that I never thought it would happen to me. But then, after a couple of months, you think to yourself, 'Hang on a minute.' Once the fat cells had set in during the time I was immobile, my body shape changed from lean to doughnut. Fortunately, Trevor Lea had just arrived at United as the club's first-ever nutritionist and he drew up a plan for me. It was less a case of what I was eating than the portions I was having. I wasn't eating anything wrong but the amount of time that I hadn't been able to do any exercise had taken its toll.

That was, without question, the start of the fight I've had ever since to maintain a decent physique. I've been up and down over the years and that's bound to continue, particularly now that I don't exercise on a daily basis. If I can't exercise at all at any time in the near future – and I hope that isn't the case – or I just decide that that's it, I've had enough, I will easily put weight on. Robbie Fowler is a former player whose weight also fluctuates. He can still play in exhibition games by the way, so he's fine on that score, but with everything he's achieved in the game he's probably just thought to himself, 'Do you know what? That's me. I'm done.'

Because I worked so hard not to be like that when I was playing, I want to carry on the good work. It's a bit of a vanity thing as well: I don't want people to comment on the fact that I'm overweight. I want people to say something more like, 'I'm pleasantly surprised that you've not turned into a fat hobbit.'

Switching to a knee brace was such a godsend. However, when we were approaching what was supposed to be the last day of wearing the cast, there was talk of keeping it on for another ten days. I told them I'd do whatever it took to get out of that thing. They gave me all sorts of stipulations, saying that for the first week of wearing the brace I had to move around as little as if I still had the cast on. After that I could gradually build up to going for a walk around the block but they certainly weren't suggesting that I start doing squats.

It was such a relief to get that cast off. As soon as it had gone I wanted to get myself back to the football club. There still wasn't a massive deal I could do but I just wanted to be in and around it, even if it meant going in and only working on my upper body.

I was fortunate in that I had strong legs but as soon as I could get started they needed to be stronger still, to compensate for the fact that my anterior cruciate ligament (ACL) hadn't been replaced. Yet here we are 24 years later and it's exactly the same one as when Dr Noble sewed me back up. According to him, the fact that he was able to successfully repair my medial meniscus, which is my inner knee cartilage, is one of the main reasons that I'm yet to show signs of osteoarthritis.

That said, my knee has certainly restricted my movement and I will probably suffer with arthritis in later life. It's things like bending down to put something in the dishwasher (though my partner, Lesley, will tell you that doesn't happen very often). I know if I'm down there for any length of time – and I'm talking seconds – it's easier for me to use the worktop to haul myself back up using my hands. Coming up off my haunches puts unnecessary pressure on my knee – you can hear it crunch and it hurts. And when I'm cleaning the wheels of my car I use a toothbrush to get in all the grooves, so I lie something on the floor and kneel down rather than crouch. Though even getting up from a kneeling position is sore.

It doesn't bother me when I'm playing football though. I can still run – if not as fast as before – and I'm not in any pain whatsoever the following morning, even if I've played 90 minutes. Say I'm told I need a replacement ACL when I'm 60, I might decide I'm not bothered. Though I probably will get it done, even if it's just to stave off arthritis for another few years. My joints are fucked as it is but if there's a chance to avoid more discomfort, I've got to consider it.

I couldn't have done it without Jonathan Noble and I'm so grateful to him for saving my career, but I also like to think that I couldn't have got through it without putting in the work to give myself a chance. When we spoke to him for the book he said, 'You were a very positive patient. If it hadn't been for your enthusiasm, industry and sunny disposition I don't think that the result would have been anywhere near as flattering to me as it seems to have been.'

He's not alone in thinking that I dealt really well with a career-threatening injury: my coaches and team-mates would say the same thing. Impeccably well in fact, considering that it looked like I might never play football again. Yet the truth is that beneath the surface, I wanted to tear strips off *everything*.

Nicky Marker will never say, 'Yes, I meant to do Ben Thornley,' but I blame him 100 per cent. He was a professional footballer, with plenty of experience, who knew exactly what he was doing. The tackle that he put in on me was late, it was high and it was calculated. Some 18-year-old had been giving him the runaround all game so he took it upon himself to dish out retribution. That decision cost me a potential career with the club I love. I'll never forgive him for that.

So those initial six weeks were life-changing, not just in the interim but the long term as well. People forget that. It's not a case of, 'Oh, I've had a knee injury, I'll be injured for six months but then I'll be fine.' It's everything else that comes with it. And it wasn't all as plain sailing then as it is if you have that type of injury now. Though to be honest, most of my problem was mental rather than physical. I'd never been in that situation before and it didn't help that I'd read my case notes and so knew the full extent of the injury.

People are understanding up to a point but they expect you to snap out of it after a while. The day I snapped out of it was the day I knew I could go back into United's training ground.

4

Growing up
1986–88

Anthony Rouse: So eager was Ben to play football that come break time he would be legging it out with the ball. On one particular occasion, he and I were the first to burst out of the doors, just as two grown men came running through the school grounds in the opposite direction. They were (fairly) closely followed by an out-of-breath old-age pensioner, who said, 'Run after them!' And we were like, 'Why, what's happened?' And he said, 'It doesn't matter, just run after them!'

So me and Ben – though I don't know what we thought we were going to do – started chasing these guys. Ben was quicker than me, though I was centre-half and he was centre-mid so he was going to be, wasn't he? Regardless, they lost us. But it was lucky we didn't catch them because only on our return to school were we told they'd just robbed a bank. They were *armed robbers*. And, of course, the real story here is that it was Ben's fault we were even in that situation because he was too keen to get out and play football.

Ben: I started at secondary school in 1986. It was called Ellesmere Park High School but at the end of my first year we amalgamated with Winton High School to become Wentworth High School.

Our PE teacher was Geoff Ogden. He had played for England Schoolboys, was a Cambridge Blue and went to teacher-training college in Didsbury with my dad. When he saw my name on the list of pupils that would be entering the school that year, he made a point of coming to watch me play for Cadishead.

Geoff Ogden: I'd heard from Ben's primary school PE teacher, Tony Potter, that he was a good player, so I already knew quite a bit about him. He was just one of those: absolutely outstanding. As soon as you saw him with the ball for 30 seconds, you knew he was something special. He had pace, he had stamina, he had skills – and skills that were far advanced for an 11-year-old, which is when I first saw him. And as well as having all those qualities he was just a terrific lad.

Ben: Geoff held trials for the first-year team, I got in and he made me captain right the way through until my fifth year.

Geoff Ogden: It wasn't a case of just giving it to the best player; he had the authority, as well as respect from all the other lads. And I never had a cross word with him because we respected each other too. I used to join in with games once the lads turned 14 and it would be a battle for me to cope with Ben on the pitch.

Ben: Unfortunately it wasn't until my second year that all the teacher strikes were put to bed and we could get on with playing competitive matches.

Geoff Ogden: There was a lot of work-to-rule going on. After-school matches often didn't go ahead because of teachers at other schools being on strike.

Ben: Until the fourth year Geoff was always the referee when we played at home and it was the other school's PE teacher when we played away. Ryan Giggs went to Moorside High School; he was a year older than me so we never played against each other but their PE teacher was always unbelievably biased towards his own school. As far as he was concerned he had the best footballer ever at his place and, therefore, he had the best teams.

But because he found that the team he had in my age group weren't as good because I was playing against them – and he took exception to the fact that I was a bit mouthy – he did everything he could to try to make his team win. It never worked. Eventually there was a game where he completely lost his rag with me and sent me off. But that didn't really help his cause either: we were playing basketball.

Ryan Giggs: I think that would have been Mr Scott.

Geoff Ogden: I used to referee matches that Ryan Giggs was playing in, against my school, and we couldn't get the ball off him. Ben was of that calibre. It wasn't a case of being greedy, it's just that nobody could get near him. He was head and shoulders above the rest and dominated to the point where it was almost unfair. He was certainly the best footballer I ever taught.

Years later I spoke to former United player and manager Wilf McGuinness at Old Trafford cricket ground, where I was on the committee at Lancashire for 20-odd years. I'd see him at Test matches – he likes cricket, Wilf – and he told me once that Ben would have been one of the stars at United. He talked about him in the same breath as Giggs.

Ben: At school I was good at English, French and history. The PE teacher who taught me after Geoff asked why I wasn't taking PE and I said, 'I get plenty of that running around playing football so I'm not bothered. I'd rather take an academic subject.' And he said, 'It *is* an academic subject: you learn about the body.' And I said, 'Yeah, but I can do that in biology.' Which, incidentally, I was crap at; science, maths and IT were not my game. But I had a mum and dad from an educational background so they made sure I got on – and I ended up with eight GCSEs of grade C and above. So I wasn't a brainiac or anything but people could see that I was doing the work, not just tossing it off and saying, 'I'm going to be a footballer, I don't need this.'

I did play truant once – and got caught. I did it with three Manchester City fans when we jumped on a train to Bramall Lane to watch Sheffield United against City in a midweek game. At one point the ball came towards my dopey mate as someone was trying to throw it back on to the pitch; he decided to catch it and throw it back into the crowd. The stewards came and carted him out (though the rest of us stayed to watch the rest of the game, obviously), we ended up on TV, a teacher saw us and all four of us got collared the next day.

Geoff Ogden: He probably got away with it. *I* certainly wouldn't have mentioned it to anybody.

Ben: Outside of football, for a while I played cricket at a place called Monton Sports Club. It was always a bit snooty, a bit like a golf club, but Anthony Rouse convinced me to go. Anthony was a very good cricketer; he used to open the batting and keep wicket as well. I'd stand next to him in the slips because I had a decent pair of hands and one day he said, 'Do you know what, I can't be arsed with wicketkeeping today – do you want to do it?' So I said, 'Yeah, alright, I'll have a go.' I absolutely loved it.

Anthony Rouse: The bastard was very good. We'd grown up together massively sporty and with some level of natural talent, but he was always football and I was always cricket. There was a cricket tournament that the school used to put on called, weirdly, the Golden Boot: it was a single-man competition where you'd bat and bowl against another individual, with everyone else fielding.

I was up against Ben – and he bowled me with his second ball. Yet again this guy had outdone me and this time in *my* sport.

He could bat as well. What he lacked in technique he made up for with competitiveness and great hand-eye coordination.

Ben: Keeping wicket started to get a bit specialised though: bowlers got involved who were older than me and could really shift the ball. I preferred the ball to bounce, sail up and drop into my gloves. The more experienced wicketkeepers would stand a lot closer to the stumps but I thought, 'Ooh, that's a surefire way to get killed.' So that put paid to my cricket career.

Geoff, meanwhile, wouldn't let me play rugby whether I wanted to or not – and that was fine because I didn't want to. I was also the Salford schools cross-country champion, winning every race up until I was 14. But in the end I had to pack it in for football.

One Saturday in 1987, when I was playing for Cadishead Sports, a guy located my dad on the touchline, told him he ran Manchester City's school of excellence at Platt Lane and asked if he would be happy for me to attend.

Philip Thornley: Ron Atkinson had not long finished as manager at United and they had no youth policy at all. City had a good team *because* they had a good youth policy so I was quite happy to let Ben go. I knew they weren't going to exploit him.

Ben: I trained on the AstroTurf on Thursday nights and during the school holidays we'd play matches among ourselves. It just went along like that; there was nothing offered. Ryan Giggs did exactly the same thing.

It was just a case of Manchester City wanting me there and me being quite happy to go, but there was nothing set in stone, nothing in writing. Though if they'd have said, 'Right, when you leave school we want you to come and play for us,' I'm pretty sure I would have. I didn't know anything about Man United's interest then so I'd have been daft not to. Though it would have been a tough call.

Then in 1988, when I was 13, my school forwarded me for trials with Salford Boys. Harry Hackett and Paul Moseley were the managers.

Harry Hackett: We were short of a goalkeeper so we put Ben in goal after 20 minutes of the first trial. In other words, he was selected for the squad after 20 minutes. In fact, he was in after about five minutes. It was like the ball was tied to his foot.

Paul Moseley: From the first time we saw him we knew he could play. He was exceptional. He did alright in nets as well.

Harry Hackett: He just had this charisma about him.

Ben: After two lots of trials they picked a squad of 20 lads to play two friendlies at the start of September. When we got to that first game, Harry announced that Ryan Giggs – or Wilson as he was then – would captain the under-15s and I would captain the under-14s. My mates Paul Devine, Joe Lydiate and Andy Scott were all in the team too.

Harry Hackett: Ben was very adult in the way he conducted himself and was clearly the best player, so it was a no-brainer as to who was captain.

Paul Moseley: He was a clever lad so he could read the game. And he had an engine – he was involved in everything.

Harry Hackett: Part and parcel of trials is that a child will tell you he's a centre-midfielder or whatever, but you look at him and say, 'No, you're not. But I bet you could play somewhere else.' Whereas Ben could play anywhere: right, left, up front, at the back. When the team was formed we couldn't nail him down to a position so we created a free role. He wanted to be everywhere.

Paul Devine: He was such a talented lad, he always shone. He had a big personality too so there was always loads of banter. His football was flying and it was just great to have him as a mate.

Andy Scott: He was the Rolls-Royce of our team. If he was playing we knew we had a chance; if he was injured or he wasn't available, everybody knew we'd struggle. He was the lad who had everything but he was lovely with it; he wasn't big-headed or arrogant in any way. He had the good looks, the silky hair (at the time anyway), a headmaster for a dad and a mum who was even quite attractive.

Hannah Scott (née Thornley): All the Salford Boys lads used to fancy my mum. She was the milf.

Elizabeth Thornley: Just ask Giggsy.

Rod Thornley: When Ben went into the first-team dressing room at United, the likes of Mark Hughes would say, 'Ben, is your mum in today?' He'd snap and bite rather than let it go so they did it more and more – and Giggsy was one of the biggest culprits.

Ryan Giggs: She was hot, yeah. I was always winding him up: 'Your mum's looking well, Ben.' A couple of times he said, 'I'm going to tell my dad.' I said, 'Sure, tell him!' His mum used to always come and watch; his dad probably did as well but I can only remember his mum being there. I tried a little bit harder whenever she was watching. She was fit.

Joe Lydiate: Ben had his serious head on in the dressing room when we were at Salford Boys. On the pitch he was aggressive but in a good way. He just commanded the midfield completely. He was able to influence the game by getting others involved when we were up against it.

Paul Moseley: No matter what the weather – it could be freezing cold, other kids could be wearing gloves – Ben Thornley had his sleeves rolled up. And when Ben Thornley had his sleeves rolled up, you knew he was on it.

Nicky Butt: I already knew his name because you'd hear about the best players in the area. I played against him for Manchester Boys and he was head and shoulders above anyone else on the pitch; he was the difference between the two teams. He had dribbling ability but he also had end product, which is what makes the best players stand out at that age. He was top drawer from the word go.

Chris Casper: I was 13 and playing for Burnley Boys when I first came across Ben. He was by far the best player in the area – he was outstanding. I didn't see anybody else like him in the country at our level.

Ben: I never used to like Casp before I played with him at United. Now I love him to pieces but he got right on my nerves because he was like John Terry: mouth, mouth, mouth all the time, a constant gabber. He was a real pain in the arse.

Paul Moseley: Those two years were a golden period for schoolboy football in Greater Manchester, with Butt, Scholes, Neville and the rest. I coached Salford so I'm probably biased but I'd say Ben was the best of the bunch.

Philip Thornley: I'll never forget when Ben was 13 and we went on holiday to Llandudno. It has a massive promenade, half a mile long or more. We were at one end of it and Ben started doing keepy-uppies. I said, 'I don't suppose you're going to keep that up for much longer? We've got a way to go yet.' He said, 'Oh, I'll try.' The ball never touched the floor. Being a teacher, I'd seen what other kids could do so I thought, 'He's probably got something here.'

Ben: I stopped playing for Cadishead that season. I appeared in about five games for them but I realised I was playing way too much football. I was also putting a lot on my mum and dad to take me to all these different places, particularly when they had two other children and were a one-car family.

Philip Thornley: If our kids were involved, whether it was Ben's football or Hannah's trampolining, we'd be there.

Hannah Scott: They always tried to be fair. But Ben, you know …

Elizabeth Thornley: This is where the jealousy starts to creep in.

Hannah Scott: No, not at all. We were just super proud; there was never any resentment.

Elizabeth Thornley: That's probably come since.

Ben: I had to turn around to Harold, the Cadishead coach, and say, 'Listen, I've got to make time for my schoolwork. I'm playing on Saturday and Sunday mornings and I don't even have time during the week, what with training with you, training with Salford Boys and playing school matches.'

My dad was quite philosophical about it: number one, he didn't want me to get bored; number two, he didn't want me to get injured. The bigger boys didn't like some kid running rings around them. It was a bit like if I was to play Sunday league now against some hairy-arsed fellas who've been out boozing the night before: all they could do is kick me. My mum used to worry all the time.

Elizabeth Thornley: It's true, I was always worried at Ben's matches but because I was frightened that he was going to plant the linesman and be sent off. I would get very nervous.

Hannah Scott: She'd sit there whispering, 'Just keep your mouth shut, just keep your mouth shut …'

Philip Thornley: Our other concern was that if anyone in the crowd started criticising Ben, Elizabeth was ready for a fight.

Elizabeth Thornley: That's *not* true.

Ben: Even after I finished playing for Cadishead I didn't have much time to do anything outside of schoolwork, spending time with my friends and playing football. Everything was geared towards the latter because the older I got, the more serious it got. Put it this way: it would have been the wrong time to take up skydiving or rock climbing. Or skiing. Actually, I did go out on a pair of skis years later and it was the most unnatural thing in the world. I think back to that day now and I wanted to kill the girl who took me. Never again.

Still, when a match finished on a Saturday morning for Salford Boys I had the rest of that day and the rest of Sunday all to myself. Very often one of the lads would suggest getting the bus and meeting in Manchester, where we'd walk around the Arndale Centre and have a McDonald's.

Joe Lydiate: Ben didn't live that far away so our mate Jeff Kerfoot and I often stayed over at his parents' house after we'd played for Salford Boys on a Saturday. We used to wander from his place in Monton into Eccles, get a kebab from the takeaway, walk back and watch *Match of the Day*.

Ben: We could also go to the Salford Precinct, which had one or two shops, but it was a bit dingy and ropey. Salford seemed to be right plonk in the middle of a few unsavoury areas: you had Broughton, Pendleton, Ordsall and Weaste in the vicinity. It wasn't a particularly nice place to be wandering around if you didn't know anybody. Basically, you wouldn't really want to be caught out and about in the middle of Salford back in the late 80s.

George Switzer: Everyone knew everyone in Salford and it's the same now. Salford Precinct had what seemed like 200 market stalls and a pub, the Flat Iron. If I told my dad I wanted a pair of jeans off a stall and they were a tenner, which was a lot then, he'd go in the pub for a quick half, come out and say, 'Here you are, I got them for a fiver.' People would rob from the stalls, go in the Flat Iron and sell everything half price.

Ben: After we'd played our first couple of games at Salford Boys, United knew that I was captain and that we'd got off to a really good start. In fact there were plenty of people keeping an eye on me then; there would be somebody down at Salford Boys games home and away because of Ryan and me. My mum did her best to scupper my career, mind you.

Philip Thornley: Salford Boys got sponsors who brought them brand-new kit and the system was that each week a different boy would take it all home to be washed. But Elizabeth had never washed that sort of material before.

Elizabeth Thornley: Well, no, I hadn't. I looked at it and thought, 'It's dirty, I'll put it on a boil wash.' So I boiled it at 90°C and ruined the whole lot; shrank it and changed the colour. I wasn't terribly popular.

Ben: At Salford Boys it was a 10.30am kick-off and we were expected to be there for 9.45am. But I was the captain so I wanted to be there at 9.30am. Dad would make sure I was there for 9.29am week in, week out – but he used to infuriate me with his dithering. Then we'd arrive and he'd say, 'Right, there you go, you're in a bad mood, go and take it out on whoever you're playing today.' And invariably I did. I think he knew exactly what he was doing; yes, part of it was his laid-back approach but part of it was doing me the world of good psychologically.

Philip Thornley: If he was there on time, what was he worried about? But it wasn't a deliberate ploy to get him worked up, no. The whole point was that I wasn't going to leave the house at some ridiculous hour just so he could be there early.

Truth be told, we never used to talk to him on the morning of a game because we'd be wasting our time. He was a nightmare. He'd just sit in the car and stare straight ahead. Not like now when he never shuts up.

Ben: I hadn't signed schoolboy forms with any clubs at this point but various scouts were asking me along for trials, so I just thought, 'I'll go here, I'll go there and have a look at what the facilities are like.' Derek Lomas, the Northwest scout for Ipswich Town, gave me a call and invited my dad and me down for a few days in the summer. We got on the Harwich boat train from Manchester and for that week my dad was my best mate; I didn't go anywhere without him. I was really grateful because on my own I think I would have panicked. I was quite shy; there was a mix of 13-, 14- and 15-year-olds and I was one of the youngest.

We had a couple of training sessions and at the end of the week there were some games laid on. The first was against Norwich at under-13 level. I scored two, possibly three, and played like an absolute world-beater. After that they said they had seen all they needed to see and offered me a two-year apprenticeship to start in two years' time, as well as two-year professional forms after that. But it would have been a case of moving to the other end of the country. Still, I waited to see what the offer was; my dad told me and back then it was like, wow. But I wrote back, told them that I wanted to wait before I put pen to paper and then nothing ever came of it.

Around that time I also went to Nottingham Forest for a trial and even had offers to go abroad. One was from Auxerre and two lads who I later played with for England Schoolboys, Jamie Forrester and Kevin Sharp, both started there. Blackburn, Chelsea and a couple of clubs in Scotland were all lying in wait too.

But then came a knock on the front door that meant there was only one club I was going to sign for.

5

Rehab
1994–95

Once my knee brace was off it was time to get going with my rehab; Manchester United organised taxis to pick me up and drop me home. I'd go into our training ground, The Cliff, on a Monday morning and the manager would grab me to ask if I was OK. Most of the time I'd say I was fine but if I told him I was a bit tired, my knee was hurting or I felt shit he'd say, 'Go home and let us know when you're ready to come back in.'

He was brilliant like that. It goes back to what I always say about Sir Alex Ferguson: he knew exactly how to treat players. Whatever condition they were in, he knew how to get the best out of them. And if that meant letting them have a few days to themselves to stop them going crazy, that's what he'd do. Plus, he knew that I wasn't the sort of person who would toss it off. From the second my cast was off, all I wanted was to be in the club, so he knew it wasn't ever easy for me to admit that I wanted to go home for a few days.

He was never going to drag me back in either because he knew I was still a kid and that it was affecting me mentally. Especially because when I started back at the club it was July, the weather was great and all the other players were out doing pre-season training while I was stuck in the gym. The only windows in there were right at the top near the ceiling so you couldn't even see out. It was enclosed and it was *dark*.

When I got back, senior physio Jim McGregor had just left the club and his replacement was David Fevre. I liked him instantly. He had a really in-depth knowledge of rehabilitating cruciate injuries because he'd come from Wigan rugby league club and they're much more common in that sport. Though rugby league players are a different breed altogether. Dave told me that Martin Offiah and Jason Robinson, for example, never lifted a weight in their lives; they were just naturally that strong and that quick. But he says it helped that he worked me more like a rugby league player than a footballer, simply because football had been so far behind until then in terms of physiotherapy.

Fortunately for me, it was around the time that I got injured that rehabilitation for cruciates was starting to improve. Ten years earlier it would have been a lot different but between the mid-1990s and now, not much has changed. There are a few more machines but, basically, the principles are the same.

Monday to Saturday I'd clock in at 9.30am, work till 12pm, have an hour for lunch then go till 4pm. I liked the routine of going in of a morning and knowing what I was going to be doing, even though the afternoon was normally easier. I'd do stuff on my own in the gym to start with while Dave got rid of people from the treatment room, getting all their strappings done so they could go out and train. Then, from 10.30am, it was me. And it was only me: there were no other players with serious injuries at the time so I had him to myself. We'd go and do our tough bit, whatever it happened to be that day, after which he'd give me some treatment, examine me and see how I was. Then he'd say, 'I want you to go downstairs and do this, this and this, then I'll be down in half an hour and we'll finish off together.'

My rehab coincided with the arrival of a new isokinetic machine; we called it the Cybex because that was the name of the manufacturer. When Dave came to the club it was the first thing he requested. He'd been shown around the gym by the manager, who proudly pointed out four pieces of kit they'd just bought for £3,000 each. Dave was horrified. That was way behind rugby league in terms of investment. The Cybex alone cost £40,000.

At the time there weren't many of these machines in the country and I would have been one of the first footballers to rehab on it. It was like a giant chair with handles that you grabbed hold of, all linked up to a computer that could make a decision on your muscle strength in correlation with your body weight. Dave programmed it so that, with my ankles strapped in, it would take my knees backwards and forwards with a robotic arm.

It was my hamstrings that we were strengthening. I would let my legs go straight and then yank them back. The more strain I put on it, the more it would resist – like Harry Potter when he falls into the Devil's Snare. But unlike Harry, I needed to give it as much as I'd got. It was the same with my quads: there'd be resistance and I'd really have to kick against it. Then Dave would remove the resistance altogether and make me kick out 50 times really fast.

It looked like some sort of torture device and trust me, it felt like one too. Honestly, I'd get off that thing and my legs would be fucked. But it was brilliant for what I needed and Dave got the rest of the players to use it too. When you pulled back and kicked out it gave a reading, so we had a ranking of the ten strongest hamstrings and ten strongest quads across the whole club. Paul Ince was top for quads by a country mile; I was about seventh or eighth. For hamstrings I was third; Andrei Kanchelskis was top and Paul Parker second. Combining quads and hamstrings I think I had the strongest legs – along with Incey.

Talking of Andrei, that guy used to do kick-ups with a medicine ball. And I'm not talking about five – he was getting towards 30. That's quite something. He wasn't so hot with his left but he had an incredibly strong right foot.

I didn't spend the whole time on the Cybex because Dave made sure there was always something different to do. United didn't have

63

their own pool at the time so he would take me to the Y Club leisure centre in Castlefield. I couldn't do breaststroke (and I would still struggle with it now, too) so a lot of it was flipper movements (up and down, up and down), walking with weights attached to my legs and using floatable aids as resistance.

He also had me out doing long cycle rides. He might tell me to ride home, have a coffee, have half an hour and then come back. It was great because being sat on an exercise bike is monotonous and the constant pounding would start to affect me mentally: 'This hurts.' And it's not like now when you've got every TV channel in the world at Carrington, United's training facility. I was sat on an exercise bike at The Cliff staring at a fucking wall (and this was long before iPods and whatever else). Whereas when I went out on my bike it gave me a sense of freedom and I never really noticed my knee because I was too busy concentrating on cars pulling out, which route I was going to take and all that.

For one of the exercises, Dave brought his rugby league experience to bear. I'd run and he'd hit me with a tackle shield: a great big foam pad on his arm, basically. He'd also have me launching myself at tackle bags, getting up again and sprinting. I remember saying, on a couple of occasions, 'Dave, I want to do that again.' But he'd say, 'I know you do – that's why we're doing something different.' He didn't ever want me to get comfortable with something so there was a lot of switching. The idea was that I didn't do the same exercise two days in a row, so there was a Monday, Wednesday, Friday schedule alongside a Tuesday, Thursday, Saturday one.

A few months in, Dave incorporated running with the ball. There was one exercise where there were ten balls around the D of the penalty area. I'd hit one, sprint to the six-yard box, come back out and hit the next one. There'd be a goalkeeper so the aim was to score but by the time I got to the seventh or eighth ball I was dragging my feet and it would barely reach the penalty spot. It was great for getting my fitness up and it was more fun because I was doing it with a ball. As players we called that sort of thing 'disguised running': having the ball at your feet took away the emphasis on the running part.

I don't actually remember anything that I didn't enjoy doing with Dave. He kept it interesting; it was hard work but it was varied. Whereas when I broke my foot at Huddersfield in 1998, I found myself doing rehab in the car park. It's narrow but about 400 yards long and I was with a physio going around it as fast as I could – on a pair of crutches. Now *that* I didn't enjoy. And I certainly didn't enjoy what I looked like doing it, not least because the stadium is full of windows, plenty of which look straight out on to the car park. Not great.

Dave then had the idea of packing me off to Lilleshall for a week, which at the time was the FA's football school and rehab centre. It was to take me away from the bump and grind of coming into The Cliff every day, as it meant I'd be able to hear some different voices and experience different rehabilitation techniques. Phil Newton was the resident physio and I really liked him, as well as enjoying the exercises he did with me.

I was there for five days. Mum and dad came down in the middle of the week and took me out for something to eat, because while Lilleshall is a lovely place in the middle of rural Shropshire, it is also a bit like a prison. I was there at the same time as Chris Marsden, a midfielder who's probably most well known for his stint at Southampton. He'd done his cruciate and yet was back playing after four months. Incredible. He was a lovely guy who I played a lot of head tennis with. It was a great week and I was grateful to Dave for recognising that it would benefit me.

I actually went to see a sports psychologist too, which was also Dave's doing. The guy was at Staffordshire University so I drove down but I only went once. However, I can't remember if that's because it had helped and I didn't feel the need to go back or I fucking hated it and thought it was a waste of time. Let's go with the former.

At no point throughout my rehab did I say to Dave, 'I'm not doing that.' I respected him and that meant there was no way I was going to go against anything he said. I just bowed to his superior judgement. He knew what I needed and when I needed it – and if I wanted to get back playing again, I needed to do it. That was it. In fact there were times when Dave had to say to me, 'That's enough, don't overdo it. I know you want to get out there and be quicker than everybody else but you need to bide your time.' (Apparently the experience of dealing with me made it easier for him to control Roy Keane when he did his ACL a few seasons later.)

Monday to Saturday, all the players at United were keen to help me through it. In terms of the Class of 92 lot, we'd been on a journey together and my injury came at a time when we were all really close. I might go and watch a film with them or have a game of snooker. Or they'd have a chat with me when I was lying down having my treatment, taking the piss when I was doing things that were really hard work. Every little bit helped and it was a real plus for me that I had such a good group of lads who I'd grown up with. I was just gutted that it had happened to *me*. Then again, I would never have wished it on anyone else.

It wasn't just the younger lads either: Peter Schmeichel, Gary Pallister, Paul Parker and Eric Cantona would come and have a word. Bryan Robson, Brian McClair and Dion Dublin too, because they played in the game I got injured in. They all made sure that they gave me a bit of encouragement and a bit of their time, but especially Bryan Robson. With the injuries he had over the years he spent a lot of time rehabilitating and recuperating, and he would have relied on the encouragement and backing of his team-mates – sometimes just to get through the day. He knew how important it was.

When Dave said, 'You've worked hard this week – go and have Sunday lunch somewhere with your girlfriend,' or whatever, I always took that advice. In his closing weekly speeches he'd try his best to make me forget about what I'd been doing and go and have a life. Don't get me wrong, it was great for me to be around people at the club all the time but that one day a week was precious.

There were a couple of times when I overdid it during rehab and tore some scar tissue. That's good for the long term as it eases restriction but in the short term it's painful. But that just meant Dave eased down for the following day or two until I felt alright to carry on. But I certainly don't recall having to stop because I'd pulled my hamstring, done my calf or anything like that. So my muscles were in pretty good working order, which was a bonus because it's often the case that when you're coming back from one injury, you end up getting another.

Close to the time when I was going to play my first game back after rehab, I stayed out of Dave's sight at Littleton Road, our other training facility. I persuaded one of the goalkeepers to come out with me for half an hour so that I could shoot at him from distance – bang, bang, bang, bang, bang. I was whacking balls from 30 yards and they were really flying. I could feel the effects of the strength that Dave had put back into my legs. I could never strike with the power of Becks or Scholes but I was really pinging these balls and the goalkeeper was very complimentary. It felt great.

However, I came in the next day and, lo and behold, I'd strained my kicking muscles, which prevented me being able to do a particular exercise. Dave twigged: 'Were you out there yesterday kicking balls and overdoing it?' The former physio, Jim McGregor, would have bollocked me for that but Dave just said, 'Right, well we can't do what we were going to do today so we'll have to do it another time.'

Throughout my rehab the manager was always very forthcoming with his support. He knew what it would take to get into Manchester United's first team on a regular basis and even at that point, he must have known that I wasn't going to do it. I think that devastated him, I genuinely do. Don't get me wrong, there was a personal interest in it for him because I'd been set to enhance his team and help him over a number of years. But he was gutted for me because it was a terrible injury that was never going to allow me to fulfil my potential.

He's just a tremendous man – everything he did for me, the way he stuck by me and the way he still sticks by me. There were one or two incidents where I disagreed with him or he had a go at me but nothing like the level I saw him at with other people. I'm sure he would have done if I'd given him reason to, mind you. He didn't like players bringing the game or his club into disrepute but really his main concern was the football being played. His bollockings were normally focused on a player not doing what he was supposed to do – not picking up his man from a corner, for example – and those were the times when I saw him go absolutely radio rental.

He was adamant that we should proceed with the civil action against Nicky Marker and Blackburn because, on top of witnesses, we had TV footage, which was highly unusual for that level of game (the club happened to be trialling the in-house filming of reserve games in those pre-MUTV days). He wasn't going to drag a 19-year-old kid through a court case if he didn't think there was a great chance of coming out the other side on top.

The action was for my loss of earnings as a result of the tackle, and United were covering the costs. I didn't have to get too involved but something like that takes its toll when it rumbles on for so long. And, obviously, every time we tried to get things moving, Blackburn's lawyers stalled. That's why it took the best part of five years to conclude, by which time I'd left United to join Huddersfield.

I finally got to sit down in chambers in Manchester in 1999; Steve Bruce was Huddersfield's manager at the time and he let me miss training that day. The case had gone on for so long that when we were called, I had no reason to believe that it was going to end there and then. But it did.

We were in one room and Blackburn another – but not Nicky Marker as far as I'm aware. An arbitrator flitted between the two rooms, with Blackburn's offer starting on the low side and ours on the higher side. After a whole day of this going back and forth, the offer had crept up. My brief asked what I wanted to do. He was quite prepared to carry on but he could see that it was draining me.

He was called David Stockdale QC and he was brilliant, as you can imagine: Man United were footing the bill so they got the best. He was full of compliments for the way I handled myself and could understand why, at that stage, I said, 'Listen, considering what I might have to go through and the length of time it might take, with all of this hanging over not just me but my family as well, can we just go for it?' So I took their offer. I was relieved.

And I know for a fact that Blackburn were *mightily* relieved. They knew that I could have gone on and got fucking millions; other people at United who've been in a similar situation have ended up with a lot more. But as far as I was concerned I was still playing, I was at a First Division club and I'd had enough. The final settlement was nowhere near a million but it was more money than I could ever have dreamed of, miles away on the horizon in terms of my career to that point.

A large part of why I was still playing for a First Division club five years after my injury was Dave Fevre. He was exceptionally good – and good for me. When he spoke to us for the book he said, 'I latched on to Ben straight away and I could see that his attitude was so good – he was a physio's delight because he wanted to work. But some of that frustration of being on the cusp of the first team before the injury meant there was an aggressive side to him. And I even see it in him now: he's still ambitious and there's a nagging doubt that something was taken away from him.'

I can't speak highly enough of the job Dave did to get me through that summer. But he's right: I did go through a phase where I was extremely angry. Not that I was threatening to do anything untoward, I just needed calming down and reassuring. I was still a teenager, after all. Even now I have a more aggressive personality than I did before my injury. Lesley will tell you: I'm a snappy fucker. And I mean really, really snappy. She is an angel for the stuff she has to put up with at times. Times when I'm not even thinking and being reckless: slamming stuff down, smashing drawers closed, trying to get a knife out of the little fucking tray in the dishwasher.

I'd always been angry on the pitch anyway, always shouting a lot – and it didn't take much. It still doesn't, as you'd see if you were to ever get in a car with me when I'm driving. People say I've got little-man syndrome but it's got nothing to do with that; I just believe in sticking up for myself. Though you can't go round speaking badly to people without it coming back to bite you on the arse one day. That's why, as much as I can be loud, I always try to help people rather than hinder them. Because I firmly believe that one day something really good will come out of what happened with my knee, that will see me able to live the rest of my life in relative comfort physically, mentally, financially, socially – however you want to look at it. It hasn't happened yet but I'm sure it will (and if it doesn't you can call me a liar).

Anyway, my first game back after rehab was against Oldham Athletic's B team, 17 September 1994, at Littleton Road; I came on as sub to line up alongside the likes of Michael Clegg, Ronnie Wallwork, Paul Heckingbottom and Philip Mulryne. We won 2-0. I was back playing after less than six months and that was pretty good, because for cruciate injuries you're talking anything from six months to a year. I was crap, mind.

I was nervous, too. I was eager to get on with it but there was trepidation. I went from being ecstatic about completing my rehabilitation without any major hiccups to shitting myself about playing again. I wanted to get out there but then all sorts of questions, none of them positive, started going around my head: 'How are you going to feel? Are you in anywhere-near decent condition? Are you going be as good as you were six months ago? Are you going to worry when somebody tackles you? Are you going to worry when somebody comes anywhere *near* you?'

Yet the thought of playing trumped anything else that was whizzing around up there. I wanted to get back out on the pitch – I *had* to get back out on the pitch. That's what I was there for and that's what I was being paid to do. And I knew that, not long ago, football was something I'd actually been quite good at. But that was the other thing: I was expecting too much too soon and that made me anxious. I wanted to prove to myself that the rehabilitation had worked and I could get myself back to an acceptable level, ready to play professional football. Eventually I did but it took longer than I wanted.

The physiotherapy didn't stop once I was back playing because Dave presented me with exercises that he said I should do for the rest of my playing career. I did everything he told me to do (apart from hamstring curls because I hate them) in an effort to avoid having to go through an ACL replacement while I was still playing. I used the Cybex as often as I could as well, and I'd ask Dave to come and test me on it. He was always obliging. But in general he took a step back once I'd started playing again. He was always interested in how I'd got on but he didn't need a running commentary on every game.

Obviously, at some point, somebody must have tackled me for the first time since my injury once I was back, but to be honest I can't remember who it was or what team we were playing. I do remember being happy once it had happened though because it meant it was out of the way. And the more time went on, the less being tackled bothered me – in fact I used to love people trying to kick me. It improved my game because I knew that I needed to be quick enough to get out of the way.

That's one thing dad always used to say: that I had a knack for being able to shift at the last minute and not get caught. To be fair there wasn't a lot I could do about the Nicky Marker tackle. But many's the year, from when I was a kid to when the damn thing happened, that I was able to ride tackles – exactly the same way Giggsy used to. At the last minute I could flick the ball away and make the opposing player look stupid.

I know I came up against Nicky Marker again at some point too, in a reserve game. He played centre-half that day, rather than right-back as he did in that 1994 game, so we never came into direct contact with each other. We didn't shake hands or communicate with each other but that was as far as it went. I wasn't going to be Roy Keane to his Alf-Inge Haaland; violence just isn't my forte. I've never thrown a punch in anger at anybody and, at the age of 43, I'm quite proud of that.

Yes, I was bitter about the tackle and, to a certain extent, I still am. I don't think anybody would blame me for that but there was no point dwelling on it because it would have eaten me up from the inside. So what I tried to do was make the best of it. And when I realised that I was going to be able to play again, I started to rebuild. While you're still playing you tend to forget about what might have been because you're still trying to establish what could be.

My first goal after coming back was in the final of an end-of-season tournament in Bellinzona, which is a beautiful part of Switzerland. I scored the winner right at the end of the game. I was one of two overage players who were allowed to feature and I actually asked Jim Ryan if I could go. I think Sir Alex thought it was a good idea; he probably felt that it would help my confidence to play against lads who were younger than me.

Though to be honest, I didn't start getting excited about football matches again until the following season. My mood wasn't helped by the fact that before we left for the summer, the manager had a go at me about my weight. He said, 'I know you've had a difficult time of it but you need to concentrate on getting that down before I'll even consider you for the first team.' I said, 'I know and believe me, I'm trying.' And he said, 'Well you need to fucking try harder.' He was only trying to help me and he probably felt like he'd exhausted the softly-softly approach. I needed to take responsibility because I was back on my own two feet trying to play a professional game.

So over that summer Brian Kidd gave me a programme to follow. He asked me what dates my holiday was booked for, told me to do nothing for those two weeks and then get on with it. He told me to come back a week before the rest of the players so he could meet me to go running and various different things. Then when the new season started I was doing extra work with him before and after training on Mondays, Wednesdays and Fridays. I'd meet him at 9.30am to go and do eight laps of Littleton Road, just at a normal leisurely pace, before all the other lads started turning up. Afterwards I'd join up with him again and we'd do little short, sharp bursts of exercise.

After a while, everyone could see the difference in me.

6

The house visit
1988

Ben: It was a winter's night in late 1988. My parents knew we had guests coming over but they were keeping schtum about who it was. All they'd tell me was, 'We need you to be here.' And I went, 'But it's Friday night!' It's not that they didn't allow me to see my friends during the week but I'd be training; Friday was the only night that I didn't do any because I'd be playing for Salford Boys the next morning. Then I said, 'Am I in trouble?' No, I wasn't in trouble. 'Then this is weird.' And I could see that they were both smirking.

Jeff Kerfoot: We were mates from first year. From our very first games lesson I appreciated how good he was at football and I think the feeling was mutual (in the early days I had a bit of a talent but I never burst into any teams). We just got talking and that was it really. Ben was outstanding, obviously; nobody else on our team got a look-in. He used to live and breathe football so if you were a pal of his, you did the same. He wanted to win at everything. We'd play table tennis at his house and if he lost, that was it, the night was ruined.

Me, my dad and my grandad were all City fans – and there weren't many of us around in Salford at that time, by the way. My dad's still an old-school City fan so he's got no time for United, apart from when Ben started there because he made an exception to go and watch his matches. I did the same – with a big woolly hat on so that no one would recognise me.

Ben: In the semi-final of the English Schools National Trophy at Old Trafford there was a picture taken of the crowd and Jeff's dad, wearing a Pringle sweater with bright pink and blue diamonds on it, is right at the forefront. He's at Old Trafford supporting me playing for Salford Boys.

If it was a choice between Man City and coming to watch me, Jeff's dad would come to watch me every time. And then there's his mum, who is a real softie but a tough cookie; we have the same birthday and we clicked straight away. They've housed me since I was 11 years old and even if I turned up on their doorstep now, there would be a bed for me if I needed it.

Jeff Kerfoot: Ben and I would often spend Friday nights at each other's houses. In later years it was to watch the WWF wrestling on Sky; it sounds a bit embarrassing now but as teenagers, that was the thing. We used to have a houseful watching it.

Hannah Scott (née Thornley): Our house was the house that everybody came to.

Rod Thornley: All my mates as well.

Hannah Scott: Just generally. The door was open.

Philip Thornley: It was a doss house.

Hannah Scott: Everybody used to pop their head around the door, 'Hiya Liz, you OK?'

Rod Thornley: You could have a proper football match in the back garden because it was that big. You could have four vs four and we did, many times. It was great, wasn't it?

Hannah Scott: It was really good.

Philip Thornley: One day they were playing and Gary Neville let fly at the net, missed and broke our lounge window.

Ben: Did he only break the one?

Elizabeth Thornley: It was about an hour before we were supposed to go on holiday.

Philip Thornley: He could never keep a ball down, Gary Neville.

Rod Thornley: It was a good strike though. I used to nick volleyballs from the leisure centre I worked in and they were brilliant for that game because they were light and would move all over the place. But also, in theory, they were light enough to not smash windows. Yet somehow Gaz managed to smash a window with one.

Gary Neville: If a house's window hasn't been broken by a football, it's not been lived in.

Ben: Anyway, on this particular night I was still getting wound up by mum and dad so I said: 'There's obviously something going on here so you're going to have to go and get Jeff. If I can't stay at his like I'm supposed to tonight, he'll have to stay here.' So they went and got him and on the trip back, explained what was going on. I still had no idea.

Jeff Kerfoot: Phil and Liz were like a second mum and dad with the amount of time I spent at their house. We had lots of good nights and they were very hospitable; they're good people and they looked after me. But when they briefed me about what was going on that night I was like, 'Oh, right. Really? Is this a wind-up or what?'

Ben: They made me put on a pair of trousers and a shirt. Then, at about 7pm, the doorbell went. I was thinking, 'This has got to be what this is all about.' My mum made me wait in the living room while my dad went and answered the front door. That meant something had to be going on because nobody ever came to our front door. *Ever.* Everyone would come in via the back door, which meant you could see who was coming as they walked past our big bay window. Not on this occasion.

But the next thing I heard was this broad Manchester accent and I thought, 'That's fucking Brian Kidd, that.'

Philip Thornley: Previously we'd got this invitation from Brian Kidd over the phone: 'Would you like to come down for a match at Old Trafford?' So we did and when Liz got out of the car in the car park opposite the ground, Alex Ferguson saw us. He came out of his office and as he was crossing the road to greet us, Liz whispered, 'Who's that?'

Elizabeth Thornley: I expected him to be taller.

Philip Thornley: And there was another kid hanging around that day: David Beckham was there with his mother.

David Beckham: Actually, one of the main things I remember from that day is seeing this really good-looking tanned kid with really great hair – Ben.

Philip Thornley: We all went in and had a look around, watched the game and came home. It was a couple of weeks later that I got the phone call from Brian saying, 'Can we come over and have a chat?'

Ben: Next thing, I heard the manager's voice. With that my mum couldn't keep me down and I went haring out into the hallway, Jeff in tow. I was gobsmacked. My heart was pounding. Even Jeff, a mad City fan, couldn't believe that Alex Ferguson and Brian Kidd were in our house.

Jeff Kerfoot: I could remember my dad talking about Brian Kidd playing at City so that's what I was nervous about, more than meeting Ferguson.

Elizabeth Thornley: I definitely made tea. With cups and saucers.

Philip Thornley: And there was cake, I remember.

Jeff Kerfoot: I stayed out of the way while they were chatting. I was just sat there thinking, 'You're better off at City really, aren't you?'

Ben: I didn't want to sign schoolboy forms with anyone and as far as I can see, that's why Alex Ferguson and Brian Kidd turned up at my house. They probably thought, 'We need to convince this lad that he wants to come to Man United.'

I didn't want to sign anything because I didn't want to be restricted. If I'd signed schoolboy forms with Man United I couldn't have gone anywhere else. That would be it. Locked in. But it worked both ways: if I was good enough they'd still want me when I was 16 anyway; if it turned out I wasn't, they'd be glad that they weren't beholden to me.

It was an absolute dream for Man United to come in and say they wanted to tie me up to a contract at 13 but I just didn't want to do it. There was no way I was signing anything. But after that meeting I just thought, 'I cannot play mind games with the manager of Manchester United. I can't do it because I love the club and this guy really, really wants me.'

Philip Thornley: Ben wasn't there for the whole conversation because we sent him up to his room with Jeff. Alex wasn't on the hard sell though, he just wanted to say that they were interested and that if Ben was interested, they would love to have him. There was no mention of enticements or anything like that.

And apparently he had this thing whereby he wanted to see the mother of any young player he was thinking of signing. Not for any ulterior motive but because from the height and size of the mother, he could get a guide as to how big her son would be. So that was why he wanted the whole family there: so he could weigh Liz up.

Elizabeth Thornley: I couldn't tell what he was saying half the time.

Ben: What was ultimately agreed was that I would join their school of excellence and if they drew up something for when I left school, they had my word that I would not sign for anybody else. But they had to respect my decision that I wouldn't sign anything with them until 8 July 1991. They guaranteed me four years at United from when I was 16 and the only other person who got the same deal was David Beckham; Sir Alex himself told me that later on.

Jeff Kerfoot: Ben took it quite well for something as big as that. He was obviously excited but I don't remember him shouting, 'I'm going to be playing for Manchester United!' or anything like that. He was alright about it rather than being massively over the top.

Ben: I was probably one of the last of the Class of 92 to be recruited. There would have been a network of people that Sir Alex got hold of and said, 'I don't just want to know the best boy in your street or on your estate: I want the best boy in your village, town or city.' I don't know how much of a rarity it is for managers to pop round for a cup of tea but I'd like to think it wouldn't have been something he would have done for just anyone, especially at the age I was.

Jeff Kerfoot: As they were leaving, Ben's mum said to Ferguson, 'Oh, this is Jeff by the way and he's a City fan.' Brian Kidd just started laughing but Ferguson spoke to me. From when I was a young boy my dad always said, 'Firm handshake, look them in the eye and you'll never forget their name.' That stayed with me. So I really concentrated on what he was saying and I could just about understand him when he said: 'Aye, well we'll have to take you to Wythenshawe Hospital and give you a blood transfusion so that we can turn that blue blood to red.'

Ben: So yeah, it was a surreal evening.

Jeff Kerfoot: When I got home the next day my dad was made up that I'd met Brian Kidd – Ferguson, not so much.

7

Manchester United
1995–98

1995/96

Before the season kicked off we headed to Kuala Lumpur to play a couple of friendlies and I was buzzing about going. We were originally heading for South Africa before Dennis Roach (agent to Dennis Wise among others) convinced his friend Martin Edwards – United's chairman at the time – to go to the Far East instead. More money in it. But I believe Sir Alex's wife had family in South Africa so when that trip was kyboshed he said he wasn't going.

And because the manager wasn't going, me, Gaz, Becks and Casp decided we were safe to go out in Manchester the night before we flew. We bumped into Keith Fane that night, who used to be the stadium announcer at United and was a bit like Peter Stringfellow: he surrounded himself with strippers and Page 3 girls. Before we knew it we were back at his house partying with all these women. Nothing like that had ever happened to us. And I'm just trying to work out which ex-girlfriend I'll be upsetting with that story ...

Anyway, afterwards the lads came back to my parents' place; they'd all left their bags there ready to go to the airport. We got back at 5am and as we looked towards the house we saw my dad hanging out of the window reading his book, enjoying the tweeting of the birds and the sunrise. Lovely. Except he was stark bollock naked. 'Morning lads, have you had a good night?' With that he came downstairs, not bothering to put anything on, and waved us through the door. From strippers to that. Memorable night.

After our first match in Kuala Lumpur we were told we wouldn't be training till 5pm the next day and so had permission to have a night out. Just down the road from our hotel was the Hard Rock Cafe. We figured if there was going to be anything happening, it would be in there. We walked in and it was dead but we didn't know anywhere else so we stayed put.

We had something to eat and a few drinks before deciding to head back. Next came a moment like that advert where everyone turns to watch a bevy of beautiful women dressed in red walking through the airport: all these Virgin Atlantic stewardesses came pouring in. Everyone's birthdays and Christmases had come at once. I can't remember exactly how many of them there were but there were enough. We were on our way out, they came through the doors, we met in the middle and it all went 'Pow, pow, pow!' like an airbomb repeater.

And I don't know how many players flew Virgin that evening but I certainly did.

Now, Paul Parker didn't end up with a stewardess but he did end up with someone, and she took him back to hers. The next day we were downstairs at the hotel ready for training, all feeling like shit in the stifling humidity. Then one of the senior players says: 'Has anybody seen Parks?'

It turned out he'd got into bed with this girl and then sparked out till God knows when. By the time he woke up, she'd gone to work. He was in the middle of Kuala Lumpur, a sprawling city, with not a clue where he was – and he couldn't get out of the apartment. So he had to ring this woman to get her to come back and release him. As our coach pulled up to take us to the training ground he came screeching up in a taxi and legged it into the hotel to get his training kit on.

While we're on the subject of nights out, an important factor in United's success in the 90s was the dedication to 'team meetings'. We always started off at the Barton Arms in Worsley of an afternoon before wending our way into Manchester. The date would be set a month in advance so the entire squad had to show up. 'The missus won't let me' or 'I've got to do something with the kids' just did not wash. There were hefty fines.

I was an integral part of proceedings because I was in charge of the kitty; fucking Gaz volunteered me when Steve Bruce was recruiting. On the plus side, I didn't have to pay for my drink and whatever was left in the pot at the end of the night was mine. By that stage nobody cared how much it was and to be fair, if multimillionaires had started quibbling over a few quid I would have volleyed it straight down the bar and suggested they go and find it.

The downside was, obviously, the amount of time I had to spend fetching drinks. I'd have team-mates screaming at me: 'Where's my fucking beer?' The worst ones for that were Roy Keane (this was before he stopped drinking), Brucey and definitely Gary Pallister. But Pally did it in a nice way; Keaney and Brucey would bang their fists on the table. Then you'd get Denis Irwin saying, 'Leave the lad alone, he's doing his best.' Then it would come back: 'Well it's not fucking good enough.' I'd just leave them to get on with it.

In my favour was the fact that the longer the night went on, the fewer people there were so the fewer drinks I had to remember. I had no choice but to stay so I always insisted that someone from my lot (which was never Gaz, by the way) stayed with me to help. And I had to make sure that I stayed compos mentis, because the person who's in charge of the kitty can't be arseholed.

But I felt privileged to be there with those guys. Never mind playing football with them, now I was out having a laugh with them. And the manager knew about these meetings so we weren't going to get into any trouble. Although what we were doing couldn't be done now; we weren't in a private room and there was no security.

Back then it wasn't unusual to see players on a night out so people, by and large, left us alone.

There were other nights out too, involving us younger lads. Sometimes on Wednesdays we'd go to JW Johnson's on Deansgate. It was a bar and restaurant (they did an unbelievable rack of lamb), with a soul nightclub downstairs. The question around 10.30pm was always: 'Are we going downstairs?' As it happens, it's where we were in 1995 when we found out about Eric doing his kung-fu kick.

Gaz used to organise these nights. Then, once we were out, he didn't want confrontation so it was always me he looked to, not because I could fight but because I'd reassure him. Whenever I did he'd reply, 'Yeah, but you would say that because you're a Salford meathead.' Becks would always be there, more often than not Chris Casper and sometimes Mark Rawlinson. We used to stay over at my mum and dad's house afterwards; they were all more than welcome to get in bed with me if they wanted but they preferred to brave the floor.

In Johnson's they used to encourage girls to dance on the bar. One night a girl got up there and made a beeline for me; she looked like Bruce Willis's girlfriend in *Pulp Fiction*, only prettier. The bar staff started spraying whipped cream around and Gaz said, 'Ben, you've got to get up there.' So I did. Only at the time I was going out with a girl called Kim (who was the spit of Pamela Anderson) and a friend of her brother saw me do it – and disappear into the club with this girl. (Which was strange because once I'd had a few drinks, I thought I was invisible.)

I got to Kim's house the next day and when her parents and brother came home, not one of them spoke to me. Kim said, 'What's all that about?' At that point I had no idea but once she went and asked, it suddenly all became a lot clearer. I went home and she then got the full low-down on what I'd been doing the previous night. Oh my God.

I had the number of this girl from Johnson's so I phoned her to try and sort it out. She said, 'I won't stitch you up, don't worry.'

Now, yes, we'd had a kiss and a cuddle downstairs – and, football cliché alert, it was in a fucking toilet cubicle – but she said, 'No one actually saw us doing anything, apart from what we did on the bar, which was just a bit of fun.' So that was that. And I was forgiven. Just.

Back then I didn't care though: I saw one girl and then I saw another. Kim, for example, was really lovely, it's just that I was an arsehole. I finished with her when I met another girl at the end of 1995. I was out with Becks around Christmas time and we were in the midst of a phase of going to different student nights. I met this girl, Catherine, who didn't live far away from me; I told her I was with somebody else but that I wasn't planning on it going much further. That said, on Boxing Day I left Kim's house and went straight to Catherine's. As I mentioned: arsehole. Catherine was a great girl too but again, it didn't work out between us because I was horrible (more on which later).

There was another night when me and Becks decided to go out and it was my turn to drive. I'd just bought a Renault Clio Williams, which was a blue car with gold wheels. Anyway, Becks ended up the worse for wear. The night had finished and we were halfway down the East Lancs Road because I was driving him back to Worsley. But he couldn't take his eyes off my dashboard: the back of it was blue, the dials were white and there were all sorts of lights. It must have sent him doolally because suddenly he piped up: 'Ben, pull over, I'm going to throw up.'

The truth is, nights out tended to be with fellow players because football is an antisocial job. The evenings when friends might be going out somewhere, you can't because you've got a game to play that night or the next day. You also play at Christmas, Easter and New Year. And in July and August you're in for pre-season and the season itself, so your summer holiday doesn't coincide with school summer holidays. People don't give top-flight footballers any sympathy for that because of the amount of money we can earn and I get that. It's the sacrifice you make. But it's still shit.

The downtime that I did have – in the afternoon after training, for example – I should have made the most of with something fulfilling. I could have been taking my coaching badges or doing a course completely unconnected with football. But I didn't and that's because a) the motivation wasn't there and b) I was young and assumed I was going to be playing football until I was 72.

You should always listen to people who have been there ahead of you, like your parents – but, at times, you don't. I've been trying to tell my 14-year-old son Lucas that because he's got no concept of it. I want to shake him and say, 'You need to listen because I didn't!' I wasn't disobedient and I didn't do it deliberately, I just didn't think that it applied to me. But it did and it does. I had time to add many more strings to my bow but I sacked it off. That disappoints me.

Anyway, football. As the 1995/96 season proper started I was trying to get back to being happy with the way I was playing. I needed to feel like a man in a man's game again, rather than a little boy. I played a match in the reserves before getting some more game time for the first team on 23 August. It was against West Ham again but at Old Trafford this time. It was the game when Marco Boogers got sent off for a horrendous lunge on Gaz; he came on in the 73rd minute and was off in the 88th. We won 2-1. I wasn't expecting to be in the first team again that soon, though I was only on for the last six minutes. What I really needed was what came next.

I already knew that the idea of sending me out on loan was in the manager's head. We'd recently played a friendly behind closed doors and unbeknown to me, Shrewsbury Town were there to watch because they wanted to take me. After the game the manager came into the dressing room and, pointing at me, said, 'You! Do you not like fucking running?' It ended up being the worst bollocking I ever got from him. And it was because he was embarrassed that he'd invited somebody to come and watch me and had to say, 'Sorry about that, he was fucking useless.' Apparently they left at half-time; Shrewsbury isn't the easiest place to get to, to be fair.

So yeah, I didn't go on loan to Shrewsbury. However, in the November of that season I did go on loan to Stockport, who were in what was then the Second Division. Their manager, Dave Jones, came in for me and Sir Alex said, 'It's not far for you to travel so why don't you give it a whirl?'

It was a culture shock. You had to wash your own kit – though that didn't bother me – and we didn't get anything to eat, whereas at United I'd got used to a canteen. But the worst thing was the timekeeping. At United you knew that training started at 10.30am sharp but at Stockport you could be taken aback and start at 10am or sit around not doing much and not be out until 11am. I hated that. It's about being professional.

In one of my first games for Stockport we won 3-1 down at Twerton Park in Bath, where Bristol Rovers were based for ten years before they moved to the Memorial Stadium. It was a muddy shithole of a pitch and it never stopped raining. But at one point I found myself on the right-hand side of the area as the ball came over from the left. I controlled it – or, rather, miscontrolled it but it looked like I'd intentionally flummoxed the guy marking me – span around and belted it into the far corner with my right foot.

That was my first professional goal and it won me Granada goal of the month. When they gave me the award they got me out on Stockport's pitch to try and re-enact the goal – but I never got close. I miscontrolled it plenty of times though.

A couple of my biggest regrets are that I never scored for Man United's first team and that I never scored anywhere near as many goals as my early years indicated I might. I was quite prolific when I was in United's youth team and I didn't do too badly in the reserves either. But whatever team I played in, I should have been hitting double figures. It still eats away at me. Arsehole.

My mum and dad came down to watch me play for Stockport in our game away to Brighton on New Year's Day. Unfortunately they came a long way to see me play like a twat and get substituted. It's the first time I can remember being taken off because I was having a poor game. I was more gutted for mum and dad than I was for me.

I had Chris Marsden for company at Stockport – the guy I'd rehabbed with at Lilleshall – and then there was Sean Connelly, who was a super lad. He's still in football with the Welsh squad and Cardiff City as head physio. I remember him pulling me to one side after a couple of training sessions and saying, 'We're buzzing to have you but what the fuck are you doing in this division?' It never occurred to me at the time but why would it? I was 20 years old and I wanted to play.

Mike Flynn was captain and he always ended up starting arguments whenever we were allowed to drink booze on the coach during long journeys back from away games. When Mike started up, Sean, down at the back, would say to me, 'Come here mate, sit with me and let this play out.' Sean hated it when Flynny got like that and he did it all the time. It wasn't too bad when we'd won but if we'd lost he'd really start laying into people.

I was originally slated to be at Stockport for a month but then Dave Jones asked to extend it to two. However, that got cut short when he left me out of the starting line-up for a game against Burnley and Alex Ferguson went ballistic. As a one-off Jones had allowed me to travel in my own car rather than on the team coach (I can't remember why I needed to) but I got stuck in traffic. I contacted him to say I'd still be there in time for the warm-up but to spite me for being late he put me on the subs bench, then only played me for five minutes. Sir Alex went nuts. I got a message from Brian Kidd to be back at The Cliff for the Monday morning and that was that.

Talking of Kiddo, we tried everything to get hold of him for the book but, unfortunately, we never heard back from him. As I understand it, he has had offers to speak about different things in his career – scoring a goal in the European Cup Final at 19, for example – and has always declined, so perhaps that's what stopped him from doing it. He's also a member of Manchester City's backroom staff these days so perhaps they were steering him away from doing it? Who knows.

I certainly hope it wasn't anything personal because I've never had a problem with Kiddo. In fact, he was an integral part of my time at the club, so it would have been a real privilege for me if he could have got involved and said a few words. It's a real shame that he couldn't but such is life.

I'd only been back a couple of weeks when the manager told me about Huddersfield's loan approach. I was keen: it was a step up from Stockport because Huddersfield were only a division below United, plus they'd recently moved into a new stadium. The training facilities weren't great but the stadium had huge dressing rooms and nice showers, and everything got washed for you. An elderly couple, Jean and Brian, used to do all the laundry and also made sandwiches that you could buy for lunch. You'd order what you wanted in the morning and it would be wrapped up with your name on a sticker when you came back after training.

I instantly felt at home. I loved the manager, Brian Horton, and I could see I was going to be happy there. There were characters in the dressing room too, like Ronnie Jepson. He took to me straight away. Then there was Lee Sinnott, otherwise known as Sinbad, who used to room with a guy called Darren Bullock (he was the only one who would) when we went on away trips. One time someone said, 'Is anybody going to call Bully down for his meal?' Sinbad replied, 'No, it's alright, I just chucked a bunch of bananas through the door.'

He used to call Bully a gorilla: he had long arms, he was a stocky fucker and he was only small. He was rough as a bear's arse and he had a proper West Country accent that didn't go with his frame because he sounded far too effeminate. Bully was also legendary for working out which games he needed to get booked in to miss the Boxing Day fixture and anything that fell over New Year, so that he could have the time off. This was in the days when you didn't serve your suspension straight away, so it took some working out and Bully was no academic. And if there were two games over New Year? He'd make sure he got a red.

What I loved about Brian Horton was that he was honest and would tell you what he thought of you. I'd come from Man United but, quite rightly, he treated me the same as the others. As much as he praised me, both in training and in matches, he slaughtered me when I did stupid things – like getting sent off. Twice.

The first one was at Roker Park against Sunderland. The referee, Neil Barry, had been annoying me throughout the whole of the first half. Just prior to sending me off he'd given a decision, a throw-in or a free kick, that should have been in my favour. Then the next time the ball came to me, a lad tried to step across me and committed a blatant foul – but Barry didn't give that either. The ball went up in the air and while it was there, he blew for half-time. So, naturally, when it came back down I caught it and chucked it at him. He couldn't wait to get his card out of his pocket.

I was having a really good game as well. We were drawing 1-1 with the league leaders and even went 2-1 up while I was sat in the dressing room. With 15 minutes to go I was thinking, 'I'm going to get away with this, I'm going to get away with this ...' Then Michael Bridges, who was just starting out as a 17-year-old kid, came on as a sub and scored twice in the last eight minutes to give them a 3-2 win.

Everyone came into the dressing room at full time to find me in the corner, hanging my head. When Brian had run out of things to say he pointed at me and said, 'Forget all that, just blame that fucking idiot there.' I felt terrible because I was only there on loan and I didn't want everyone to think that I didn't care.

My other red card came when we were playing Portsmouth in the last game of the season and they needed to win to stay up (which they did, 1-0). We got into a bit of a melee right at the end that involved Fitzroy Simpson, who had been kicking people all game – and, of course, he was ex-Man City. So I saw my chance and wellied him, a right whack on the back of the calf, in full view of the referee. He had no hesitation.

That night we had our end-of-season party and my girlfriend Catherine was there. Brian Horton came over and said to her, 'Ben's been absolutely great for us but I don't know how you do it – he's a fucking idiot.' Sir Alex bollocked me for those red cards too, fining me both times. Though he said he could sort of let me off the second one because it was Fitz (who I get on really well with now).

There were games I played for Huddersfield where I *didn't* get sent off though. I scored a header in my second match for the club when we got beaten 3-2 by Derby at the Baseball Ground. In the next game we won 1-0 at home to Luton and afterwards Ronnie Jepson – proper old school, was Ronnie – came up to me and said, 'You're far too good for this level.' I think at one point during that game I danced around three or four players and emerged with the ball. Ronnie said he stood there and thought, 'It's a long time since I played with anybody like that.'

A few games later we were away to Barnsley; it was a Yorkshire derby and Barnsley were doing really well. At the time they played with wing-backs and they had a lad on the right-hand side called Nicky Eaden. Brian said to me, 'Listen, we know you like to go forward but you need to keep an eye on him because he's scored a few goals this season.'

They had a corner in the first two minutes. It was cleared so I went haring off up the field – but the ball came straight back. And who did it go straight to? Nicky Eaden. He was right on the corner of the area, took one step and battered it into the bottom corner. Fuck. Fortunately he didn't score again but I had an absolute shitter and we ended up losing 3-0. Brian wiped the floor with me.

We were on course for the play-offs until we lost eight of our last 13 games (though I missed three of those through suspension, don't forget). Then Brian Horton tried to sign me at the end of the season but Sir Alex said no. Actually, I think he set the fee a little too high because he wanted me to stay, knowing that Huddersfield wouldn't pay what he was asking. Then he offered me a new contract for another two years.

I signed it because I let my heart rule my head. I wish I'd been more insistent about making the move happen there and then because I could have made more of my career. I'm not blaming Sir Alex but there was no reason for me to go back to United to play in the reserves when I now knew I could cut it at First Division level. In those two seasons I could have had another 70 games under my belt and maybe that would have provided a route back into the Premier League. Who knows.

But I stayed. That's why, in my head, I've written off 1996 to 1998. I wasn't strong enough.

I couldn't take any enjoyment from United winning the Double that season because I didn't play any part in it. I went to the Cup Final but I wasn't involved in any celebrations afterwards. Part of me was thinking, 'That could have been me.' Another part of me was thinking, 'I wish I could have been elsewhere and supporting the team as a fan.' That would have made it easier.

Not long after that I got a letter through the post with the three-lions stamp on the envelope. My first thought: 'Am I in trouble?' But the letter said I'd been selected for the England under-21s and I'd be flying out for the Toulon Tournament at the end of May. A few days earlier Becks had told me he was going so I rang him and said, 'See you there.' There was a pause while the penny dropped. 'Oh, you've been picked too!'

A lot of the names in that squad, barring Becks and a couple of others, had been drafted in because clubs didn't want their players taking part; it was an end-of-season tournament that didn't mean anything. But their loss was my gain. The moment I got my call-up, it didn't matter that it was by default; you have to take your chance when it's offered to you. I was over the moon. And it would never have come about if I'd been playing for United's reserves – I got myself noticed at Stockport and Huddersfield.

The under-21s manager was Dave Sexton, whose reputation took a bit of a beating when he was in charge at United during the late 70s. But I thought he was great. He was a bit like your grandad;

you often felt like giving him a Werther's Original. He loved his football and he knew how to treat people. He was a real gentleman.

The coach was Graham Rix, who went on to serve time as a sex offender. He'd been at Arsenal, he'd been at Chelsea and he was a bit of a cockney wide boy – the total opposite of Dave Sexton. I found him to be a nice guy and he and Sexton clicked as a pairing. In other news, our press officer was Clare Tomlinson, the Sky Sports News presenter.

Apart from me, Becks and Terry Cooke, all from Man United, some of the other lads in that squad were:

- Chris Day: He was the goalkeeper when we knocked Spurs out of the Youth Cup in 1992; loudmouth cockney, nice lad.
- Andy Marshall: Another goalkeeper. When Norwich played Huddersfield once he told me that if anybody wanted to give Craig Bellamy a kick, none of the Norwich lads would bat an eyelid.
- Chris Holland: He was the guy who had ammonia sprayed in his eye in a nightclub and came close to going blind as a result. I ended up playing with him at Huddersfield. Lovely lad.
- Ian Moore: His dad is Ronnie Moore, the manager. Nice lad, very quiet – Ian that is, not Ronnie.
- John O'Connor: He was at Everton and he was young – younger than us anyway. Nice lad, defender.
- Steve Slade: Not my cup of tea.
- Michael Brown: Nutcase, great lad.
- Lee Bowyer: Not my cup of tea either.
- Richard Rufus: He was alright but less so in Bowyer's company (they were both at Charlton at the time). He went on to become a born-again Christian, then masterminded a £16m Ponzi scheme.

We didn't win the tournament – nor were we expected to – but I loved the experience, helped by the fact that I played well. Steve Slade scored to make it 1-0 in our first game against Belgium, then Angola beat us 2-0 (but I didn't play in that game). Then we lost to

Portugal 3-1, with Nuno Gomes and Dani playing. Dani was giving it loads and was horrible but having said that, he's probably the best-looking footballer I've ever seen. He just defied belief.

Then we lost 2-1 against Brazil and went out but that was probably my best game. Getting to play against them was phenomenal. Archie Macpherson, the Scottish commentator, was working that game for Eurosport. My mum and dad told me afterwards that he'd said how much he loved me as a player but wished I'd keep my mouth shut because it was going to get me into all sorts of trouble.

1996/97

My mentality during the summer was to keep myself ticking over, get back to United and give myself a chance. I must admit, at some point I was expecting the manager to send me back out on loan but it never happened. As such, most of my games that season were with the reserves – and then I had another season of that to endure. That was tough to take for two years but I got my head down and got on with it.

I was on the bench for the first team a fair few times that season, including games against Liverpool, Arsenal and Nottingham Forest. Whenever I was a substitute at any club after Man United I was pretty confident that I would get on the field at some stage; at United it was a real surprise if I did. Whereas in the reserves that season, I started every game I played. That was good for me because while I wasn't having the best time of it mentally, physically I was OK. I made 16 appearances and scored four goals; one in four, can't argue with that. We won the Pontins League that season too.

I was on the bench for the first team when we played at Fenerbahçe in the Champions League in October. It was when Jay-Jay Okocha gave Denis Irwin a torrid time and the bugger on the tannoy never shut up, constantly trying to incite the crowd. On the flight home, Kiddo came down the plane to tell Phil Neville and me that we would be playing in a friendly at Barry Town the next day. That was the first we'd heard of it. So after a four-hour flight, which didn't land until about 4am, we then had to leave Old Trafford at 10am for a four-hour coach journey to Wales. I don't think I had a great game.

Six days later I played against Swindon in the League Cup. It was my first start for the first team and it was brilliant to walk out at Old Trafford as part of the starting line-up, but I will always remember that game for missing a sitter. I put it over the bar from Gary Neville's cross when I was five yards from an open goal. I can't blame a bobble; I should have scored. It was atrocious. It was like, 'How have I missed that?' The last action of the game was me smacking the ball into the advertising hoardings, which was frustration at not scoring. I didn't care that we'd won 2-1. Purely and simply, I'd had a chance to score and maybe that would have seen me start the next game. I felt like I'd blown it. Rubbish. Fucking rubbish.

Still, it wasn't as bad as Ronnie Rosenthal's miss for Liverpool in 1992. That provides a crumb of comfort.

I was sub again three days later for our league game at Southampton. Whenever you were named on the bench you knew that you'd be warming up Peter Schmeichel. Pressure, trust me. However, on this occasion it was going well and the final thing Peter wanted me to do was hit half-volleys at him from the edge of the box. I'd done it enough times to have a routine: he'd bowl the ball out to me and I'd catch it, put my head down and not even look at him when I struck it.

So there I was: catch the ball, head down, bang; catch the ball, head down, bang. I was conscious that Peter was getting a few jibes from the Southampton fans behind the goal and then somebody said something that he felt the need to respond to. He'd already bowled the ball back to me so he shouted, 'Ben, wait!' But I never fucking heard him, did I? So after he'd turned around to react to whatever it was, he turned back to see this ball flying towards his face. Catch the ball, head down, *bang*. Straight into his bugle.

Of course, all the fans went up with a cheer. And of course, Peter went berserk. The next thing I knew, he was running in my direction. I just legged it. He chased me right down the full length of the pitch and into the tunnel. And he was deceptively quick, by the way.

I managed to get into the changing rooms, which were really small at The Dell; you came in through a little door and the toilets were at the back, which is where I headed. Peter appeared at the door to the changing room and screamed, 'Where is he, that little bastard?' The manager had to tell him to calm down. And it wasn't like I could have a nice chat with Peter at the end of the game because he conceded six goals that day. Even if I'd gone to the manager at that point and said, 'I'm worried Peter Schmeichel is going to kill me,' he probably would have let him.

That was in the middle of one of United's worst periods with Sir Alex in charge. Between 20 October and 2 November we conceded 14 goals in four games: 5-0 at Newcastle, 6-3 at Southampton and 2-1 at home to Chelsea, plus a 1-0 loss to Fenerbahçe in the Champions League that ended United's 40-year unbeaten home record in Europe. Dreadful.

On 23 November I started another game for the first team, this time away to Middlesbrough in the league. Our team was relatively inexperienced because of injuries: Michael Clegg, John O'Kane, Nicky Butt, Paul Scholes, David Beckham and me, all 21 or younger. Derek Whyte was playing for Middlesbrough and he ended up being my captain at Aberdeen.

I was replaced by Jordi Cruyff in the 72nd minute and then David May scored a minute later. If you spoke to Maysie he'd tell you it was me leaving the scene that allowed United to go on and score. Mind you, I wasn't on the pitch when Craig Hignett scored his penalty to make it 2-2 so I can't quite remember, but maybe Maysie gave it away? Let's just assume he did.

If I'd played an evening game on a hard surface, my knee used to ache afterwards. As such, if I was in the squad for an away game that would result in a long coach journey home, in the days prior I always tried to find someone agreeable to driving me home (usually

Gaz or Becks) once we'd been dropped back at Old Trafford. I wouldn't want to drive my own car because my knee would seize up on the coach, so the last thing I wanted was it going up and down on the pedals.

On 21 December I came on for Giggsy in the second half of our 5-0 win against Sunderland at Old Trafford, which meant I was on the pitch for Eric Cantona's iconic chip. If you watch the video clip you'll see me following it up because I was thinking, 'Nah, no way this is going in, it's coming back off the bar. I'm going to score here.'

It was an amazing goal from a great guy. He was brilliant but he was lovely with it. Simple things like when you came in of a morning he'd say hello, or he'd offer you a lift back from training (and you'd think, 'Should I?'). He brought me back from Littleton Road to The Cliff once and I told him my family speaks French. I admitted that I wasn't as good as my mum, dad or sister and that when I was at school I found writing in French particularly hard. He said, 'Even for French people, writing in French is hard.' So that made me feel better.

When we finished training he was always one of the last to leave (he was one of the last to arrive as well, by the way, but he could do what he liked). And while he didn't need to teach us younger players about work ethic, he showed us that what we were doing was the right approach. That just encouraged us to stay even longer on the training pitch, working on stuff that we weren't very good at and improving things that we were.

He was a fascinating person. I never heard him raise his voice; he was driven and focused, which influenced the rest of the dressing room because of the way he prepared and presented himself. He had an aura about him, an ego, but to be at that level you need a bit of an ego. Like the Ready Brek man, he needed a shield around him to set himself apart from the rest. That said, he was still extremely approachable.

He left at the end of that season and, like everybody else, the first I heard of it was on the news. I think it was completely and utterly out of the blue. If you've read the manager's book, *Leading*, you've read the letter he sent to Eric Cantona, which basically said, 'Don't go but if you are going to, know you're always welcome to come back.' I've also had a letter from the manager. It wasn't as complimentary as the one he sent to Eric but still, I'm in esteemed company. A letter basically saying, 'I like you and thank you.' I'm happy with that.

Before we broke up for our holidays, the club asked me and Michael Clegg to go and play in a game being fronted by Versace in Milan. It was a decent standard: Kubilay Türkyilmaz – who scored for Switzerland against England in Euro 96 and played for Galatasaray against Man United – was involved, as was Daniele Massaro, the pointy-nosed fella who played for AC Milan and won two European Cups.

We didn't get any money for it but we did get a trip to the flagship Versace store in Milan to pick out any outfit we wanted. I found this electric-blue suit with snakeskin shoes and belt, complemented by a mesh T-shirt. I was 22 and thought I had the body for it so I decided I looked pretty cool at Donatella's penthouse after-party. Apparently not. When my partner Les saw it for the first time years later her reaction was: 'You obviously lost the game then.' My mate Paul Devine said I looked like something out of Showaddywaddy. Never mind, I still think I looked the dog's bollocks.

Cleggy was my room-mate again when we went on our 1997/98 pre-season tour of Bangkok, Hong Kong and Tokyo. And it was while we were on that tour, lying on our hotel beds, that it came up on the news that Gianna Versace had been assassinated on the steps of his house in Miami. We both sat bolt upright when we saw that. The image of the sheet over his body, with blood barely dried on the steps, is still vivid in my mind.

The season ended with a testimonial for former Coventry City player David Buust, who was playing at Old Trafford in 1996 when he suffered a dreadful leg break that ended his career. I came on as sub in a game that saw the likes of Les Ferdinand, Ally McCoist and Paul Gascoigne playing for Coventry at Highfield Road. It also turned out to be Cantona's last game for United before he retired, but nobody knew it at the time; he scored twice in a 2-2 draw. And, would you believe, my co-writer Dan Poole was in the stands watching.

After that I went on holiday with Catherine, my girlfriend at the time, to Barbados. It was one of these Teletext ones where you paid £800 each for two weeks and were guaranteed to stay in a four-star hotel. When we got there we found out we were staying at the Almond Beach Club, which happened to share the same stretch of beach as Sandy Lane. And as nice as the Almond Beach Club is, Sandy Lane is worlds apart.

Anyway, the day after we arrived in Barbados I took a walk down to the beach. I looked around to see if there were any restrictions in terms of where you could go; there weren't so I wandered down in front of Sandy Lane. I turned back when I reached the end of the peninsula, looked up and saw someone walking down towards the sea. I thought, 'That's fucking Gazza, that.'

The David Buust testimonial was the first time I'd met Gazza and he recognised me from that. He'd been in Florida and said he was full of ice cream and doughnuts, so he'd come to Barbados to chill. We must have been stood talking in the sea, water up to our calves, for the best part of two hours. Easily enough time for me to have to try and ignore my back turning red raw in the Caribbean sun. Thing is, I didn't really want to say, 'Gazza, this is great but I'm getting burnt to a crisp here – any chance we could switch places?'

It was a surreal situation but he was so fascinating to listen to; I just wish I'd been able to record our conversation. He told the story of Alex Ferguson laying into him on the phone in 1988 because he'd signed for Spurs instead of United. The manager had gone away thinking it was done and dusted and as a result, Gazza said he got the biggest bollocking of his life. During the crescendo he was holding the phone at arm's length yet could still hear the manager clear as a bell.

If we'd have been anywhere else he would probably have said, 'Hiya, how you doing?' and walked on. But it was only me and Gazza. It's something I'll always remember – and not just because my back got burnt to a cinder.

1997/98

I didn't get off the bench for the Charity Shield against Chelsea but I got to go up the steps to receive a winner's medal. It was brilliant to be on the Wembley turf again, seven years after I'd played there as a schoolboy; I never managed to get on it again after that mind you, which is less good.

I was on the bench again for our game away to Bolton in September. There wasn't much to write home about when it came to the football; more interesting was the head-tennis court just off the main dressing room. The Reebok was the first ground I'd been to that had one. A game of that easily killed 45 minutes, until the manager came in and said, 'You lot will be fucked before you've even gone out for your warm-up. Calm it down.'

Gary Pallister got sent off in that game after a tussle with Nathan Blake. Nathan was an awkward customer: strong, quick and physical. And Pally didn't like physical; he liked it easy. To be fair he very often made it *look* easy but from time to time there were players who got on his nerves, shall we say. That's how this one ended up.

I got on the pitch when we lost 1-0 away to Leeds a couple of games later. That was the one where Roy Keane did his knee and I was virtually right next to him when it happened. It was really innocuous but if he ever stayed down you knew it was because he couldn't get back up. He understood that most of the time he was in a physical battle but what he took exception to was Alf-Inge Haaland's reaction. It would have eaten away at him; he hadn't done anything wrong, he was going to miss the rest of the season and he had someone leaning over him accusing him of cheating. That's why Keaney got him back in 2001 and was walking off before the referee got anywhere near his cards. That was what Roy wanted to do and he did it.

In early October I played in Paul Lake's testimonial at Maine Road. I didn't get chance to speak to him but it would have been nice to because we suffered a similar injury. The difference with him was that he had a succession of operations that weren't successful; surgeons going in and out of his knee like that weakened it too much. He was still so young when he had to stop playing. Although he got to progress further with his career than I did before injury struck, I'm sure he'd have swapped that for being able to carry on afterwards, like I did.

Next up were Ipswich in the League Cup. Kieran Dyer had only recently come into the team and was playing right-back. I started and gave as good as I got against him but I ran out of steam and came off after 66 minutes. We ended up losing 2-0, which was doubly disappointing because whenever we were out of the League Cup I was left wondering where my next first-team appearance was coming from. To be fair though, by now I knew that it was never going to happen at United. If it was down to me this was going to be my last season at the club.

I was on the bench again when we played Feyenoord in the Champions League in the November. They've got a notorious following and the atmosphere in their stadium was outstanding. Andrew Cole bagged a hat-trick that night but all I can remember is the horrendous challenge by Paul Bosvelt on Denis Irwin. It kept Denis out for a couple of months, though the fact that he didn't have more damage to his knee is incredible. I played in his comeback game for the reserves against Leeds at Gigg Lane on 30 December. It was a good, entertaining 1-1 that was really competitive. Denis came off at the end and said, 'Bloody hell, that was as hard as any first-team game I've played in for a long time.'

I was in the first-team squad for our third-round FA Cup match against Chelsea on 4 January. I shared a room with Becks at the Chelsea Harbour Hotel the night before and we watched *Planes,*

Trains and Automobiles; when we looked at each other at the end we both tried to hide the fact that we were wiping a tear away. After we'd composed ourselves and gone to bed, I woke up in the middle of the night needing a wee. I got up to go to the toilet and found something unexpected propped up against the door to the room: Becks. He'd been sleepwalking and was fast asleep with his duvet wrapped around him. He scored twice the following day in a 5-3 win.

Talking of Becks, that season he sorted a few of us out with a box so we could join him to watch the Spice Girls at the MEN Arena. There was an after-party back at his house in Worsley and they were all there. Well, I think they were: I don't remember seeing Mel C. Mel B I definitely saw because she was a lunatic. I stayed the night at Dave Gardener's, the ex-football agent who's with Becks everywhere he goes and now has a family with Liv Tyler.

My next start was against Walsall in the fourth round of the FA Cup but I only lasted 65 minutes before I was subbed off. They had a player called John Hodge who was quick but a few years older than me. He went on one run that wouldn't have seen me bat an eyelid before my injury – but I couldn't catch him. So I knew then that something needed to be done. I was carrying too much weight again and my confidence was low so it was back to extra training with Kiddo to get back into shape.

That went well and a month later I played in the next round of the Cup in our replay at Barnsley (we'd drawn the first game 1-1 at Old Trafford). They won 3-2 but they were so lucky. They just managed to hold out and that was my fault because I missed a sitter near the end that would have made it 3-3. Well, maybe not a sitter but I should have scored. Oh God. If I had put that in and it had gone to extra time, they were dead on their feet. From 3-3 it could have been 6-3 quite easily.

I was really disappointed because otherwise I'd had a good game and felt a lot better compared to the Walsall match. Plus, I took that missed chance off Andrew Cole's toes. Considering he ended up scoring 187 Premier League goals, I might have been better off just getting out of the fucking way.

Come March I was on the bench for our first-leg game at Monaco in the Champions League quarter-final. Their stadium, the Stade Louis II, is nice, if very small and built on a car park. The pitch was rock hard and we drew 0-0. That was the first time I saw Thierry Henry in action and they had Fabien Barthez in goal, who ended up at United, of course. Apparently he used to light up in the dressing-room showers like he was in a hashish bar.

I was on the bench for Sheffield Wednesday at Hillsborough that same month. Peter Atherton and Paolo Di Canio scored against us and Des Walker played brilliantly. The manager was really, really, really fed up and the lads weren't much better at full time when they had to wash themselves in a couple of sinks. The showers were taking their skin off and there was nothing anyone inside the ground could do about it, apparently. In those sorts of situations you sometimes wonder if it's genuinely the case that they can't help or it's been done deliberately. We'll never know.

Four days later we were away at West Ham. I came on at half-time for Brian McClair and was up against Trevor Sinclair, who's from Salford. Trevor was powerful and never stopped but he wasn't super quick. Not that he was slow. Actually, I guess he *was* quick but I didn't have any major problems with him anyway. It was a really good 1-1.

Next up were Arsenal at home. That team in 1998 was so powerful: Adams, Petit, Viera, Parlour, Overmars, Bergkamp. Viera had five strides to my 25. At one point during that game I tried to turn on the edge of their box but he saw me coming, wrapped his leg around me, took the ball and was away. Once they broke they were quick too but nothing came of it, thank God.

Lee Dixon was a very good full-back; he's also a nice fella and a very good pundit. But as a player he could be quite rash. I remember getting the legs on him, going as if to put a cross in from the byline with my left foot but faking and turning back; Lee skidded straight past me and ended up on his arse on the touchline. Then I fluffed the fucking cross.

That was the game when Overmars scored and they won 1-0. From our dressing room we could hear the Arsenal players screaming and shouting. I was thinking, 'How could this happen?' I didn't play badly but that match sticks in a lot of United fans' throats because Arsenal won the league by overturning our 12-point lead. You just wouldn't expect a Man United side to crumble like that but we did.

It was a *great* few days actually because next we drew 1-1 in the home leg of our tie against Monaco to go out on away goals. David Trezeguet smashed it in early and the manager slaughtered Nicky Butt for it at half-time. So much had gone on between the ball going in the net and Nicky giving it away but Sir Alex didn't care. It's one of the worst bollockings I ever heard him give to anybody. I was sitting right next to Butty and honestly, it was brutal. A you'll-never-play-for-me-again kind of rant. Harsh.

I was involved straight after in a game against Wimbledon at Old Trafford, so I couldn't have done too much wrong against Arsenal. I came on in the 82nd minute when it was still 0-0 and there was real concern that we weren't going to score. But we managed to from a corner (that I played no part in) within seconds of my arrival so I must have made all the difference.

The game was still nervy because Wimbledon looked like equalising – but fortunately I created a second goal. I picked up the ball in our half, found myself in some space, ran at the defence and knocked it past Chris Perry, one of their centre-backs. The touchline seemed to be hoving into view a lot quicker than I was getting to the ball but I made it and saw Becks at the far post. Rather than fire it in I just clipped it to him at the far post; he nodded it back across goal and Scholesy put it in.

I wound up on the floor because my momentum had carried me over the touchline. If you watch the clip of the goal, the camera goes to the bench and you see Mike Stone, who was the doctor at the time, pointing – that was in my direction to check that I was OK. I was looking up thinking, 'Thank fuck that's gone in.' Scholes was probably just offside, which Gaz kindly mentioned in his and Phil's United diary that came out that season. Thanks for that, Gaz.

It was nice to get a bit of the adulation. It was the highest league attendance that season as well so the paying public must have known I was going to be coming on. It wasn't a particularly great goal but it was a decent run and a decent cross. And I remember thinking, 'I'm so glad I didn't come on any earlier than this because I'm bollocksed.' From one run! Before I came on Kiddo said, 'Go and change the game for us.' That was still ringing in my ears when I thought, 'Fuck it,' and went past Chris Perry.

It was my most rewarding moment in a United first-team shirt. I got a big hug from Kiddo at the end because we'd been doing the extra training together and it had really paid off. And the manager told us all that it was going to be a great result for us – though it wasn't because we still lost the league. In fact, we didn't win anything that season.

I was back on the bench for our game away at Blackburn, which we won 3-1. Chris Sutton scored a penalty for them. Next we played Liverpool on the same Good Friday as the Good Friday Agreement. I came on for an injured Giggs in the 39th minute. Michael Owen scored to make it 1-1 but then got sent off, so we played the entire second half against ten men. That made it all the more gutting that we couldn't capitalise. Though I did manage to do the same thing to Steve McManaman that I had to Lee Dixon: sat him down on his backside. I probably fucked up a cross immediately afterwards as well.

And with that, as the final whistle blew, I'd made my last ever appearance for the Manchester United first team.

8

Signing up 1988–91

Ben: Manchester United's school of excellence was run by Brian Kidd and Archie Knox. Almost as soon as I arrived, Kiddo said to me, 'Don't get me wrong, we've got you here because we've seen you playing as a central-midfielder but we can also see that you're quick and skilful. Do you want to try playing on the wing?' Straight away I said yes and from then on it was taken as read that left-wing was my position.

Then there was Archie. He was also assistant manager for the first team and he was a fiery character with a broad Glaswegian accent. We used to train in the indoor gym at The Cliff, which had a tin roof – and my God it made a racket when it rained. It meant that when Archie was giving out his instructions there was a melee of shoving someone, *anyone*, to the front to listen, because we couldn't understand a word he was saying. Invariably, whatever he asked us to do, we then got wrong. Worse still, he seemed to be as unforgiving with a group of 13- and 14-year-olds as he was with the first team. And all the while you've got Kiddo taking the piss in the background. He was a nice guy Archie, he really was, but boy what a temper he had. He and the manager were definitely two of a kind: old school.

George Switzer: Archie just scared me. If he was training us I'd think, 'Oh shit.' When you're young and you've got a big hairy Scotsman in front of you ... But what a character he was.

Paul Devine: He was strict, Archie, so we were in fear of him really. And sometimes he'd say things and me and Ben would look at each other like, 'What on Earth?' One time he passed the ball towards us and shouted, 'Leave it!' So we just let it go behind us. Then he went off his head: 'What the fuck are you doing?' And me and Ben went, 'Well you just told us to leave it!' And he said, 'What do you mean? You control it!' There was no point discussing it any further because *obviously* we were wrong.

Paul Scholes: We definitely had some difficult training sessions.

Ben: During the Easter and summer holidays we'd have training weeks and play matches against other teams. That's when Keith Gillespie would come across from Northern Ireland, Robbie Savage would come over from Wales and Becks would come up from London, and they'd all be put up in digs at Salford University.

Paul Devine: I remember Becks turning up for the first time: here was the new kid, cockney wide boy, bit of a dream boy. Me and Ben were stood there like, 'Who the fuck is this?'

Ben: I found myself in The Cliff three times a week because we'd train there Mondays and Thursdays with United and Wednesdays with Salford Boys; Paul Devine's mum used to drive us in most of the time. Paul's in business with Gary Neville now.

Paul Devine: These days Ben and Gaz are equally hard work, just in different ways.

Ben: Where Salford Boys played, Lower Broughton Playing Fields, was a 50-yard walk down the hill from The Cliff; in between the two was where Becks had his digs a few years later. In that 1988/89 season I played in the English Schools National Trophy; it was the under-15 schools FA Cup, if you like. In the third round Ryan's team, the year above me, were playing against South Nottinghamshire. Ryan's manager, Steve Kelly, asked me to step up an age group and play, which then became a regular occurrence for that cup run. Ryan played on the left wing, I played left-back and all I did was give him the ball.

Steve Kelly: That was the instruction to the entire team. Coaching Ryan for a year was a gift: all of a sudden people thought I knew what I was talking about. And that was a really wet, horrible night in Nottingham but Ben was superb in that game.

Ryan Giggs: I knew Ben wasn't going to end up as a left-back but he was intelligent so it was a piece of piss for him. He went behind me and we had a really good relationship right from the beginning. You don't get many players who are intelligent at that age – they normally just kick it and run. He could do a bit of everything and he was tough.

Steve Kelly: Ben was as good as I'd seen since Ryan. He was feisty and very competitive but with a lot of quality; he didn't just win the ball, he knew what to do with it when he got it. I never saw Ben Thornley anything other than 100 per cent at it.

Ben: We played the semi-final and second leg of the final of that competition at Manchester United. The semi was the first time I'd played at Old Trafford and the pitch was massive, to the point that I got cramp for the first time in my life. We played Plymouth in the semi and beat them 6-1. In the final, May 1989, we played against St Helens and lost 3-2 on aggregate, having won the first leg at theirs 2-1.

Steve Kelly: We won that first leg despite not playing very well, so I told them they needed to play better in the second. But we didn't really perform; we were subdued, a bit nervous. Overawed by the situation, maybe? I don't know. But it was desperately disappointing.

Ryan Giggs: It was a massive disappointment because we'd beaten South Notts, who had a few England Schoolboys playing for them, and we'd beaten Islington, who were the top team in London. But we didn't play well in the final and they deserved to win.

Ben: St Helens's boys, because it's a rugby league town, were huge. And I mean *huge*.

Paul Devine: They were murderous, massive. They were all 6ft and brutal with it; there wasn't much ability there. It was just ridiculous.

Steve Kelly: Yeah, they had a couple of bullies who, in all honesty, shouldn't have been playing in that second leg because they should have been sent off in the first. We had a First Division ref who was bloody hopeless. After the game he said to me, 'They're only kids.' I said, 'Sure, but they can't go around kicking the life out of other kids, can they?'

Tony Potter: I saw Ben play in that game at Old Trafford. At one point the ball was looping over his head and he stuck his foot out behind him to control it on his heel. Now you don't see that very often.

Steve Kelly: Ben was top, top class. He would have played an awful lot of games for Man United's first team and there's no doubt that he would have played for England. He would have gone as high as Nicky Butt, Beckham, the Nevilles, Giggs and Scholes, no question. And that made it so hard to see him after the injury because it wasn't Ben anymore.

Ben: At the end of the 1988/89 season I was put forward by Paul and Harry for trials with Greater Manchester County. I was chosen and it was Nicky Butt and me in central midfield, with Paul Devine playing on the right and Andy Scott at left-back. Then, in the summer of 1989, I got a letter from the FA asking me to attend a trial for England Schoolboys, who were managed by Dave Bushell.

Dave Bushell: I had a lad called Ryan Wilson in my England Schoolboys team so I knew about Ben, because he'd been playing a year up in Ryan's age group at Salford Boys. I saw Ben play lots of times.

Ben: The following season, in October 1989, United sent out my contract offer: a two-year apprenticeship and two years pro, which was torn up after we won the Youth Cup in the first year. There was a small signing-on fee too, alongside a basic YTS wage of £29.50. Plus, my mum and dad were to be paid £40 bed and board.

Elizabeth Thornley: I don't remember that.

Philip Thornley: I don't think we ever were.

Hannah Scott (née Thornley): He brought it home or it came direct from the club?

Philip Thornley: Did he pocket it?

Hannah Scott: Clearly.

Ben: Did I bollocks. So United invited me to a game and I signed the contract at the club – in the manager's office mind, not on the pitch or anything. Then we received another letter finalising what we'd need and what time we needed to report by on 8 July 1991: 9am.

Meanwhile, the first part of the England Schoolboys trial lasted a week and was at Trent Polytechnic in Nottingham, before term began in September of 1989. It started with 256 boys and I got through that. Then it was halved to 128 boys and I went back for a three-day trial in October. I got through that and it was reduced to 62, plus the 18 lads who were already at Lilleshall, the FA's school of excellence at the time, to take it up to 80.

That trial was in November at Lilleshall itself. It was another three-day stint and it was in term time, but because it was such a prestigious thing for your school to say that you had been selected, my headmaster said it wouldn't be a problem.

Dave Bushell: What we also used to do was have trial games between areas, and in Ben's case it was the Northwest versus the Midlands.

Ben: It was down at West Brom's ground, The Hawthorns. Because I was the captain of Greater Manchester, the most recognised county in the region, they made me the captain of the Northwest – and oh my God, it was like somebody had sewn my knees together. I was awful. Only the fact that we ran out winners masked the fact that I was so, so bad. Fortunately there were no repercussions. If anyone ever offers me a video of that game I'll politely suggest where they can stick it.

Paul Devine: He was terrible and I'm sure I slaughtered him. He certainly didn't do himself any favours.

Ben: At the Lilleshall trial we went from 80 boys down to 40, then from there down to 24 – another three days. After that you were told within a week whether you had got into the final squad of 16. For that week Geoff, my PE teacher, gave me special dispensation to leave school in the first break every morning so I could go home and check whether I'd got the letter.

Geoff Ogden: I did it on the quiet. But I was a head of department so I would have got away with it if I'd been found out.

Ben: One day I went haring off in the rain, slipped and went arse over tit on the grass, soaking my trousers.

Jeff Kerfoot: I was in one of the prefabs when I saw him leg it past. I thought, 'Where's he off to at this time?'

Ben: When I came back one girl said, 'Are you alright?' And I said, 'Yeah, why?' She said, 'I saw you go head over heels – were you wagging it again?' It was worth it though: when I got home there was an envelope with a three-lions stamp on the seal. I was panicking like mad when I opened it but inside it said I had been selected for the squad.

Philip Thornley: That December, Ben was captain of Salford Boys under-15s and they had a quarter-final in the National Schools Trophy against Barnsley – but he got flu a few days before and it floored him. He was in bed when Paul Moseley phoned to ask if he was alright and I said, 'No, not really.'

Hannah Scott: He couldn't move.

Rod Thornley: Man flu, was it? Worse than giving birth.

Hannah Scott: No, no, no, it was proper flu. His body wouldn't work.

Philip Thornley: Then Paul Moseley said, 'Can we come and see him?' So he and Harry came to find out how Ben was fixed.

Harry Hackett: I knocked on the front door and said, 'Jesus, Phil, you've got to get him fit for this game. It's the most important of the season.' And Phil said, 'No chance.'

Philip Thornley: Come 4pm the following day, Ben hadn't had anything to eat and I asked him how he was feeling. He said, 'Oh, a bit sick but I want to go.' Paul had been ringing up saying, 'Is he coming? Is he coming?' Kick-off was 7.15pm at Oakwell in Barnsley so we took him; he played a stormer and they won. He was taken off once they went 2-0 ahead midway through the second half.

Ben: I'm not sure I played a stormer.

Paul Devine: When I scored that second goal I ran past Ben and he just fell to the floor. He didn't have the energy to grab hold of me. I think it was relief, as if to say, 'Fucking hell, I think we've won. I'm done.'

Philip Thornley: We took him home and he went straight back to bed.

Paul Moseley: I named my son Ben. That's because it was a special team and Ben was the leader of that team. He was a special lad, a clever lad. And the way he's dealt with adversity, the way he's moved forward with his life ... If my son is half the guy he is, he'll do alright.

And my son has turned out to have some sporting ability too: he's been ranked 25th in the country over 200 metres and has a professional contract with the Salford Reds rugby league team. But here's the weird thing: at the age of 18 he's just done his ACL.

Dave Bushell: Ben was not only technically good, he had two good feet as well. His ability made him stand out.

Ben: Of the players I went to those England Schoolboys trials with, plenty never made it into the squad; Paul Scholes and David Beckham, for example.

Paul Scholes: You can see why: at that age Ben was a level above all of us. He was very mature for his age; he was almost like a man at 15. And with the ability he had to go with it, it was no surprise that he was getting picked for England and we weren't.

David Beckham: I was always one of the slow starters but it was soul-destroying seeing kids like Ben go through on a higher stage.

Ben: Julian Joachim was another one and I thought he was a certainty. There was a brilliant lad who went on to play for Everton called Tony Grant: super, super footballer, played for Liverpool Boys, looked like Rodney Trotter – didn't get selected. Robbie Fowler was another one; Gary Neville too. And Darren Caskey: he was a year older than me and played a few games for Spurs. Massive things were expected but, for whatever reason, it didn't happen for him.

And do you know what: the lads who I played with for England Schoolboys who were at Lilleshall, by the time they got to 16 they were either no good or injured. Or they had fallen out of love with the game because they'd just had football, football, football hammered into them. Even I didn't want that. Sometimes I wanted to be able to come home, put my bag down, have a chocolate biscuit and watch TV. Those lads had no choice. They'd finish school lessons at 3.45pm, get changed, go on the training pitch for an hour and a half, have a meal, do homework and go to bed. Then do it all again the next day. You can count on one hand the boys who did well. One of them was Sol Campbell – though he never got picked for the England Schoolboys team.

Philip Thornley: It was an unmitigated disaster. Most of the boys who came through Lilleshall never got anywhere.

Ben: And I actually could have been one of those lads at Lilleshall. Earlier that year I'd been getting all my stuff together one Sunday morning, ready to get on the train at Manchester Piccadilly to go to a trial. Then my dad said, 'Do you know what you're doing?'

'Yeah, I'm going for a trial,' I replied.

'Yes, but to do what?'

'To go to Lilleshall!'

'Yes, but then what happens?'

And I thought, 'Oh shit, yeah: I'd be leaving my mum and dad at 14 years of age to basically go to boarding school.'

Philip Thornley: My thinking was, what can they give him that he isn't getting at United? But there was almost an obligation: because you'd been invited, that meant you had to go.

Dave Bushell: The lads who stayed in county football were better prepared. At the England Schoolboy trials, each time the bus was leaving to go to Stafford Station to take the county lads home it was as if they were going to freedom and the Lilleshall lads were stuck there. To live in halls of residence 24/7 must have been awful for 14- to 16-year-old boys.

Elizabeth Thornley: Plus, it was a pig of a place to get to.

Ben: In the end I didn't go to the Lilleshall trial. I didn't even make a phone call; I didn't do anything, knowing that somebody was going to ring me as a result.

Philip Thornley: Only they didn't ring. The guy from Salford who recommended Ben for Lilleshall came to the school – uninvited, by the way – knocked on my door and launched into me. 'You should be ashamed of yourself, standing in the way of your child. There's an opportunity of a lifetime here.' He was really having a go and I was so angry with him, which made me even more adamant that Ben wasn't going. I told him to get out of my office.

Ben: My first game for England Schoolboys, in 1990, was at Hillsborough against a Northern Ireland side containing Keith Gillespie. Then I got an ankle injury playing for my county against Lancashire, which put me out of a game against France at Wembley. I came back into the team at Filbert Street to play a Wales side featuring Robbie Savage.

Robbie Savage: I scored.

Ben: So did I but then I got a whack on my ankle and got carried off. Fortunately I was fit enough for what came next, which was a trip to America with Salford Boys to take part in a tournament called the San Diego Spring Classic. We spent a year fundraising to be able to go and it was the trip of a lifetime.

Harry Hackett: It was the first time we'd been and we've been doing it ever since.

Paul Moseley: We played two or three matches per day with short gaps in between. It was competitive because we were the English team, so everyone wanted to beat us.

Ben: It was April in southern California so it was *hot*. Playing in those temperatures, when you've got a load of Mexican kids running around who are used to playing in it ten months of the year, meant we had to acclimatise in a short space of time. But we played the first couple of rounds and I was flying, everything was going great and we got to the final. But during that game some lad stuck his knee in my thigh, a completely innocuous challenge, and gave me a dead leg.

It was a bad one. When you have a dead leg it can get so severe that you can't move it; it's called calcification and it's serious. You have to get all the scar tissue out of the muscle and eventually – as long as you keep stretching it out, having warm baths, stretching it out – it heals. If it doesn't you have to have it sliced and drained and I was close to that on this occasion.

I was distraught because there was another England Schoolboys game coming up when I got back and, yet again, I wasn't going to be able to play. Prior to the ankle injury and the dead leg, I'd never been injured before. Hadn't known what a muscle pull was, hadn't known what a bad tackle was. I've certainly learnt about them since. Bugger.

However, there was one compensation that came out of that trip. One of the families I stayed with in San Diego was friends with another family whose daughter had just won the Miss California Teen pageant – and she asked me out on a date. Straight up. Me and Paul were sat in a booth with her at a pizza restaurant having a chat when she said, 'We should hook up.' I was just shy of my 15th birthday and this 18-year-old, who'd just won *Miss California Teen*, was asking *me* out on a date. And she was stunning. I'd never clapped eyes on a girl so gorgeous. Unbelievable.

Andy Scott: She was amazing.

Paul Devine: Thornley, that stuffy bastard. To this day I'm gutted about it. Miss California Teen. I said to him, 'I can't believe she fancies you – you're fucking horrible.'

Ben: Anyway, even though I was injured, Dave Bushell kept me in the England Schoolboys squad every single time despite pressure from above to take me out. One of the games I had to miss was against Scotland and we were playing in a place called Dingwall, at some shitty little stadium that is now Ross County's ground.

Dave Bushell: We had a trip to Italy and Germany coming up after that. I knew that Ben had an injury and I knew he was struggling – but I decided not to tell anybody. We had just got a physiotherapist in called Mike Dickinson and I said to him, 'Look Dicko, Ben can't play. I know he's injured but give him a go and see whether we can get him fit for ten days' time because I'd love him to go to Italy.'

For away games you used to fly in, do your training session and have dinner with the dignitaries – the England schools councillors, as they were called. Then the next day you'd prepare for the game, play it and fly home. I knew these councillors wouldn't come to watch the training session because it would be *boring*; they'd want afternoon tea and scones instead. So I thought, 'It'll be alright. Ben can go on the subs bench and nobody will know any better.'

But the buggers came to watch training, didn't they? I'm doing a session with 15 boys and there's Dicko jogging around the pitch with Ben. Oh shit. Then sure enough, at teatime: 'Dave, we'd like a word with you afterwards.' They took me to one side and said, 'Young Ben Thornley, he's injured. What's happened?' I had to lie through my teeth then, didn't I? I said, 'Well, we got up here, we'd just started the warm-up and he felt a twinge. With the game in ten days I thought it was better to check him out. Unfortunately he's not going to be fit for this game but he's OK for Italy.'

And they said, 'Well you shouldn't be bringing someone who's injured.' I replied, 'Well he's just felt a twinge. He's obviously not fit enough to play but nobody knew. The young lad thought he was fit, I thought he was fit.' I just had to take the stick.

Ben: My mum and dad hired a minibus to come and watch me in that game and travelled all the way up with a load of their friends and my brother and sister, staying at some B&B. But on the day – my birthday, no less – I had to phone them and say, 'My leg's not right, I can't play.'

Hannah Scott: It was a long way.

Ben: I did come on against Italy and Germany in the end, as well as getting to play against Holland at Wembley.

Geoff Ogden: I took a load of pupils down to watch Ben at Wembley because we were so proud of him.

Phil Neville: My first sighting of Ben was for England Schoolboys and he stood out: he had a busy style and was a stumpy little lad. Not stumpy, that's the wrong word … stocky. He wasn't Giggs-esque, in that Ryan used to glide past players – it was more about his tenacity.

Ben: When I was injured playing for England Schoolboys, Alex Ferguson rang me up and said, 'You come in at 11am and Jimmy McGregor will have a look at you.' So my school used to allow me to go and have an hour's physiotherapy – and my grandad Tommy, who loved his football, used to come in with me. He'd see all these players that he'd only ever watched on TV before and start mithering the life out of people like Mark Hughes, Neil Webb and Norman Whiteside. He was so proud of his grandson being a footballer and I was heartbroken when he died. He was diagnosed with lung cancer and eventually, in 2003, it was pneumonia that got him. To this day it's the only time I've seen my dad cry.

Dave Bushell: Ben was a positive young man with a really nice personality and he had a great mum and dad – there was a good support network there. He could dribble past players, he could excite people and he could affect a game. And I suppose he is a true 'leg end', rather than a legend: he's been injured that bloody many times and it's all been around the end of his leg. I just thought he was a smashing player.

Ben: By the time I went into my final year at school, starting in September 1990, I was too old to play for Salford Boys and Greater Manchester. That meant the only competitive football I was getting was with my school and the 14 occasions throughout that season that I played for United's B team. I scored in my first game for them:

a header, unbelievably, against Merseyside's Marine Youth, who we beat 3-0 on 22 September 1990. So that means I scored on my debut for Man United, essentially.

And I was actually still at school when I made my first appearance in the FA Youth Cup: I was on the bench against Sheffield Wednesday in April of 1991 and got on. The youth-team manager, Eric Harrison, was off with a stomach ulcer so B team manager Nobby Stiles (former United player and England World Cup winner) took the side. I was playing against one of the Linighan brothers, Brian; I was only on for 20 minutes but I tore him to pieces.

Nobby came into the dressing room after the game and went nuts. I'm pretty sure Alex Ferguson was in there as well. Nobby said, 'Every single one of you let a 15-year-old come on and show you how to play.' He put his arm around me at the end and said, 'I'm sorry for making an example of you but you were brilliant out there and I wish you'd been on for longer.' I came off the bench for the second leg too – but we lost 1-0, making it 2-1 on aggregate. Such is life.

Paul Devine: There's another game that springs to mind. A United youth team played a Lilleshall team in November 1989, when we were 14. I walked into the dressing room at The Cliff in the morning and said to Ben, 'What's up with you?' He said, 'What do you mean?'

'Ben, what's up with you, I can tell.'

'I got pissed last night.'

'What? *What?*'

'Yeah, I went to this party and I come out bladdered. I can't believe it.'

'Right.'

'And there was this girl there …'

'Oh fucking hell, Ben.'

Ben: It was the first time I'd ever tried alcohol, let alone got drunk.

Paul Devine: He ended up throwing one in, saying he wasn't feeling too well. We beat the Lilleshall team 4-2 without him. And that sort of behaviour – football, a few beers and a few girls – has been a thread throughout the rest of his life.

Ben: At school our exams went on until the middle of June 1991 and after that I went on holiday with Joe Lydiate and his parents to Tenerife. His older brother Jason was at United already; Joe, who I played with for Salford Boys, was about to start as an apprentice with City.

Joe Lydiate: One of the main things I remember from that trip is arriving at the airport for the flight home and the woman at the check-in desk saying, 'Ooh, um, I'm sorry but you've missed your flight.' Ben, his face a picture of total shock, said, 'Well you're going to have to tell it to turn around!' We spent the next ten hours in Tenerife airport waiting for a flight.

Ben: Once I got back it was time to report for my first day as an apprentice. Before United, the only person who had ever worked on fitness with me was me, which meant a professional pre-season was gruelling. None of us knew what the hell had hit us. I remember Eric Harrison coming downstairs with Nobby at The Cliff and we were all stood there holding our football boots. Eric laughed and said, 'I don't know what you've got them for – you won't need them for a fortnight.'

And sure enough, we didn't – it was just run rabbit, run. And it was *hard*. United did realise that we had only just come out of school but by the same token, if we were going to step up into the higher echelons of the club we would need the basis of a pre-season, even at such an early age. And it was only going to get worse: pre-season with the first team was even harder. The staff expected more of you because you were more physically able.

Everyone did their pre-season over at Littleton Road, which was a big expanse of pitches. Apprentices, reserves, first team: they all had their sections there. And one Friday we had a five-a-side competition involving the whole club, from first team to juniors. That was a real eye-opener. Mark Robins was on my team and he called me Speedy Gonzales.

Nicky Butt: Great lad, Ben. You meet as young lads and you don't always click straight away but I got on with him right from the word go. He never took life too seriously but he took his football seriously. I don't think anyone could speak badly of him. He was a good kid.

Ben: In late July we played in something called the Milk Cup in Northern Ireland and stayed in a hotel that was owned by former United goalkeeper Harry Gregg. I remember that tournament for two things. First, it was probably the one and only time that Gaz has played left-back, directly behind me, and we argued like cat and dog throughout every game. Nobby Stiles loved it.

Gary Neville: Ben was the snappy one.

Ben: I also remember it for Keith scoring a hat-trick in the quarter-final against Liverpool, in a game we won 4-1.

Keith Gillespie: It was a long week in that we played Monday, Tuesday, Wednesday, Thursday and Friday; six games in five days, 40-minute halves. It was a great beginning for us all.

Ben: The atmosphere was brilliant and we got to line up against teams we'd never heard of, like Akureyri from Iceland. In the group stages one of the teams we played was Hearts; we drew 1-1 and I scored. I ran from inside our own half and beat about five men before putting it into the net – Giggsy-esque. It won goal of the tournament.

Gary Neville: At that age we were all starting on this journey. It was competitive, it was pressurised; you felt a little bit intimidated by the whole thing. But Ben was very confident. He really got on with everybody, he had a bubbly personality and that smile – and he was a brilliant player. If you were to liken him to someone, he had the style and change of direction of Eden Hazard. He had a low centre of gravity and he could beat a man. He had that two or three yards to get through someone – the quick ones go under defenders' armpits.

Ben: Our semi-final was against Motherwell and it went into extra time, by the end of which it was still a goalless draw. We had to take penalties and I was penalty-taker number five. At 4-3 to us, they stepped up and the guy skyed it. So it was up to me – and I took a terrible penalty but the goalkeeper did everything he could to help me. Having scored I started running, everyone jumped on me and somebody gave me a dead leg. After everyone had got up I was sparko, thinking, 'I've got to play a final tomorrow.' Oh my life. I was icing it constantly. It wasn't too bad in the end though and we played Hearts again in the final, I scored again and we won 2-0.

Jimmy Curran: It was in that tournament that I first saw Ben play and he was outstanding in the final. He was a brave lad who got stuck in.

Ben: Even when we won, it didn't really register that it was an international tournament. The big scalp was when we beat Liverpool, because there are a lot of United and Liverpool supporters in Northern Ireland; Keith scored a hat-trick in that game. Actually, that reminds me: I'm not one for blowing my own trumpet but I was, by a country mile, player of the tournament. But, strangely, they gave the award to Keith Gillespie of Northern Ireland.

Jimmy Curran: Ben should have been man of the match in the final too but they gave that to Keith as well.

Keith Gillespie: I wouldn't disagree with any of that.

Ben: But never mind because I think I kissed Keith's sister that night. He doesn't know that yet.

The next day we all got the coach to Old Trafford and arrived back at lunchtime. The first team had been at pre-season training and I remember Sparky saying, 'Well done, lads,' as he got in his car. He had a blue Mercedes with the number plate LMH 123 (his first name is actually Leslie, in case you're wondering).

After the Milk Cup it was time for the season proper to kick off. It's so different now but when I started we had a B team, an A team, a reserve team and the first team. The B team was made up of mainly first- and second-year apprentices, the A team was made up of mainly second-year apprentices and young pros, and the reserves was made up of mainly young pros and players from the first team who the manager deemed in need of a game. But there were no age restrictions for any of those teams; Lee Sharpe and Paul Parker, for example, played in B team matches while I was there.

When it came to home matches, the B team would play at Littleton Road, the A team would play on the pitch at The Cliff and back then the reserves played all of their matches at Old Trafford. A team and B team games were always Saturday mornings apart from, in the A-team league, Morecambe, who for some reason played on a Friday night. It was only once a year but you always thought, 'I don't want to play in that.' The other one you never wanted was Carlisle away. That's a killer. And do you know what? I avoided it for two years. Though I did have to go to Morecambe once. That wasn't nice.

Nobby was in charge of the B team and he was a lovely, lovely fella who was very enthusiastic. And bless him, he's struggling with dementia now. But it was brilliant to have him around and he actually retired at the end of the 1992 season. When he was doing his half-time team talks he'd grab hold of lads to show them where he wanted them on the pitch and if you hadn't done so well he'd normally try to find a way to tell you that meant you didn't feel like you wanted to go and cry in a corner.

Joe Lydiate: My dad tells a story of when he and my mum had a friend who owned a wine bar in Sale called the Brook, which was frequented by footballers and staff from United and Man City. My dad was a friend of Ned Kelly, then head of security at Old Trafford, and on this particular Sunday in the early 90s they shared a drink with former United manager Sir Matt Busby and former players Shay Brennan and Nobby Stiles, among others.

My dad was sat next to Nobby and on the other side of Nobby was my dad's friend Myles, who owned the bar. At some point Myles said, 'Come on then, Nobby, who is the best young player out of all the up-and-coming lads at United?' Without a moment's hesitation Nobby replied, 'Ben Thornley.' Myles, surprised, said, 'What, even including Giggsy?' Nobby paused and said, 'Ben is the closest I've seen to George Best in all my time at the club.' Sir Matt, apparently, didn't bat an eyelid.

Ben: I actually met George Best in 1998, at a sportsman's dinner when I was at Huddersfield. When I got there, panic ensued because they'd got him into a B&B across from the stadium at 2pm but he'd gone missing. They found him at 6.30pm, got him to the ground and all he did was drink whiskey after whiskey after whiskey, all night.

He didn't have anything to eat but he seemed fine. I was sat there with a sparkling water making sure I didn't make an arsehole of myself. And George had heard of me, which was great. He was very well schooled in the Class of 92.

Chris Casper: Ben was a joy to play with. He always wanted the ball in any position; he used to get kicked a lot but he was able to deal with it.

Ben: I played in my first game proper for United, as an apprentice, on 24 August 1991. It was for the B team against Wigan Athletic; I played on the left wing and scored. I squared the guy up, went to go on my right foot, came back on my left and smashed it in the bottom corner. I used to do that week in, week out when I was playing for Salford Boys and Cadishead; I'd dance round three or four players at will at times.

Admittedly it was going to be more difficult now because I was up against better opposition but I didn't see it as that big a challenge. I didn't really know any different because it was what I'd always done.

John O'Kane: He always looked forward. He was very attack-minded, which I loved to watch.

Philip Thornley: In addition to the football, United paid for Ben to go to sixth-form college.

Ben: I went back and did my maths, because I didn't pass it at GCSE, and I also did French and history at A-level. None of my teammates were doing the same thing; they'd go to college as apprentices on Thursdays and do a BTEC in something. My going to college meant I was there slightly less than the rest of the lads; I wasn't in on Monday afternoons, Tuesday mornings or Thursdays. Well, in theory: the problem was that I spent more time at the football club than I really should have done.

Philip Thornley: He'd go to Eric Harrison and say, 'Do you need me for training on such and such a day this week?' And Eric would say, 'Oh, yeah, I need you for training.' But what Ben didn't tell Eric was that he'd got a lecture that day, so he'd just not turn up for college.

Ben: I took the exams but didn't pass them, despite being more than capable. I regret that now but as a kid you don't realise the implications of something like that. It was a stupid decision but what can I do? You live by your mistakes.

Around October time that season, United were quick to get our crop of apprentices into the A team; from the off it was imperative to Sir Alex that he kept us together. Because we were beating everybody, you'd get teams like Tranmere and Morecambe playing their regular first-team players against us – and they still couldn't win.

Ryan Giggs: Even if he was having a bit of an off day he contributed to the team; he'd work hard and end up making an important pass or cross.

David Beckham: He'd get kicked all game but he'd still put in a great cross. He put it in the right position every single time. He also had one of these engines that meant he could run all game and he could tackle – actually, he couldn't tackle that well.

Keith Gillespie: Ben was a great finisher from early on. And he always had a good trick; I was a bit different on the other wing in that I'd drop my shoulder and use my pace. The advantage he had over full-backs was that because his left and right foot were as good as each other, they didn't know which way he was going to go.

Ben: Before we both joined Man United, Gaz didn't know what to do with me when we came up against each other. I was his worst nightmare when he was playing for Bury Boys. He knew I was quicker than him, he knew I had two feet and so he did with me exactly what he did with Marc Overmars: he fucking kicked me.

Gary Neville: When I look back at the left-wingers who I struggled against most, it was the ones who had a change of direction and could turn both ways. If I knew they only had a left foot, simple: I just showed them that way and they ran into a cul-de-sac.

However, if they're coming directly at you and they can go one way or the other, you're in trouble. You're also in trouble if they can play with their back to goal and beat you by wriggling out of a challenge – and Ben could. His movement was good, his reading of the game was good and his understanding of his position was good. His speed was good, he had acceleration off the mark, his crossing was good with both feet, he was a goalscorer – he had everything. He had absolutely everything that you could want in a winger.

Ben: Once I did start playing with Gaz, I soon realised that he never stopped asking questions. He always wanted to know the ins and outs of a cat's arse and it started from such an early, early stage. Hence that nickname you've probably already heard of: Busy.

Keith Gillespie: Talking of nicknames, I came up with Ben's: Squeaky.

Kevin Pilkington: God yeah. I wasn't going to mention that but yeah, Ben had a proper squeaky Salford accent.

Paul Scholes: You could always hear him shouting during a game and his voice just used to go.

Colin McKee: It was ... unique. Sometimes what he was saying wasn't that funny but the way he said it was.

Nicky Butt: I don't think his balls had dropped yet, to be fair.

Andy Scott: He talked at 100mph, loudest voice ever, with every other word a swearword. Obviously not when parents were around – then he was nice as pie.

Joe Lydiate: He always had a voice to match his middle name.

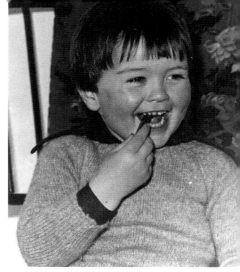

The infamous, and deceptively dangerous, hippo. *Severe fringe. Cute, mind.*

With my mum, dad, sister and brother. Me and Rod must have come straight from a boy-band audition.

Salford Boys under-11s: I'm front row, far left, with Paul Devine next to me; George Switzer is front row, fourth right; Ryan Giggs is back row, third left; coach John Chappell is at the back on the right.

the MANCHESTER UNITED FOOTBALL CLUB plc OLD TRAFFORD MANCHESTER M16 0RA
Registered Office: Old Trafford, Manchester, M16 0RA

Registered No. 95489 England
Telephone:
061-872 1661 (Office)
061-872 0199 (Ticket and
Match Enquiries)
061-872 3488 (Commercial
Direct Line Mgr.
Fax No. 061-873 7210
Telex: 666564 United G

Chief Executive	Manager	Secretary	Commercial Manager
C. Martin Edwards	Alex Ferguson	Kenneth R. Merrett	D. A. McGregor

KRM/LL

16 October 1989

Mr & Mrs Thornley
30 Stafford Road
Monton
Eccles
Salford

Dear Mr and Mrs Thornley

On behalf of Manchester United Football Club I have pleasure in confirming a Two Year Trainee Players Contract for Ben with our club, when he leaves school.

This will be followed by a Two Year Professional Contract, terms to be mutually agreed. In addition a signing on fee of £4,000 when Ben reaches 18 years, we will also pay a 'Once Only' payment of £6,000 when Ben has played in a Competitive First Team game. Ben will also be covered by B.U.P.A.

We will also pay the equivalent of £20 per week into a Pension fund. This will be paid in Two Instalments of £1,040 each, covering the two years of his Professional Contract.

We are delighted that Ben has decided to join us.

Yours sincerely

K R Merrett
Secretary

President: Sir Matt Busby CBE.
Directors: C.M. Edwards (Chairman), J.M. Edelson, R. Charlton CBE, E.M. Watkins, A.M. Al Midani, N. Burrows. R.L. Olive.

I've received worse letters.

The family and me with Sir Alex Ferguson when I signed for United as an apprentice. Try not to be distracted by the ginormous television.

Playing against Crystal Palace at Old Trafford in the second leg of the 1992 Youth Cup Final (we won).

With Gary Neville and the wonderful Eric Harrison in Malta, 1993. My tie wins.

With David Beckham, Chris Casper and Gaz in Malta, 1993. We're in Joe Farrugia's museum – but we're not permanent exhibits.

Making my debut against West Ham, 26 February 1994.

Walking down Stafford Road in the very early stages of the comeback trail.

Spot the 9.5 inches going down my leg. By which, obviously, I mean my scar.

My perfectly reasonable choice of attire for Giggsy's 21st birthday.

With Paul Scholes, Michael Appleton and Terry Cooke in Juventus's Stadio delle Alpi in 1996, clearly having a lovely time.

On tour with the first team in Malaysia in 1995.

F ... iddlesticks. Playing for the first team against Arsenal at Old Trafford, 16 November 1996.

We're probably watching Gary Neville in shooting practice.

On your marks…

Versus Wimbledon at Old Trafford, 28 March 1998. My most satisfying game for the first team (apart from my debut).

The manager and me.

Playing against Liverpool at Old Trafford, 10 April 1998. This would turn out to be my last appearance for the Manchester United first team.

MANCHESTER UNITED

The Manchester United Football Club plc, Sir Matt Busby Way, Old Trafford, Manchester M16 0RA

AF/LL

21 August, 1998

Mr B Thornley
C/o Huddersfield Town Football Club
The Alfred McAlpine Stadium
Huddersfield
HD1 6PX

Dear Ben

I am sorry I have not been in touch with you earlier, but you know how hectic things have been. I am delighted to hear that you have settled down well, and I know that you will give 100% to everyone at Huddersfield, both on and off the pitch.

Ben, I am sorry that your career didn't take off the way we all had hoped, through your injury, but I am delighted that the tribunal is now settled, and you can get on with shaping your future. Your determination to make your career in the game, says everything about your character, which I hope in some small way that the staff here at Old Trafford help to form, and I am writing on behalf of all of us to wish you good luck and good health.

In any relationship between a Manager and player there will be differences and I know that we had our share, but I always knew that I could count on you. You never gave me any cause for sleepless nights and I thank you for that!

I hope your days at Huddersfield are good ones, and most importantly that you enjoy it, and should you ever need me, at anytime, I will always do my best to help.

Yours sincerely

Alex Ferguson C.B.E.

Telephone: 0161 872 1661; 0161 930 1968. Ticket & Match Enquiries: 0161 872 0199. Facsimile: 0161 876 5502
A subsidiary of Manchester United PLC. Registered office as above. Registered in England No. 95489. VAT No. GB 561 0952 51

This piece of A4 means a lot to me.

HUDDERSFIELD TOWN FOOTBALL CLUB

Huddersfield Town AFC Limited The Alfred McAlpine Stadium Huddersfield HD1 6PX
GENERAL ENQUIRIES (01484) 484100 FAX (01484) 484101 TICKET OFFICE (01484) 484123 COMMERCIAL (01484) 484140

FACSIMILE TRANSMISSION

TO: Mrs E Thornley

FROM: Ann Hough
Huddersfield Town FC

FAX NO: 01706 357079

DATE: 17th June 1998

TOTAL NO OF PAGES: 6

MESSAGE:

Dear Mrs Thornley,

Further to our telephone conversation earlier this afternoon, I have pleasure in attaching a copy of Ben's contract with Huddersfield Town AFC Limited.

I would be grateful if you could ask your husband to read through the documents just to confirm that the terms detailed are what was agreed.

I have made contact with the Hotel in the Bahamas and have left a message for Ben to contact Alan Sykes asap.

Any problems, please do not hesitate to contact me.

Kind regards,

J Ann Hough
ASSISTANT SECRETARY

OFFICIAL CLUB SPONSOR

CHAIRMAN Malcolm Asquith VICE-CHAIRMAN David Taylor
DIRECTORS Geoff Headey Robert Whiteley ASSOCIATE DIRECTOR Trevor Cherry PRESIDENT Lawrence Batley O.B.E. LIFE VICE PRESIDENT Clifford Senior
TEAM MANAGER Peter Jackson COMPANY SECRETARY Alan Sykes COMMERCIAL MANAGER Alan Stevenson
REGISTERED IN ENGLAND No 129960

Sign for Huddersfield while on holiday in the Bahamas? Don't mind if I do.

Reserved celebrations after my last-minute winner against Wolves in 1998.

I had a lot of time for Peter Jackson.

In action for Huddersfield in the Yorkshire derby against Barnsley in 1999 (we won 2-1).

Just one of many polite enquiries over the years.

Celebrating with Steve Jenkins and David Beresford after scoring against Wrexham in the FA Cup, 3 February 1999. I wouldn't have played if I hadn't bought the manager, Peter Jackson, a bottle of champers.

*Consoling
Jamie
Vincent after
we'd lost
to Fulham
and missed
out on the
play-offs in
2000.*

One of my Best moments.

My wedding day at Mottram Hall in 2005.

A fab picture of me playing for Aberdeen.

This was after scoring on my home debut against Motherwell in 2001.

My debut for Blackpool against Huddersfield in 2003 (that's Steve Jenkins again).

Lining up for Manchester United legends for a game against Barcelona in 2017. I'm front row, far left.

Lucas, Les and me — my favourite line-up.

Phil Neville: If he got tackled really hard, he'd scream.

Mike Phelan: It stood out in a male environment. It was a child's voice in a grown-up world.

Rod Thornley: I mean, yeah, he has got an annoying voice. He still pulled loads of birds though.

Mark Rawlinson: Even now it goes higher when he gets excited – and he's quite an excitable character. Everything seems to be brilliant with Ben.

Ben: Yep, I had a high-pitched voice. It was a high-pitched Salford shriek, in fact. Not pleasant to listen to.

Paul Devine: He was always chirping away. He still does now when he's commentating on the radio.

Ben: At that time divisions one and two of the Lancashire League – the A- and B-team leagues – were regional competitions. So when you were an apprentice, the FA Youth Cup was great because you came up against lads who you didn't see week in, week out. There was a chance you'd end up playing the likes of Arsenal, Chelsea, West Ham or Tottenham. That made it the pinnacle.

The 'youth team' was made up of the players who United deemed best out of the two-year apprentice cycle. By and large it was mostly first years that season: there was me, David Beckham, Gary Neville, Chris Casper, John O'Kane, Keith Gillespie, Nicky Butt and Robbie Savage. Now, we loved that but the lads who had already been there a year had a nightmare. They'd been thinking, 'In our first year we're not going to get a look-in but in our second year we'll have a real chance.' Then us lot turned up.

9

Huddersfield, Aberdeen, Blackpool & Bury

1998–2004

1998/99

When I went in to see Sir Alex at the end of the 1997/98 season I put forward a stronger argument for leaving than two years previously – and his resistance was weaker. To his credit, he then did everything he possibly could to help me get away. I wasn't available on a Bosman because of my age, which was a stumbling block for some clubs, so I suggested it might be worth contacting Huddersfield.

They paid £175,000 up front, plus an extra £25,000 for every 25 appearances up to 100, making a grand total of £275,000. Meanwhile I got a £75,000 signing-on fee and my wages started at £1,500 a week, going up by £100 each season.

I gathered my stuff together at The Cliff before walking out as a Manchester United player for the last time. I'd spent the best part of ten years there and was leaving with nothing but fond memories, so to a certain extent I was looking over my shoulder and thinking, 'It's never going to be that good again.' But I was buzzing about what lay ahead, especially because I was leaving with the manager's blessing.

I'd never had the experience of knowing that I was going to be in the starting line-up on the first day of a new season.

My mum has always said I should have made more effort to stay in touch with the Class of 92 lads. I did take a step back once I left but it's also hard when you go in different directions. That said, I can still pick up the phone to George Switzer and Keith Gillespie, I see Nicky Butt around the club all the time and I bump into Robbie Savage, Gaz and Scholesy when we're fulfilling our media duties. So I haven't lost any friends over it.

The Huddersfield contract was faxed to me while I was on holiday in the Bahamas and it was great to know I'd signed a three-year deal because I could relax. I loved the summer of 1998.

Well, most of it. After the Bahamas I went on a three-day jaunt to France to watch England play Colombia in the World Cup. Jeff Kerfoot, Paul Devine and his brother, Phil, came in my BMW; we drove down to Dover and hopped on the ferry. The game was in Lens but the fans knew Lens was dry so they – and we – started in Lille. It was a lovely day and we were having a good time but then we noticed that some England fans were starting to take over the shops, putting banners up. As the day went on, the locals were becoming fewer and fewer. Then the taxis started to stay away. Then the trains stopped running. Then there was nothing.

We were prisoners. And the England fans in question, with no locals to berate, started turning on each other; you had the Birmingham Zulus and West Ham's ICF going looking for their club rivals. When a pint pot smashed on the floor next to me while I was on the phone to my mum it was my cue to say to the lads, 'We've got to get back to my car if we want to get to Lens. I'll speak French to someone and ask where the nearest train station is that's still running. Then we can get back to our hotel and pick up the BMW.' We were four hours out from kick-off.

A pharmacist gave us directions but we ended up walking through an area where we might have had trouble if anyone had picked up on the fact that we were English. And I'm sorry but four lads from Salford wandering through some random French estate? We must have stuck out like spare pricks at a wedding. But we made it. And our seats turned out to be right behind the goal where Becks scored his free kick.

Because of that trip I missed the first three days of pre-season at Huddersfield. I'd booked it before I signed so they'd given me permission to start back late but it wasn't the best of first impressions. Still, I was there in time for a week with the Royal Marines down in Poole, which was brilliant because we all bonded (even if it did involve sinking to the bottom of a swimming pool with a rifle around my neck).

One Huddersfield player I'd already bonded with was Kevin Gray, who I first met when I was at the club on loan. We soon became a double act. I made him laugh – he used to call me 'fool' – and his missus, more fool her, actively encouraged him to make me feel welcome, which he did on numerous occasions by introducing me to the locals. We'd still be mates now if we saw each other but I don't know where he is or what he's up to.

I also got on with the manager, Peter Jackson, who'd replaced Brian Horton in 1997. Because Peter had played in the lower leagues, he thought I must be a millionaire because I'd arrived from Man United: 'Come on Ben, how big is your house?' It was like he was still a player, wanting to be one of the lads; it was his first management job and he was only 36. Whereas Terry Yorath, his assistant, had managed for years, including Wales. There was a bit of a Welsh contingent at the club actually because we had Barry Horne and David Phillips in the squad and Neville Southall was goalkeeping coach. He was a funny fella and an exceptional head-tennis player. He'd take the mickey out of me, mainly for being small and from Manchester.

There was one bone of contention and trust it to be with the hardest person to have ever played football: Andy Morrison. Andy, or Jock as he was known, was Plymouth born and bred but moved to Blackburn Rovers in the early 1990s in a double deal that involved, of all people, Nicky Marker. And he actually played in the game when Nicky tackled me.

I was nervous. Jock is an intimidating character: he talks like Jethro, he's got a head the size of a Rottweiler's and everything else follows suit. But when we spoke about what had happened there was no issue, in that he was never going to start hating Nicky Marker and I was never going to start liking him. So it was what it was, we forged our own relationship and got on brilliantly.

I made my debut against Bury at Gigg Lane, which was the ground where I'd got injured. But going back there never bothered me in the slightest – in fact I enjoyed playing there. I had a really good game but we lost 1-0. In the September I scored the winner against Wolves in the fourth minute of injury time and the *Daily Express* called it a 'quite magnificent lob'. It was a lob but it wasn't magnificent; I just didn't have the energy to run anymore so I needed to shoot. I took my shirt off and got mobbed by Peter Jackson and my team-mates. I was booked for that and Huddersfield got a letter from the Football League about my behaviour. Excellent.

Against QPR in October I scored from 25 yards; I was playing against Tim Breacker, who I was up against when I made my debut for United in 1994. I was *The Sun* Star Man for that game but next came an example of how, although I did like Peter, there were times when he was naive. He was normally really jovial with me but in the hotel on the Saturday morning of our next game, at Norwich, he barely looked at me. I thought that was a bit off and my instincts were right: he dropped me. We got hammered 4-1.

He called me into his office on the Monday to see if I'd be alright for the following Saturday; I think I'd got a slight knock when I eventually came on against Norwich. I told him I wasn't happy that he'd left me out with no explanation but he said he wasn't planning to leave me out again and that was good enough for me. So I played the next game at Birmingham City and after a week of not training I felt fresh as a daisy. But then, from a throw-in, I let the ball go across me and as I went to hook it on, Darren Purse, the idiot (though I know he didn't mean it), came through with his studs and went straight into my second metatarsal. Snapped. Gone.

After the game some of the lads helped me on to the coach. A group of Birmingham fans saw them walking back to the dressing room and I heard shouting: 'Huddersfield scum!' Then they spotted the coach and threw a brick through the front window. The driver ran off, which meant I was totally on my own – until these fans decided to get on and join me.

I thought I was a goner. I was sitting at the back in the middle seat, with my foot on the armrest in front. They started giving me abuse but, fortunately, once they saw my foot they stopped coming towards me, then got off anyway because they heard the police arriving. If they'd thought I was capable of putting my dukes up they probably would have given me a beating. It was scary.

I drank half a bottle of Jack Daniel's on the way back because I was in so much pain – and that night I went out. I wasn't even on crutches, I was literally dragging my foot around Wakefield town centre. The next morning I woke up at Kev's house and my foot was ginormous. John Dickens, Huddersfield's physio, was a very nice guy and when I told him what I'd been up to he said, 'I won't say anything, let's just get you to hospital.' They confirmed that it was a break so John rang Peter to let him know and he was gutted. So was I: I was out for three months. During that spell I ended up carrying a bit of weight again, disillusioned with the fact that every time I seemed to be doing alright I'd get injured. The team had been playing well and so had I; it felt like people were relying on me again and I hadn't really had that since winning the Youth Cup.

Once my ankle had healed, Peter was umming and aahing about whether to start me in my first game back. It was an FA Cup replay against Wrexham in early February that was also the game when they announced that Bradford businessman Barry Rubery was taking over as owner; there was a firework display and all sorts. Anyway, Peter said, 'Tell you what, bring me a bottle of champagne and I'll start you.' Next day I stopped off on the way to the ground to buy him a bottle of Laurent-Perrier rosé – and he picked me. Not only that but I scored our second goal in a 2-1 win. It was shown live on ITV and you can imagine the reaction: 'What a great decision by Peter Jackson to take a gamble on Ben Thornley.' He took all the plaudits for it as well so I said, 'If I hadn't bought you that champagne, would you have played me?' He said, 'No, would I fuck.'

We had a bad end to that season. We went out to Derby in the next round of the Cup and from 9 March we only won one league game in 11 (I scored in that one win, 3-2 at Bradford). Our last match, 0-0 at home to Crewe, was the worst game of all time. We finished tenth, having been top in October, so Barry Rubery sacked Peter. We saw him leaving the ground in tears and that wasn't nice because he was a proud fella. I don't know what he's up to now but if we were to see each other again it would be a happy meeting.

Post-season, me and my girlfriend Catherine flew to Malta for a week's holiday. While we were there John Buttigieg, then president of the island's supporters club, said, 'We're chartering a plane to Barcelona on Wednesday night – why don't you come?' United were playing Bayern Munich in the Champions League Final. I said, 'Well John, mainly because I've not got a ticket.' He said, 'We can sort that.'

There was no need to pack: we were flying back at 7am the following morning. So we took off on this chartered Air Malta flight and nobody sat down for two hours. There were people doing the conga up and down the aisle; I've never seen anything like it. Once there we met up with Neville Neville, who had all the tickets, then inside the Camp Nou I saw Steve Bruce a few rows up, who'd just been confirmed as Huddersfield's new manager. I waved and he gave me a thumbs-up, then pointed at my beer and made a cut-throat gesture. But he laughed because he was (fortunately) only joking.

After the game (United won, by the way) we went to the Hotel Arts and the team came back to start the party at about 2.15am. At 5.30am we left for the airport. It was one of the most energetic yet tiring days I've ever had.

Soon after, I took Catherine to Antigua. I'll let Chris Casper set the scene:

'In the mid-90s I went away with my girlfriend Karen to a Sandals resort in St Lucia, then Antigua the following year; we liked Antigua so much that we went back there for our honeymoon in the summer of 1999. Not long after it was booked, Ben said, "Chris, you've been to Sandals – which did you prefer, St Lucia or Antigua?" I said, "They're both nice but to be fair we're going to Antigua on our honeymoon." And he just said, "Oh, right."

'A few days later I was round at his house, about to head off for a night out, when his dad said, "Chris, how do you feel about Ben coming on your honeymoon?" Ben had scarpered out of the lounge so I found him and said, "You're not going when we're going, are you?" Of course he was. I'm sure he planned it.'

I promise I didn't – I'd already booked it before I knew Chris and Karen were going. And Casp also had Kevin Gray and his then wife Debbie for company because they came with us. While we were there it was Debbie and Kevin's anniversary and Catherine's 21st on the same night, so the two girls went to bed early because they were paralytic. That was when me and Kev got talking to two female tennis coaches from Germany. The conversation went so well that we ended up disappearing with them: he went to an outdoor gym with his new companion and I was stark bollock naked in the sea with mine.

As it turned out, fellow footballer Kevin Phillips was also at the hotel with his wife Julie, and it was his missus who told my missus (who was awake by this stage) that she'd seen us leaving with two girls. Ultimately I've got to take some responsibility for what happened but Julie's got a certain portion of the blame in all this too – as has Kevin Phillips for bringing her.

So Kevin (Gray) was rattling away on this crash mat behind a partition wall when he heard voices, and realised it was the girls. Just as he thought he was done for, my missus shouted to his missus, 'Come on, they're not here.' Kev poked his head up to watch them walking away towards the beach – and that's where they caught me, otherwise engaged, lying down in the surf. Debbie came racing into the sea, I jumped out of the way and she went straight for the tennis coach and banjoed her. To add insult to actual injury, I couldn't find my clothes afterwards. I never did, in fact. Ridiculous.

More ridiculous: I proposed to Catherine on the flight home the next day. Even more ridiculous: She said yes. We never got married though. And while I look back now and laugh about what happened, I'm genuinely not proud because it must have been horrible for her. Catherine I mean, not the tennis coach.

Some time after that I jetted off to Tenerife to hook up with a girl from Huddersfield who I met in a showroom selling high-performance cars, where she was a part-time sales girl. We never went out in the city as a couple because she had a boyfriend, so we'd just meet up in different places – like Tenerife, where she was working this particular summer. On another occasion I was at a hotel in Huddersfield called the Old Golf House, which is where I'd often spend the night if I was staying over and I wasn't at Kev's house. One evening the night porter rang up and said, 'I've got a young lady at the door asking to see you.' I said, 'Right, what did she say her name was?' In the background I heard this voice say, 'Don't tell him.' So I double-checked she was on her own and then asked him to send her up.

When she knocked at the door, all I could see through the peephole was this wave of long blonde hair going down the back of a long coat, as she had her back to me. When I opened the door the girl from the car showroom walked in and I said, 'How did you know I was here?' She said, 'You're not disappointed are you?' I replied that I wasn't, to which she said, 'No, you wouldn't want to be either,' and opened her coat to reveal that she was entirely naked. To which my reaction wasn't, 'If you can just wait for this last game on *Match of the Day* to finish, I'll be with you.'

Our fling officially came to an end when, a few weeks into the following season, she marched over to me in a Huddersfield nightclub called Visage. I was with yet another girl so she said, 'Is that it then?' I could tell she wasn't that bothered but then she added, 'Right, well don't think you're ever seeing your kid again.' This girl with me was gobsmacked because she hadn't spotted the smirk.

1999/2000

Before the season started, a journalist interviewed me and asked what was stopping me getting a call-up to the England team. It got me thinking. Even though it was unheard of to have First Division players in the squad, I'd had my grounding at Man United and was part of a team that had been challenging for promotion. Could I kick on and get myself involved, ready to be picked for Euro 2000? Then it all went tits up.

I thought Steve Bruce's appointment would be a positive development because he knew me. Then I get back from Antigua and the next thing I hear, he's signed Scott Sellars, a left-winger. Nothing wrong with a bit of competition but it meant that, chances were, I wasn't going to start. He brought in more lads too and the club paid them upwards of £200,000 per year, which was a lot for a First Division side. We suddenly had a big squad with a lot of players on a lot of money – and I wasn't one of them.

The season started and so did Scott Sellars. But I came on during our first game, against QPR, and ran their backline ragged. I should have scored to draw us level at 2-2 but I also created countless chances for other people. Despite that, Steve Bruce came into the dressing room after we'd lost and started having a go at me. Before he could finish, Kenny Irons, another new signing, jumped up and said, 'Fucking hell gaffer, get off his back. The lad was only on for 25 minutes and he was our best player. It was the rest of us who fucked it up.' Steve was being deliberately 'anti-Ben' because he thought people were expecting a version of nepotism. All it needed was a 'Well done'.

I managed to get back into the team in the October when Scott Sellars got injured. Yet while Scott was out he worked with me in his own time after training to help me maintain my place at his expense. I couldn't thank him enough because not many people would do that.

On 19 October we played at Stockport. On the morning of the game we were practising free kicks at Mottram Hall and even though I wasn't in the team that day, I took one. I walloped it and it whacked our Greek winger George Donis, who was in the wall, right in the hooter. Steve Bruce found me in the hotel afterwards and said, 'Will you do anything to get a game? George feels sick after you battered him in the head with a ball so you're now starting – in his position.' Whoops.

I played well at Man City in the November and we beat them 1-0. Paul Devine had come to watch and after the game we were driving down to Croydon in my BMW M3 to go out with a girl I'd met in Manchester's gay village; she was bringing a mate for Paul.

Somebody had written to me when I was still at Old Trafford to say he'd seen me in my M3 and did I want to buy a number plate off him for £300. So I did. But I hadn't thought of the consequences of having a number plate that said M500 BEN: everybody knew it was my car and there were too many times when I was in too many wrong places.

I'd be with Catherine and somebody would say they'd seen me in such and such a place, when I'd told her I was elsewhere (I took a few 'detours' during my relationships over the years; I was even known to be unfaithful to the people I was being unfaithful with). She never put two and two together but I needed to get rid of the plate.

However, I hadn't done that yet when I met Paul in the players' car park after the game. We needed to get on to the Princess Parkway, the main drag that takes you towards the M6, but there was a backlog of cars trying to get out of the junction. To further complicate matters, when you came out of Maine Road there was a pub on the corner called The Claremont that was notorious on matchdays and this line of traffic went straight past it. If anyone clocked my registration plate, chances were that we wouldn't get to the M6 because there wasn't going to be any of my M3 left.

I started panicking as we inched closer to the pub. But Paul, a few beers down, said, 'Not to worry. Jump in the back, cover your head and I'll drive.' As we crawled along, all he kept saying was, 'Geezer! Geezer! I've had a drink you know!' And in the back of an M3 there's a ridge in between the two seats, so lying down was like being in traction. After a while Paul, getting twitchy, said, 'If anyone even looks like approaching this car I'm going up the wrong side of the road.'

I said, 'Next time the lights change, just fucking do it.'

'But I've had a drink you kn–'

'I don't care, we've been sitting here for 20 minutes and it's the lesser of two evils. How many people are going to drive in this direction towards a stadium that they know is going to be hammered?'

With that he zipped up the outside and cut right in like we were in *Wacky Races*. Then as soon as we saw a petrol station he jumped out, I jumped in the driver's seat and off we went to Croydon, where we both had an enjoyable evening.

We lost 2-0 to Liverpool in the FA Cup in mid-December and they had a lad at full-back called Steven Gerrard. He was only 19 so I didn't know who he was but he had energy, pace and power; you could tell he was going to become a top player. Not a top, top player though, obviously. We were top of the league come Christmas Day but I didn't play against Crewe on Boxing Day because I got flu. Steve Bruce put me back in for the game against Charlton on the 28th but I wasn't ready, I didn't play well at all and by the 65th minute I couldn't run anymore. More frustration.

January brought the Club World Championship, which was the tournament that United missed the FA Cup for. I was asked to go to a studio in London to join the BBC's coverage; Steve Bruce, meanwhile, actually went out to Brazil to cover it, which was far from a universally popular decision among Huddersfield fans. I covered United's game against Vasco da Gama; United lost and Gaz had a nightmare. In between times I got chatting to Ray Stubbs about the darts; Matt Smith was presenting too. I've seen him since and he hasn't recognised me but next time I'll say hello. I'm sure he'll remember the tournament and if he doesn't, I'll just look a twat.

When I came back I did my hamstring, then my form dipped and I couldn't get back in the team. I used being pissed off as an excuse to get pissed but in the end Brucey pulled me into his office and said, 'You are exactly like me: with your body shape you can't afford to have weekends on the beer. It means you spend all week working to get yourself back to where you need to be for a game on the Saturday.'

So I did extra training and a couple of weeks later I came on as sub in a few games. My agent phoned and said clubs were circling because they knew I was unhappy, but on the Monday morning Brucey said, 'I've had phone call after phone call but I'm not selling you so just continue to perform like you have been.'

I came back in for the penultimate game of the season against Stockport and the fans were brilliant with me. We needed to win that game, and our next one at Fulham, to be guaranteed a place in the play-offs, but Stockport beat us 2-0. I created umpteen chances though, to the extent that their manager, a guy called Andy Kilner, made enquiries about me after the game, but nothing came of it. Then we went to Fulham knowing a win would still get us in the top six – and got hammered 3-0 to finish eighth. It felt like – and ultimately was – my only chance to get within a shout of being back in the Premier League. I wasn't looking forward to next season.

2000/01

My pre-season went really well. We went up to Scotland and beat Motherwell, then we went to the JJB stadium and beat Wigan. If I do say so myself, I was tremendous in both games and Brucey was particularly complimentary about the performances I was churning out. Then, first game of the new campaign, he benched me. That told me that no matter how hard I worked, I wasn't getting a look-in.

There was so much negativity surrounding that season, not least because we only won once (sorry, Sheffield Wednesday) in our first 21 league and cup games. I've got no explanation for how and why we were so bad. It was a spectacular fall from grace. Unsurprisingly, Steve Bruce was sacked in the October when we were second from bottom.

We knew what was going on when he didn't turn up for training, then he appeared midway through the session to say goodbye. As he walked off I ran after him to thank him and say that I hoped he'd get another job soon. He looked me in the eye and knew I meant it so we parted on decent terms, but prior to that there hadn't been many other occasions when we'd been in each other's company and exchanged words.

Lou Macari, who'd been knocking around with the reserves for a while, was next in the hot seat. He'd previously managed Stoke City, Celtic and others but Brucey brought him in when he was on his chinstraps. Lou appointed Joe Jordan as assistant manager, which meant we had two Man United old boys at the helm to replace the outgoing one.

Joe, a super coach and nice guy, took most of the training sessions. Lou only took us for the physical stuff, the running and what have you. Though even when he became manager he still watched the reserve team, home and away, which I admired. There was one thing he did that was a bit unusual though: whenever he announced a line-up he would just read out 11 names; he wouldn't say the formation or who was playing where. That meant we'd spend the lead-up to kick-off having this conversation:

'Are you playing?'

'Yeah.'

'Where are you playing?'

'Not sure.'

Lou initially played me a lot, more on the right than the left. And even though we were in the mire in the league he never referred to it and never panicked. He didn't go over the top with praise and never slaughtered anybody either. That said, if you're ever going to improve you need some sort of feedback after every game. As much as you don't want a bollocking, it's good as long as it's justified and constructive. And although Lou included me from the start in a lot of games, if there were substitutions to be made in midfield or up front, I was always the one to make way first. I needed to perform at an exceptionally high level before he'd consider removing somebody else first.

We had a burst in December where we won five and drew two, mainly down to signing Peter Ndlovu on loan. He was a good lad, Nuddy, really bubbly and carefree, which was what we needed. He must have been ten stone wet through and he was deceptively quick; he transformed us for a little while, scoring four goals in six games. But then Neil Warnock signed him for Sheffield United and even that run of results had only got us up to 19th; in January and February we went another seven games without a win and were right back in the relegation places.

A few of us weren't covering ourselves in glory off the pitch either. Me, Kevin Gray and Chris Holland were playing in the reserves one week and games kicked off on Wednesdays at midday. I said, 'Listen, we *always* get tomorrow off, they'll have us back in training on Friday and then we'll just be in the squad for the first-team game on Saturday. Let's fuck off on an all-dayer after the game today.'

Huddersfield's ground is just off the main Leeds Road, on which there was a place called Ricky's Bar. It was one of these pubs where all the downstairs windows are blacked out and this place was packed out at 3pm on a Wednesday, primarily by old men wearing macs. The stripper appeared and made a beeline for Kev. Then she got on all fours, reached for what we'll call her 'condiments' on the side of the stage, came out with a bag of marshmallows, stuck one on each arse cheek and indicated to Kev to crawl around after her and try to bite them off. The only thing missing was Kev's wife walking in.

After that we went to the Head of Steam, which is right next to the station and the only pub I've ever come across serving absinthe. Chrissy Holland said we should have some and this was at 6pm. People were waiting for their trains or having a quiet drink after work while me and these two balloons, already on the wrong side of six pints each, sat there with these ridiculous drinks in front of us. I tried mine and thought it was alright so I said I'd get more. I stood up and fuck me, I was all over the place. Once I'd ordered the second round the barmaid said, 'You can't have another one after that.' I said, 'I'm fine!' She said, 'That isn't the point: legally I can only serve you two. And you're not fine, by the way.'

We finished those off and went to Pizza Hut. We were steaming so we could only assume that the rest of the night passed uneventfully because none of us could remember it the next day. Then, as expected, all three of us were named in the matchday squad so we travelled even though we weren't going to play.

On the Friday we'd been out training and come back to the hotel, where me and Kev, as usual, were sharing a room. Then, a knock on the door; I opened it and Joe Jordan was stood there. I said, 'Hiya, Joe!'

Then I shouted through to Kev: 'Kev, Joe's at the door!'

Kev, the thick Yorkshire twat, said, 'Fucking Joe who?'

I said, 'You know, Joe ...'

Joe said, '*Kevin.*'

Then, as Joe stepped forward to come in, I saw Chrissy Holland stood behind him in the corridor wearing his dressing gown, head bowed. I thought, 'Oh fuck.' Joe, a teetotaller, sat down on my bed and addressed the three of us: 'What happened on Wednesday?' It turned out that I was caught on CCTV picking olives and mushrooms off my pizza and lobbing them over the top of a newspaper being read by a woman wearing jam-jar glasses.

Somebody in there had recognised us, seen what I was doing and reported us to the club.

I said to Joe, 'In all fairness, I had no idea that I was going to be involved in the squad so soon.'

'The squad? We've named you and Kevin in the *team*.'

We got a proper, proper bollocking and the following Monday I had to apologise to the manageress of Pizza Hut (apparently she'd told me to stop three times and my language in response was a bit choice). And I did play on that Saturday – and had an absolute shitter.

As did the rest of the team when we needed to beat Birmingham City on the last day of the season to stay up: we lost 2-1 and went down. Getting relegated was horrendous. I went to see Lou and he said that he didn't know exactly what was going on but he didn't think I was going to be offered another contract. To be honest, even if we had stayed up I was ready to move.

So that was that. The next day I walked out and never heard from Huddersfield Town again.

2001/02

It was the end of the season and I was out of contract. I was looking at my career, my life, and nothing was happening. It was a barren place. I was thinking, 'I'm only 26. Is this it? It can't be, I'm too good a player. Aren't I?'

Gaz took my mind off things by inviting me out to Malta to do some coaching for a soccer school he was running for the first time; he looked after my flight and accommodation as payment. The school never established itself, which was a shame, but the trouble is that the facilities in Malta aren't great. While I was out there I got a call from Alan Pardew asking me to come along for a trial at Reading so I left straight away. I had two weeks of pre-season with them in the July and Chris Casper was on their books so I stayed with him. We played a friendly at Aldershot and a game behind closed doors against Charlton.

I went to see Alan Pardew afterwards and he said he'd call me. I got home on the Friday night, went upstairs to unpack and got a phone call. But it wasn't Alan: it was Aberdeen's chief scout, who said, 'How do you fancy flying up and having a trial with us?' I never even asked the guy where he got my number because I didn't care. They wanted me there that weekend because Scotland's season always starts two weeks before everyone else's.

Their first game was at home against Rangers the next day, so they flew me up in the morning to be there in time to watch (Rangers hammered them 3-0). I then took part in a training session on the Sunday and on the Monday night we played a friendly at Arbroath. It finished 2-1; I scored one and won a penalty. The manager, Ebbe Skovdahl, offered me a two-year contract and said I'd be in the squad for the game against Hearts that weekend. It didn't hurt that Sir Alex had put in a good word for me; he knew everything that went on in and around Aberdeen because he managed them prior to United.

My agent by this point was a guy called Francis Martin, who was working with the manager's son, Jason, and Becks's mate Dave Gardener, at Elite Sports Group. Franny was a local lad who'd kept goal for a Sunday team called MSS, in the same side as my brother. He sorted me with a contract for £800 a week, with the rest based on bonuses: if you played you doubled your money, if you won you tripled it. I'd never heard of that system before and I frowned upon it at first but it was a brilliant way of doing things. If the team weren't doing well it gave you an incentive to try harder.

Pardew eventually decided that he wanted to sign me but Casp had to tell him I'd already committed to Aberdeen. I was grateful for those two weeks of pre-season at Reading though because they got me into decent shape. It meant I could play the full trial game for Aberdeen and not be breathing out of my arse after 45 minutes.

Having said that, things happened so fast that I didn't have time to breathe. In the space of eight days I'd gone from playing for Reading on Charlton's training pitch to making my debut for

Aberdeen at Tynecastle. Mad. Colin Cameron scored a blinder for Hearts in that game and we lost 1-0. Then we played at Hibs and lost 2-0. *Then* I made my home debut against Motherwell, we won 4-2 and I scored the first goal midway through the first half; the ball came out from a corner, I swung my left foot at it and it took a slight deflection on the way in (though it was heading in anyway). My mum and dad were there to watch so it was brilliant.

Our next game was against Kilmarnock and I scored both goals in a 2-0 win. I was buzzing; I had a new lease of life. All of a sudden I felt like loads of good things were going to start happening. They didn't but you know what, having been slightly apprehensive about leaving home for the first time I found that I loved being up there.

When I signed my contract I got a relocation fee of about £4,000. Straight away I put myself in the Marcliffe Hotel for three weeks, which is one of these olde-worlde places with an open fire. Once I left there, two of the lads put me up: first the captain, Derek Whyte, and then vice-captain Darren Young. Then I bought myself a two-bedroom apartment on the river. It was a new-build and I was in the fortunate position of not needing a mortgage, so I was straight in.

The first things I bought were a bed and a TV but my mum said, 'Is that it?' I seemed to have stopped there. So I bought a beautiful leather sofa – but dickhead here didn't measure anything. When it turned up I said, 'It didn't look as big as that in the shop.' I persuaded this builder across the road to lend me his crane so we could try and swing it through my second-floor window, having got a glazer round to take all the windows out. It didn't fit so we had to try and get it up the stairs. I soon had half the Aberdeen team at my apartment, supposedly to help but mainly taking the piss. In the end we managed to get it in via the stairs, though I had to get plasterers and painters in afterwards because of all the holes in the wall on the way up. Expensive business, sofas.

It was a brilliant little apartment and I even had an Australian stripper as a flatmate for a while. The lads took me to a gentlemen's club one night, I got chatting to her and she told me she had to move out of her place. Having had a few I said, 'Why don't you come and live with me?' She stayed for two months but by the end I was trying to get rid of her because my mum and dad were coming for Christmas; I didn't fancy trying to explain that one away.

I liked Aberdeen's manager, Ebbe Skovdahl, but he was an odd character. He also had a way of trying to translate words and phrases that didn't quite work. For example, once he was talking about Peter Løvenkrands, the Danish guy who played for Rangers, and said, 'Be careful, because he is as fast as a sack of cheetahs.'

He smoked like a chimney. If you were to go into his office and move a picture, the wall underneath would be a completely different colour.

And apart from smoking, another thing he took an interest in was one of my coats: it was heavy, long, cream, furry and unbelievably lovely, just not anybody's scene whatsoever. I don't know what the fuck possessed me. One particularly cold night at Pittodrie I walked into the dressing room wearing this thing. Ebbe saw me and said, in his Danish drawl, 'Ben Thornley, what is that you are wearing? You do look like you have killed an *ice bear*.' I said, 'Gaffer, do you mean polar bear?' And he said, 'Ah, you know, you *know*. An *ice bear*.'

He did piss me off at times, mind you, because his decisions could be baffling. For example, after I'd scored against Motherwell and Kilmarnock, he put me on the bench against Celtic. Why? I did get on the pitch but they beat us 2-0. They were far too good for the Scottish league. They had a right wing-back called Didier Agathe and fuck me, he ran like lightning. Worse than that, you never knew he was there because he didn't make a sound on the football field. He didn't *breathe*. It was as if they had this ghost haring up the right-hand side.

After Celtic we played Queen of the South in the Scottish League Cup; I played a blinder and scored. I even remember Gaz commenting on it because he saw it on a highlights show. I ran a long way with the ball up the right-hand side and then stepped on to my left foot and bent it in. A little bit like (if nowhere near as good as) Ray Wilkins in the 1983 Cup Final. We won 2-0.

Next up were Dundee in the league and that was one of my best games for Aberdeen, on a shit pitch at a ground that felt like a morgue. Our striker, Hicham Zerouali, was unplayable in that game; we won 4-1 and he got a hat-trick. He was frustrating because, a bit like Nani when he was at United, he had bags of talent but you only saw it intermittently. I got on really well with him but, tragically, he died in a car crash back in Morocco a few years after I left Aberdeen. He'd only just had a child as well.

My mate Paul Devine used to come up from Manchester to visit and there were times when he told me I needed to rein it in. When I wasn't in the team, as was increasingly the case as the season progressed, he could see that there was a spiral happening and it wasn't an upward one. He wondered what might come next. Though I should point out that it didn't affect my football because I always put 100 per cent into whatever I was doing at the club and behaved professionally.

I can't remember one Saturday night in Aberdeen when I stayed in, nor that many Sundays. Ebbe almost invited it because he gave us Mondays off, which was the oddest day of the week to pick. I think it was because a lot of the time he had family coming over from Denmark and they couldn't fly back to where they needed to go on a Sunday. So if they were staying till Monday, he didn't want to have to miss out on time with them.

I used to sit in the dressing room counting to myself: 'Right, who's going to be out this weekend?' I was always in control but I knew it was excessive. When I was on my own I'd rarely go out during the week and if I did, I wouldn't drink. But come Saturday night, and all day Sunday, I'd more than make up for that.

Although, now that I think about it, there was one weekday night when I went out drinking. I rang one of my team-mates to see if he fancied it and he did, so we ended up going to one of our local haunts that was always busy on a Wednesday night. This one girl in there spent most of the evening with us – and me and my fellow player sensed an opportunity.

We had a threesome. It was incredibly surreal. It was the first and only time I've been with a girl and had another guy's knob in my face and to be perfectly honest, it's not a spectator sport. In fact it was that funny – and she was laughing too – that in the end my team-mate said, 'Listen, I'm going to have to go.' I said, 'Fine, no problem.' Then I gave her a proper seeing-to.

Hey, this is a book about a footballer – a bit of debauchery is to be expected.

Going into our last game that season we were guaranteed fourth, which meant we got into Europe. Us lads pre-empted that with an end-of-season trip to Magaluf; we went straight there from our last game of the season, at home to Celtic. Before we kicked off there were sombreros hung over dressing-room pegs and carry-on suitcases everywhere you looked.

In Magaluf one night a girl came over with a strange chat-up line: 'I really like your shoes.' They were lilac. Anyway, she told me she was on a hen do – and she was the bride-to-be. She said she was with a couple of friends and her future sister-in-law so she couldn't take me back to her hotel but she'd come and meet me at mine. I said, 'Yeah, brilliant!'

She left my hotel the next morning but not before I'd told her I was going out to Malta the following week, which I duly did. I was having a great time with my mates from back home, including Gaz, when I received a phone call. It was the girl from Magaluf, who said, 'I'm at the airport.'

'Oh, right.' I said. 'On your way back from Spain?'

'No. I've booked myself on a flight to Malta. I'm coming to see you.' And that was how The Malta Incident began.

I drove to the airport and sure enough, there she was. Her wedding was three days away. I brought her back to Gaz's apartment (I was able to stay there because he used to stay in the Hilton next door) but booked her into a hotel, the Westin Dragonara, so she had a base. That night she stayed with me in the apartment but the next morning we went to her hotel and the Canadian concierge, who I knew, said, 'Ben, the young lady you're with was getting phone calls to her room at all times of the night.'

I said to her, 'I've got a funny feeling your other half has been ringing.' She was gone for a couple of hours to thrash it out over the phone, then she came back and said it was sorted. Fine. But to be on the safe side we went out early for something to eat that night and went back to drink in her room, on the balcony – that way she'd be there when he called. But it was getting on for 11pm and she still hadn't heard from him. She decided to give him a ring but got no answer, so she tried his mum and dad's house. His job was hiring out JCBs and his mum said, 'Oh, he's had to go to the yard because the alarm was going off.'

With that we went to bed. But then, an hour later: KNOCK, KNOCK, KNOCK.

We sat up in bed with a start. I said, 'It's your room, you'd better go and find out who it is. But I wouldn't open the door if I were you because I can fucking *guess* who it is.'

She looked through the peephole, looked back at me in horror and whispered, 'Ben, it's him!' Now her fiancé was banging on the door, screaming, 'OPEN IT! OPEN IT!'

I figured that my only means of escape was doing a Spider-Man impression: I threw on as many clothes as I could and headed for the balcony, planning to nip over on to an adjacent one. But I'd forgotten that in their lovely wisdom, because I booked the room and they knew me, the hotel had given us a sought-after spot on the corner. That meant there were no adjacent balconies to climb on to as the next one along on either side was separated from ours by 6ft of sheer wall. Nor could I risk going up or down because we were six floors up overlooking the sea – and rocks.

I had nowhere to go. But I'd told her what my plan was, so with me disappearing on to the balcony, and net curtains preventing her from being able to look out and check, she assumed I'd gone. Thus she opened the door to her future husband who, naturally, was built like a brick shithouse.

'Where is he? I'm going to fucking kill him! Where the fuck is he?'

She said, 'I don't know what you're talking about.' I thought, 'This guy is going to marmalise me.'

Eventually he came out and found me, at which point I gave him a cheery, 'Alright?' Magic. Maybe that threw him because what he did next saved me. I was sat on a chair in the far corner of the balcony with only a table stopping him from coming straight for me. But instead of coming towards me on the side of the table that would have blocked my exit to the balcony door, he inexplicably decided to walk around the other side and leave me with an escape route. His next move was to pick up an ashtray (one of those big, thick, glass numbers) that was on said table and try to smash me over the head with it. I put my arm up, it cracked against my elbow and I screamed at the top of my voice. Then he lunged for me but, again, around the wrong side of the table – so I bolted. He threw the ashtray after me, which whizzed past my head and smashed against the door that his wife-to-be was holding open for me. I got out just in time: half a second later and I'd have been running through broken glass with no shoes on.

My God, the adrenalin was pumping. He started chasing after me and must have thought I was heading for the lift, but I went for the service stairs. Next the Westin Dragonara, a five-star hotel, saw an ill-soled Ben Thornley, dressed only in a pair of jeans, tearing across the lobby floor and legging it straight through the middle of a pristine orchestra because it was the shortest route to the exit. The Canadian concierge, who knew exactly what was going on, shouted after me, 'I tried to ring to warn you but you've blocked incoming calls!' (Why did I do that? Dickhead.)

I ran up the street to my mates because I knew where they were. I explained what had happened (my elbow was huge by this point) and then stayed up all night, drinking anything I could get my hands on. I eventually got to bed in Gaz's apartment but stayed wide awake; when I got up the bedsheet was covered in sweat, despite the air-con. Thankfully I was able to contact John Buttigieg, my mate, who owned a lot of bars at Malta Airport. He was able to get hold of a list of that day's passengers and confirmed that the happy couple had got on a flight that morning. I was shaking by the time I finished the call.

She phoned me on the Monday morning; her fiancé had taken her phone but she'd got my number on a piece of paper. The first words out of her mouth were, 'I'm so sorry.' She also told me that he was outside listening to us for half an hour – and we weren't having a chat at that point – before he started banging on the door. Then she said, 'You'll obviously never hear from me again but you're probably thinking what I'm thinking: why he went around the other side of that table. I've no idea but I'm glad he did because he got loaded on the plane on the way over and, without any question, he'd have killed you. He'd have picked you up and chucked you on to those rocks.' Here's the best part: they still got married.

2002/03

After all that I was looking forward to the new season starting. But Ebbe started leaving me out again and alright, I'm not saying I should have gone straight into the team but I was training as well and as hard as anybody. Yet before long he wasn't even putting me in the squad sometimes and that angered me because he never told me why.

There was no point flogging a dead horse so I went to see him in the November to ask him to allow me to find another club come 1 January 2003. He agreed and once he did, he didn't involve me in anything. I was literally going in, training and having every weekend off. I had a couple of meetings with my agent, Franny, and straight away he asked if I fancied Blackpool for six months. He said the manager, Steve McMahon, was desperate for somebody who could cross a ball and they'd pay me £1,400 a week. I said yes.

I also ended up saying yes to Claire, my now ex-wife who I met in Aberdeen around the same time. We spent a lot of time together over Christmas and then I needed to make a decision because I was moving back down to Manchester to play for Blackpool. She ended up coming with me and initially we lived in a place Gaz had in No 1 Deansgate, then I bought an apartment in what was once the Hacienda and we moved in together.

From day one our relationship was very rushed and never really worked. Which is a shame, not least because I spent a fortune getting married. It was one of the best days of my life but it was to the wrong person, which is a big regret. I have no regrets about the fact that Lucas was born as a result of us being together but we should have called time on it rather than getting married. That's mostly my fault because I got carried away with the fact that we'd had a child and so getting married was the right thing to do. It wasn't. And people were telling me as much so I've only got myself to blame.

Our personalities clashed because we're both hot-headed. She just wasn't for me. We came back from our honeymoon in Mauritius and I thought, 'This is it now and I'm not so sure I can do this for another 40 years.' I only just managed four months: we got married in June 2005 and split up in January 2006. We (mostly) get on these days but it was hardly a match made in heaven.

Neither was my relationship with Blackpool's manager, Steve McMahon. I had an initial chat with him in which he told me what he expected but after that, we didn't see him that often. He had a place in Spain that he would disappear to after the game on the Saturday, returning Thursday the following week. And us players didn't train Monday to Friday: it was more like popping in Monday morning, having Tuesday and Wednesday off and going back in Thursday and Friday.

I have huge respect for what Steve achieved as a player with Liverpool and England but I hardly ever spoke to him at Blackpool, not only because he wasn't there but because he was difficult to get along with when he was. To be honest, he wasn't a nice guy. He wasn't unfair towards me but he treated some of the other lads incredibly badly. I sat next to Graham Fenton, a great lad who'd played for Villa and Blackburn; Steve treated him like shit. When we were getting changed for training, Graham would say, 'Fucking hell, just get me through today.'

Whereas Steve's assistant Mark Seagraves, who was otherwise known as Ziggy and had been a centre-half for Bolton, was there throughout. He got along with everyone, did all the training and kept morale up. I also saw Jimmy Armfield in the gym a lot; he was a nice fella and Blackpool through and through.

Essentially it was a holiday club in a holiday town. We were a middle-of-the-road Second Division team that was never going to improve. There wasn't much of a vibe to the place and it showed on the field. The difference between Blackpool and every other club I played for – even the non-league ones later on – was the lack of togetherness.

There were a few players there I already knew, including John O'Kane and Richie Wellens, former United team-mates who were good lads and good players. Mike Flynn too, who was the captain of Stockport when I went on loan in 1996 – the one who used to start all the arguments on the coach. Someone I hadn't met before but who was a great lad was Paul Dalglish, Kenny's son. Scottish legend Colin Hendry was there too but I found him hard work.

I made my debut against my old club Huddersfield on New Year's Day and we drew 1-1. I came on at half-time and had one of my most effective games for the club, even though I played centre-midfield. But Steve brought me into the team so that I could put crosses in for big John Murphy up front, so for the rest of my time there I played on the left wing.

I made 13 appearances for Blackpool and they finished 13th. If I'd been offered a new contract I'd have signed it but I was released, along with eight other players. That meant I was going into the summer without a club again. And frankly, because I'd only played a bit part that season and Steve McMahon had done little for my self-esteem, I was falling out of love with football.

I was still only 28. I needed someone to stick their neck out for me – or maybe I didn't try hard enough. I should have done more because I had at least another four years in me playing at a decent level, but I never fulfilled that. I could have gone knocking on doors but I'm just not that sort of person. Nine years prior I'd made my debut for Man United and now I was … I don't want to say 'on the scrapheap' but I suppose, technically, I was.

Chris Casper came to my rescue. He'd become youth coach at Bury and suggested to the player-manager, Andy Preece, that he should take a look at me. If Casp hadn't done that, bearing in mind I hadn't heard from anyone else, that could have been it for my football career.

2003/04

My trial was in August and Andy Preece liked what he saw, so I agreed to non-contract terms on 5 September; I was on about £350 a week appearance money, no bonuses. There was a decent set of lads: David Nugent was there, as was Gareth Seddon (later of Salford City) and Tom Kennedy, Alan's nephew. Gary Neville's mum and dad, Neville and Jill, were both there at the time – Jill was, and still is, the secretary.

I played the day after I signed and, bizarrely, it was against Huddersfield again, who had dropped down to the Third Division. I provided two assists in a 2-1 win at Gigg Lane and thought, 'Do you know what, I can do this.' I hadn't had a pre-season though and needed to get fit, so I did extra sessions with assistant manager Graham Barrow. He was a lovely guy who I had loads of time for; he was later Roberto Martinez's first-team coach when Wigan won the FA Cup.

I played in a few games, things were going really well and I was getting my love for the game back because I felt appreciated. Then one day Andy Preece pulled me into his office and said, 'I'm really sorry but you were last in so you're first out – we need to cut the wage bill.' They had the smallest budget of anybody in the league; Andy himself left in the December for the same reason.

So it was October and I was back not playing again. Now what?

10

Youth Cup run 1991–92

Ben: We made the most of all the time we were given at United. And anyway, under Eric Harrison there was no chance we were going to be disappearing after lunch. We were apprentices and as far as we were concerned, we were in before everybody else and left after everybody else.

On Mondays, Eric stayed to take evening training at The Cliff with the lads who were still at school; before long three-quarters of our team was there as well. It was nothing to do with currying favour, it was just that we enjoyed being there so much. When there was an opportunity for us to have another training session, we loved it – simple as that. We'd say to Eric, 'Some of us are going to stay behind, is that OK?' and he'd normally say, 'Yeah, brilliant, no problem.' But there were times when he'd say, 'No, get your rest.' And that would kill us: 'What do we do now, lads?'

Jimmy Curran: I don't think they could keep away from the place. And they were a rare breed because no one had ever turned up for extra training on a Monday night before.

Ben: Eric didn't think badly of anyone who didn't come along. However, if he had a bee in his bonnet about something he might say, 'It's no surprise that there are a few of you here that I've never seen before at evening training.' Even though he couldn't care less, it was a stick to beat them with; he had something that he could pull out of the bag.

With Eric, if you made a mistake – and it could be the very first game that you'd ever played – you'd come in and get absolutely screamed at, even as a 16-year-old kid. A dressing room is a bit like working in a garage: there are a lot of expletives, often all in one sentence and some of which you've never heard of before. So there was fear there but you wanted to listen to him and you wanted to make sure you did everything he asked of you. He realised that some players were more talented than others but he didn't treat anyone any differently. I had my bollockings along with everyone else and there were some brilliant quotes.

For example, in our first year we had an A team game coming up against Chester City but we had a few injuries. Normally when I looked for my name on the team sheet of a Friday lunchtime I was always number 11. But on this occasion the team was pinned up and me and Butty were nine and ten. This is back in the day when we played 4-4-2 so we were the two centre-forwards. Yet he was a centre-midfielder and I was a winger; we'd never played up front in our lives.

The game was the next day and we came in at half-time with Butty having scored a hat-trick – two of them set up by me – and me having scored another two. We were all sat in number order so me and Butty were directly opposite Eric as he walked in. Straight away, the first sign that something was up: as he stood there waiting for everyone to get settled he was sweeping his foot back and forth across the floor. That always meant somebody was getting it. Me and Butty were sitting there proud as punch. 5-0! Then: 'You two! I don't give a fuck if you've never played in those positions – the fucking lights are on but there's nobody home!' Butty and me didn't dare look at each other. 'I'll let you two work it out,' added Eric, and walked off.

Nicky Butt: I was convinced he'd got me mixed up with someone else. I'd never played there before in my life, we'd both played well, I'd scored a hat-trick in the first half and I was still getting a rollicking at half-time. I didn't have a clue what I'd done wrong but I didn't dare go and ask him.

Maybe we were fannying about with it too much rather than doing the basic work. I think that day was all about, 'Don't get carried away – you're only playing Chester City, not Liverpool. Do your things right, don't take the piss out of kids who are not as good as you and be respectful.' Certainly that's what I would say now to kids at that age.

Ben: I'm pretty sure Eric pre-planned who he was going to have a pop at. It seems too much of a coincidence that it didn't fall on the same person week in, week out. Sadly, with Eric having dementia now, it's too late to ask.

Gary Neville: It was like they decided during the week in the coaches room: 'Right, he needs bringing down a peg or two.' I always thought that and more so on reflection now, knowing them as I do. You were tested all the time.

Ben: Another memorable game was against Blackpool's A team, who used to play right near the airport; it was very open and so, at the best of times, it was very windy.

Gary Neville: It was windy as fuck.

Ben: There was one goal we conceded because no matter how many times we tried to clear it, we just kept kicking it against each other. We were like the Keystone Cops. I'll never forget the look on Gaz's face; it was priceless. If he could have laughed out loud as everyone was trudging back to restart, he would have done.

Gary Neville: There was another game we played where I was alongside Mark Gordon, away to Bolton. They kept lumping it on top of us and this big centre-forward kept elbowing Mark. We just started laughing and couldn't stop for the next ten minutes. Now, I was really serious when I played football – you've probably never seen a picture of me laughing on the pitch, ever, in my life – but there was a period of about six months in the A team when we were winning that easily and got that comfortable that we were maybe in danger of becoming a bit complacent.

Ben: At half-time in that same Bolton game, which was being played on Horwich RMI's muddy-as-hell shit-tip of a pitch, Simon Davies came in looking pristine. Eric took one look at him and growled, 'You're a good fucking advert for Persil.' Then, in the second half, Nicky Butt was having a nightmare. Eric screamed at him, 'Right, I'm going to count every time you kick the fucking ball away.' So of course, the next pass to Butty went under his foot. Straight away: 'There's one!' He must have got up to about 18.

Nicky Butt: It was probably around that, yeah. Eric was always on to me about giving the ball away too much. That was probably my downfall as a younger player.

Ben: Then, with 70-odd minutes gone, Butty was having a fight with the ball in the centre circle. Just as he went to volley it forward, a Bolton player managed to get hold of him and they interlocked arms. Butty made perfect contact but by that point he'd been spun around. He hammered the ball, it bounced and went just over our goalkeeper's head on to the roof of the net. Oh my God – Eric went absolutely mental.

Nicky Butt: That was the way to get to me. Eric was different with Ben, with Ryan, with Becks and all those players. He'd realised that I'd react better to being dug out rather than having an arm around me and discussing it. It wasn't nice but it certainly helped me get my head around what I had to do.

Ben: Eric wanted to make sure we stayed grounded, that there was no chance of us getting carried away. Players leaving early, players driving fast cars: that sort of thing used to drive him up the wall. He always referenced the Liverpool team of the 80s and he loved Ian Rush. And bear in mind that he was at Man United and came to the club from Everton, yet it was Liverpool under Bob Paisley and Joe Fagan he admired because they worked and worked and worked. He loved Liverpool through the 80s as much as he loved Man United through the 90s.

That was the work ethic that we had to aspire to and I'll always remember one of his quotes: 'None of you are good players until I fucking tell you that you are.'

Nicky Butt: He was a genius, really.

Ben: When we first arrived, Eric took the A team and Nobby Stiles took the B team. Plenty of players used to say, 'I hope I'm not with Eric tomorrow.' But us lads who knew we wanted to get somewhere would all say, 'I hope we *are* with Eric tomorrow.' That was even if you'd had a bollocking the week before, because it was a case of wanting to get back into his good books. He was the only person who I wanted to see because I wanted him to tell me what I hadn't done well.

Think of him like Simon Cowell or Craig Revel Horwood: you're seldom going to get praised to the hilt, and rarely are you going to get a ten out of ten, but they are the ones you want feedback from. You took on board what Eric said. For the first 18 months at Man United that was all I cared about. And beyond that too, actually: when things weren't going well for me after I got injured I often asked Eric if I could play in his A team. Straight away: 'Yes, course you can.'

I haven't been able to speak to Eric Harrison for the book because of his struggles with dementia but one thing I do hold dear is that he had this to say about me in his 2001 autobiography: 'Serious injury can be devastating for any player. Ben Thornley ... would have been playing in Manchester United's first team now but for a cruciate ligament injury. He was one of the best young wingers that I ever worked with.'

Jimmy Curran: Eric was very pro-Ben and thought the world of him, as he did most of the lads. But he had an affinity with Ben, definitely, because he was a workhorse, he never stopped running and he was brave. If you did all those things with Eric, you had a great chance.

At that time Ben was as good as, if not better than, one or two of that group who made the first team. He could have made it to international level, he was that good. He was a fantastic lad too; if I'd had a daughter I'd have been pleased if she'd gone out with him. He was that type of lad, you know?

Ben: Thanks, Jimmy, but you probably wouldn't have been that pleased ... There was another A team game we played in 1992 against Oldham at The Cliff. It had been well documented that Bryan Robson was going to play and there were a couple of other pros too, so we had a good team playing and a good crowd in. But at one point Oldham's right-back tackled me and it was unbelievable that he didn't break my ribs; I had stud marks all round my torso. Bryan Robson went ballistic.

Bryan Robson: There are a few people who get naughty with kids because they try to frighten them. I wasn't going to let that happen to my team-mates.

Ben: He said to me, 'You just come infield a minute and let me go out there on the wing.'

Bryan Robson: When I broke my leg three times in two years at West Brom, a guy called Alan Merrick took me to one side in the gym and showed me things he did to protect himself during a game. And right from when I was 17 and got into the first team, Len Cantello always looked after me on the pitch. So it was something that I was brought up with.

Ben: When we weren't playing or training, a few of us would go to the snooker hall in Salford.

Gary Neville: It was a dark warehouse of a snooker hall but we didn't know any different because we were 17; we just went. It was round the corner from The Cliff so we all jumped in together and drove there.

Ben: Listening to Chris and Gaz on the field was great comedy value because they had some belting arguments, so it was brilliant playing snooker with them too. They were ultra-competitive – and mainly between themselves. Each one would be talking the other through his shots; Gaz would expect Casp to listen to him and vice versa. But neither did.

Chris Casper: We're very similar Gary and I and yes, we had the odd fallout. We still do actually.

Nicky Butt: They were the Steve Davises of the group: so boring.

Gary Neville: Six-time world champions, you mean? Yeah, we used to think about our shots a *lot*.

Nicky Butt: Scholesy was like Alex Higgins: he had a bit of flair.

Paul Scholes: I did? Really? I just used to smash them as hard as I could, that's probably why.

David Beckham: Ben was decent but if there happened to be a girl in the snooker club, he was easily distracted.

Ben: I'd normally partner up with Becks or Keith – and it was between Keith and Sav in terms of who was the best.

Keith Gillespie: It probably was but we weren't brilliant; it was more a case that Ben and the others weren't that good.

Robbie Savage: I was certainly the best. I was making 70-odd breaks back in Wrexham at club level. Ben was alright but I was the best.

Nicky Butt: No chance.

Paul Scholes: Um, no. Definitely not. And he knows that. He must be taking the piss.

Nicky Butt: John O'Kane was probably the best.

David Beckham: He was the silent assassin.

John O'Kane: All the team know I was the best on the green baize. Savage can fuck off! He was only good at brushing his golden locks.

Nicky Butt: It was important for us because it's where we came together away from football. It was really fun. Well, it started out fun and then it would get aggressive. Ben was always shouting the ball into the pockets and calling out fouls.

Gary Neville: When I'm going to watch Salford City play I drive past where it was – it's not there anymore.

Ben: Something that's received a bit of press coverage in recent years is the 'hazing' that went on at United: initiation ceremonies like chatting up a mop, and punishments like being hit over the head with a ball wrapped in a towel if you refused or 'failed'. For me, it wasn't troubling. But bear in mind that I was doing my A-level course, so I wasn't there full time. It's possible that there was more of it going on that I wasn't privy to.

Chris Casper: It wasn't fun, I can tell you that much. There was a culture that had been allowed to develop over a number of years and I first saw it when we used to go to the club in school holidays, before we'd signed. It wasn't very nice but it's sometimes part of sport: you're going into an aggressive, hostile, challenging environment.

Nicky Butt: You didn't want to chat up a mop – it wasn't the ideal afternoon – but once it was done it was done and that was it, you were part of the dressing room. In that sense it was a really good grounding for us.

Keith Gillespie: It was character-building. I didn't particularly enjoy it and you were made to look a fool at times but it put things into perspective: you were a first-year apprentice with a long way to go.

John O'Kane: People nowadays call it abuse and bullying but it wasn't. It was a laugh and it built team spirit. It made us tight.

Kevin Pilkington: You wouldn't get away with it now but nor do policemen give kids a clip around the ear anymore. I was on the receiving end so I'm in a place where I can say that it was all part of our education. We learnt how to handle ourselves. I didn't see anyone struggling with it and I know I certainly didn't.

David Beckham: Did it go too far at times? Possibly. But it made us stronger.

Gary Neville: I found it nerve-wracking and unpleasant when it was my turn but I found it funny, at times, when there were other lads doing it who were more comfortable in that sort of scenario – like Ben. It was the culture of an era, in that there are a lot of things that wouldn't happen now that did happen 30 years ago.

Robbie Savage: At lunchtime you used to be a bag of nerves. There were one or two who didn't like it; people used to hide. But Ben was like me and just got on with it – if you did then eventually they'd leave you alone. But in this day and age I don't think you could have an initiation ceremony like that.

You look back and some of it was wrong; it would be unacceptable now and rightly so. But it was a ruthless place and I'm sure that part of the reason that the lads went on to achieve what they did was what we went through as a group.

Paul Scholes: At the time you think it's serious. It was no fun. It was horrible really, embarrassing. It made you feel like you didn't want to go to training.

Colin McKee: It was only fun if you were a second year. It was no fun when you were a first year and it was happening to you – it was a nightmare. I'd come from Glasgow, I didn't know anybody, and it's not like I could say, 'I'm not doing that.' If you didn't do it Tuesday, you'd do it Wednesday; if you didn't do it Wednesday, you'd do it Thursday.

Yes, it made you stronger if you dealt with it. But some people *didn't* deal with it and that was the problem. The more timid ones never could. It was brutal. So perhaps people should have backed off sooner but it had been going on for years. If it happened today there would be severe consequences.

Ben: There was an incident involving Steven Riley (otherwise known as Riser), who played behind me at left-back during the

1992/93 season. All these lads set about him at once with balls wrapped in towels and he snapped. He shouted, 'You're fucking pricks, the lot of you!' and stormed out. The next day he didn't come into training and all the second-year apprentices were called into Eric Harrison's office, including George Switzer and Simon Davies. So if you put two and two together, the hazing was probably called to a halt because of that incident. Not least because Riser's dad was friends with Brian Kidd and they didn't live too far from one another.

Paul Scholes: We were just grateful that it got stopped.

Ben: George Switzer later told me that Eric said, 'Any more of this and you lads, the lot of you, will be out the door.' And he pointed at Simon and said, 'You're the captain, you should know better.' Not that Simon really took part anyway; his nickname was Shaky because if someone was having a go at him, he'd panic.

And Giggsy wasn't included in that talk by the way because he'd already moved into the first-team dressing room (though he didn't get involved on a regular basis either).

It was the older pros who were the worst for it: lads like Lee Costa, Sean McAuley and Deiniol Graham. Sean's party trick was to walk around with his tackle pulled over the top of his shorts. One day Butty was sat in the dressing room and Sean – who by this time had given his cock a pet name and was, in no way seriously, asking people if they'd like to stroke it – was coming towards him. Butty, in every way seriously, said, 'If you come anywhere near me with that I'm going to punch you.' He was seething.

Nicky Butt: I'm the academy director at United and it's all done totally different at the club now – we sing songs and that sort of thing. It's a way of trying to get young players to come out of their shells.

Ben Thornley: On a happier note, every year the apprentices did a Christmas pantomime, which was organised by the head physio at the time, Jim McGregor.

Jim McGregor: It was one of my joys. I loved acting when I was young but my father said no because it wasn't a profession for 'men'.

Originally the boys used to be asked to sing a song or do something else daft in front of the senior players while they were having their Christmas lunch at the training ground. I felt it would be far more interesting to involve all of the apprentices at once so that they weren't making arses of themselves individually but as a group – much better than being embarrassed on your own.

Ben was handsome, a nice young man from a very nice family. He was not from a typical footballer's background, I would say. He never got into trouble, never swore, never did the wrong thing. So I cast him as Prince Charming. Whereas Robbie Savage, with that surname, believe you me he was trouble. So I cast him as Snow White.

Ben Thornley: Playing Snow White is the sort of thing that Sav would have been buzzing about.

Robbie Savage: At the time there were plenty of girls out there who would have loved to have been Snow White to Ben's Prince Charming. I count myself as one of the fortunate ones.

Denis Irwin: The panto was one of the highlights of Christmas and that group had a great camaraderie. They were a really happy bunch of players.

Kevin Pilkington: Ben was great. Chirpy, very chirpy. Just a pleasure to be around because everyone got on with him and he always had a very positive outlook.

Jim McGregor: Ray Wilkins was the nicest human being I've ever met in football. When I arrived at Man United he was United captain and England captain. And Ben, if he'd really made the grade, could have been a Ray Wilkins. He might have become someone like that at United because he was always a young gentleman to me.

Ben: Meanwhile, every Monday morning we did work experience: we'd go over to Old Trafford and do filing in the office, work in the megastore, stuff like that. Gaz and I used to work for Ken Ramsden, the secretary to the secretary, who was Ken Merrett at the time. Ken Ramsden's office was along the corridor from the manager's – and Sir Matt Busby's. Sir Matt's door would always be open and he'd raise his hand if anyone walking past said hello. But on one particular occasion he actually invited us in. It was just like, what do we do? So far we'd only had limited dealings with Alex Ferguson and now here was *Sir Matt Busby*. It was unbelievable and surreal. I couldn't tell you what his office looked like because I just locked eyes on him till he'd finished talking, turned around and scurried out.

Gary Neville: I can't remember exactly but I wouldn't be surprised if Ben said, 'Hiya!'

Ben: On 27 November 1991 came the first round of the FA Youth Cup against Sunderland at Roker Park. We'd been playing together as a team for three months and we were beginning to realise what we were capable of. But it was a particularly tough draw and they had some good players: Michael Gray was playing left-back and David Preece, who was later my Aberdeen team-mate, was in goal.

It was the first time we'd played in a first-team stadium. We were used to playing at places like Rochdale, whose A team played on a school pitch, so we were wandering around Roker Park thinking it was brilliant (even though it was a shithole). There was a buzz surrounding the fixture but at that stage it was a more about where we were playing than the competition we were playing in; that never dawned on us until later on.

We won 4-2 but the most memorable thing about that game is that when we came out for the second half, the pitch was covered in snow. There was no sign of it when the half-time whistle blew; it was in those 15 minutes we were in the changing rooms, which didn't have windows so we didn't see anything until we came back out. We had to use an orange ball. It was really strange – and really, really cold.

Robbie Savage: Freezing night. I scored.

Nicky Butt: Yeah, it was absolutely freezing. And we all played crap, I remember that. We got a rollicking off Eric Harrison.

Keith Gillespie: Sir Alex Ferguson came into the changing room afterwards to congratulate everyone so he was obviously taking great interest if he had travelled all the way up to Sunderland to watch the youth team.

Ben: The next round was at Old Trafford against Walsall, who were in the Fourth Division at the time. They didn't half give us a tough game though; in fact it was the toughest game I can remember us having all tournament. It was fucking freezing again and really wet. Butty was the best player in that game, he was tremendous; I scored early on with a tap-in but I was crap. I played alright against Sunderland but against Walsall I was useless. It was only because I scored that I thought I'd be in the team for the next game because my performance didn't merit it at all.

Nicky Butt: They were like men. We were just kids playing football and trying to do the right thing but they were very physical.

Ben: In the changing room afterwards Eric said, 'You're lucky, you're lucky! You're still in it but you're lucky!' And it was true. You could never take any of these teams lightly because they could spring surprises – and youth teams aren't representative of first teams. They're unknown quantities.

Ryan Giggs came on in the second half; even though he was training with the first team more often than not by that point, he was still eligible for the youth team. People used to say that I was on a hiding to nothing on the left wing with him around and when I heard that he was going to feature in the Youth Cup, I went to see Eric Harrison. I said, 'I completely understand that there's talk of Ryan playing and I just want you to know, as much as I appreciate what a player he is, I'm obviously going to be disappointed to miss out.' Eric said, 'What the fuck are you talking about? As long as you're fit you'll be in my team.'

Gary Neville: Ryan Giggs comes in? Ben Thornley plays. Stick Ryan Giggs up front.

Ben: And that was it. Robbie Savage made way.

Robbie Savage: I thought Giggs would be in for Ben. But there's no resentment from me because he deserved his place. He was brilliant.

Paul Scholes: Robbie used to run everywhere and he was a nuisance, pretty much like he's been for the rest of his life. He could play but when you're talking about Giggs and Becks, Ben and Nicky, as far as I'm concerned he wasn't at that level. And Ben was a step above all of us really. He could do everything.

Ben: Alex Ferguson spoke to me too. He said, 'If you keep progressing like you are I will incorporate you into my team so don't worry about it. It might be that you play on the right-hand side if

Giggsy plays on the left, or Giggsy can play up front if you're on the left. There will be times when I'm going to rest one of you, or one of you won't be playing well. But the fact that you and Giggs play in the same position is the easiest thing I have to worry about. It won't keep me awake at night.'

John O'Kane: Obviously Ben had Lee Sharpe to contend with as well.

Ben: But if the manager wanted to play me on the right-hand side I had Andrei Kanchelskis and Keith Gillespie in front of me. Whatever position you play, you're at Manchester United: it's never going to be easy to get into the first team. But then before you knew it, Andrei Kanchelskis had gone to Everton, Keith had gone to Newcastle and Sharpey had gone to Leeds; the path would have been cleared.

John O'Kane: Ben was as good as anyone in his position. He was ruthless and knew how to win games on his own sometimes.

Dave Bushell: I actually had the feeling, because he was good with both feet, that Ben should have gone for being a right-winger. Because if Ryan Wilson is only a year older than you, why fight? Why not complement him on the other side? I really thought it would upset teams to have Ryan on one wing and Ben Thornley on the other. But for his injury, that might have happened.

Ben: The truth is that I preferred being on the left. When I was crossing the ball from the byline, I was more comfortable doing that with my left foot. I could put it across the floor, I could put it in at the exact height for somebody coming in to head it and I could clip it to the far post. I had a greater degree of accuracy. I was also better at coming back on to my right foot and whipping the ball in than I was when I checked back on to my left foot from the right-hand side.

If I was crossing the ball with my right foot from the right, I tended to do it with a lot more pace than was necessary, maybe because I was on my stronger foot. I concentrated more when I was crossing from the left-hand side because I knew it was my weaker foot.

Nicky Butt: Ben was at his best when he was getting to the byline and crossing it. Or checking in early: he had a great knack of checking on to his right foot and hitting the far corner of the box.

Ben: Eric used to say, 'First and foremost, go on the outside of the full-back. Test him out, see what he's like. He's expecting you to do that anyway so just see how quick he is, whether he's alert to you.' And that's the advice I'd give any winger: get the ball at your feet and drive for the byline. If he's quicker than or as quick as you, that's the time to square him up, do your tricks, go one way or the other.

Keith Gillespie: Ben was so good on the left wing and because he was two-footed, you didn't know if he was going to go outside or inside. He had a trick, he could go past players with ease and deliver a great ball. Throughout the whole of that cup run he was as good as anyone.

David Beckham: Along with Giggsy, Ben was in the top two in terms of the most talented players that we had in that youth team.

Ben: Man City were next in the Youth Cup and we destroyed them. We played it at Maine Road in February 1992 and I embarrassed their full-back Nevin Riches with one of my goals: he underhit a backpass and I nipped in, nicked it off the keeper, took it round him and slammed it into the empty net. (Nev, an Irishman with the strongest accent you've ever heard, is now a mate of mine.)

For my second goal I picked up the ball on the left and beat a couple of players by running parallel to the goal, then just hit it with my right foot and watched it fly into the bottom corner. We won 3-1 and I have to say it was a particularly good game for me; I really enjoyed it.

In fact, with honourable mentions of the away leg against Tottenham in the semi and the away leg against Palace in the final, it was my best game in the cup.

Robbie Savage: I had a good game as well. But yeah, Ben was tremendous.

Kevin Pilkington: Ben was good at carrying the ball, beating players then putting great deliveries into the box. He was an outlet for us because he got us up the pitch quickly with his pace.

Ben: In the next round at Old Trafford, Tranmere were hopeless. It was the quarter-final yet it was the easiest game of the whole tournament. When we realised we were in the last eight of the competition we were expecting Arsenal, West Ham, Liverpool, Everton – and then we got Tranmere. And they put on a poorer show in the Youth Cup than they ever did in the A or B leagues. Seriously, they were bad. Giggsy sorted them out. Danny Coyne was their keeper and he kept it to two when it should really have been five or six. I nearly got a goal but Giggsy made sure when the ball was on its way in anyway. Could he not have just shepherded it over the line? Shocking.

Ryan Giggs: I don't remember that at all; I don't even remember playing Tranmere. So I'll take Ben's word for it.

Ben: I was subbed off in that game, which didn't happen very often. They must have been resting me. Surely.

Robbie Savage: We got Spurs in the semi-final and they were the favourites.

Ben: They were a bloody good side: Sol Campbell, Darren Caskey, Nicky Barmby, Andy Turner, Neil Young (Luke's older brother), Danny Hill, Paul Mahorn. A really strong outfit.

George Switzer: We saw some of them and thought, 'Look at the size of these kids.' Sol Campbell: wow.

John O'Kane: But we knew if we kept Barmby quiet we could win.

Ben: And then Barmby was sent off in the first half of the first leg for dissent! Between that and scoring three quick goals we were done and dusted after half an hour at Old Trafford. Barmby was a petulant little sod; lovely lad, by the way, but petulant on the pitch. Then it was just a case of, 'Come and take the ball off us' but they couldn't do it.

Having said that, would it have remained 3-0 if they'd had 11 men on the park? I'm not so sure. Irrelevant now, of course. Mind you, they had 11 players on the pitch for the second leg and they didn't win that game either.

George Switzer: We absolutely mullered them.

Ben: I even scored a header in the second leg and I couldn't head for shit (I could jump but my timing was crap). But this one was from about 18 yards and it skidded right along the surface. It was a really wet night, the ball came over and as it bounced in the area and out towards me on the left-hand side I met it and nodded it back where it had come from into the far corner. And because I'd crossed for Butty to score a minute prior to that it meant that with 73 minutes to go, Spurs had to score six.

George Switzer: They put Sol Campbell up front because they were chasing the game but we still kicked their arses. Leathered them.

Ben: When I got subbed off I think it was a case of it being 5-1 on aggregate and not risking me. I suppose they could have chosen anybody but I presume it was because I played well in that game. Maybe.

Robbie Savage: For us to have beaten them ... That was the one where everyone thought, 'This is something special here.'

George Switzer: It was just mint.

Ben: Having played together for a whole year it was evident that we were a good team. And at the start of the season everyone had said that if we could beat Spurs we'd probably win the whole thing – but nobody held out much hope for us beating Spurs. Yet we breezed past them. And that had a lot of people in football taking note of the emergence of this Man United side, a club that hadn't won the Youth Cup since 1964.

Paul Parker: The boss was creating a buzz around the youth team, talking about the players all the time, telling us who was going to be taking our places. He didn't mean for the next game, he was looking long term.

Denis Irwin: The Cliff was a small place so these lads were *there*, they were right in front of us.

Mike Phelan: As senior players we knew who was in the ranks and who was coming through. We had a nice understanding at The Cliff whereby the senior players used to mix with the coaches, so we got a good idea of what all the talk was. With Ben the potential was there, it was just a case of how it was going to come through and when. It was a matter of time.

Ben: You should enter the world of football with trepidation because you don't really know what to expect. So when I walked through those doors on 8 July 1991 I could not have envisaged that in nine months' time I'd be part of a team challenging for a national trophy that United hadn't won for 28 years. Yet slowly but surely, with the people you're playing with and the people in charge, you start thinking. I knew I was a half-decent player before I came to the club but being in there every single day and listening to, watching and playing with people who were more experienced than me, was making me a much better one.

Brian McClair: Senior games were starting to be played on Sundays so quite often we would be training on a Saturday morning. The youth team would be playing in the A league at The Cliff with an 11am kick-off, so a few of us would usually stay and watch the first half. It was a very good group of players and you could see that they enjoyed playing, and playing with each other.

But certain players will always stick out and when I went to watch, as a forward I'd be looking at the attacking players. You'd notice Savage, for instance, because he ran all over the place – except where he was supposed to be. But I liked the way Ben played football. He was a very exciting player who wanted to go forward and be positive. And he was always a happy chap with a smile on his face.

Clayton Blackmore: I used to go and watch the youth teams because you'd hear about these players, you'd be interested. But I only watched the home games, like.

Bryan Robson: I'd watch the FA Youth Cup games at Old Trafford and that's when I first saw Ben. He had a good touch on the ball and even though he was playing wide, he didn't just stand out on the touchline. He knew when to go and join in with the midfield and the strikers. You've got a good football brain when you can mix up your game.

Jimmy Curran: The Cliff on a Saturday morning used to be packed to the rafters. These were only 16- and 17-year-olds but the fans were coming in droves. We'd never seen anything like it. I used to sit on the touchline with my sponge bag just enjoying the football.

Hannah Scott (née Thornley): The best thing, and the thing I remember most, is that as soon as Ben got the ball there would be a collective intake of breath. Everyone would be on the edge of their seats thinking, 'Here we go, something's going to happen now.' That always got me, I loved it. I was like, 'That's my brother.'

Rod Thornley: Around the semi-final stages, Granada TV were down at Old Trafford interviewing fans. When they were asked who their favourite player was, loads of them said Ben.

Ben: We started to get more attention. If you had Beckham, Butt and Gary Neville playing in the B team and Thornley, Savage and Gillespie in the A team, some people would watch the first half of one game at Littleton Road and the second half of the other at The Cliff.

You became aware of female attention as well. *Just Seventeen*, or someone like that, ran an article on the hottest young footballers – and me and Becks were both in there. You start advancing into the latter stages of competitions and the next minute, before you've turned 18, you're in a national magazine. You don't quite know what to think. The side effects of being at Manchester United and being successful are a lot to take in at a young age.

Rod Thornley: Yeah, he could nick a bird, there are no two ways about that. Every girl in our school loved him. Every. Single. One.

Hannah Scott: I wasn't Hannah, I was 'Ben Thornley's sister'.

Elizabeth Thornley: I was 'Ben Thornley's mum'.

Rod Thornley: From the age of 12 to about 28, I was 'Ben Thornley's brother'. Don't get me wrong though, I got a few off the back of it.

Robbie Savage: Ben was a bit of a heart-throb. Whereas when I look at photos of me in the youth team – wow. I've certainly matured like a fine wine. Yet Ben was probably shaving when he was 14.

David Beckham: He played on it because he found out very quickly that girls liked a hairy chest.

Ryan Giggs: He was hairy before I was. I wasn't hairy till much later.

Paul Scholes: He was like a little gorilla.

Rod Thornley: The opposite of me, really. I've only just started puberty.

Ben: There wasn't anyone who got anywhere close to how hairy I was – and still am. I saw the mess that waxing can leave and decided against it. Rawly – old Body Beautiful – used to do it but it wasn't for me.

Mark Rawlinson: No I didn't, I just matured late. Whereas Ben had more hair than all of us combined.

Ben: I was covered from head to toe. The only place I never had it was on my back, which I was happy about.

Philip Thornley: Well, when he was born it was a sort of semi-horror because he had black hair across his shoulders. I've never seen a baby with black hair across its shoulders before nor since.

Elizabeth Thornley: It was really weird.

George Switzer: He was a wolf. He must have been shaving when he was one, let alone 14. A few times, when he had a shirt on and there were chest hairs coming over the top button, I grabbed them. The sight of it really wound me up so I just had to grab the hair.

Ben: I first played with George, our left-back, at Salford Boys and he was a dream to play in front of. Very similar to Denis Irwin, although I didn't get to play in front of Denis very often. George would get the ball, as Denis would, and pass it to you straight away. And George was brilliant that season, so tenacious. And he was really unlucky actually. He did get one more year but then the manager said he was worried about his height. So he had a season at Darlington when they were still in the football league, then he played a load of games for Hyde United before dropping down the leagues.

George Switzer: Until that season when we won the Youth Cup, I'd never played left-back – I always played left-mid. But that season we didn't have a left-back so I got put there. Ben and I clicked straight away; sometimes I didn't even have to look up because I knew where he was. And if I overlapped – *if* I did – he was always covering me. We were telepathic or something.

Ben: Everyone inside the football club knew George. He was a joker and he had an answer for everything, typical Salford street kid. He was one of those people who would shout 'Boss!' and then hide behind a wall in the corridor, leaving you to face Sir Alex as you walked out of the dressing room.

George Switzer: I can't just sit. If no one's talking I get bored. You've got to do something, piss about or something.

Ben: You might have noticed that there's been no mention of Paul Scholes or Phil Neville in this Class of 92 cup run. That's because

Scholesy was in our age group but never played in the Youth Cup that season and Phil wasn't even at the club yet.

Paul Scholes: Whenever I'm interviewed about it I do try to remind people that I didn't actually play. I try my best. At least I was in that year – Phil wasn't.

Phil Neville: It's something that doesn't sit well with me but because of that famous photo of us all with Eric Harrison, I always get pigeonholed. I was actually a 14-year-old still at school. It's not a bad group to tag along with though.

Paul Scholes: I just wasn't physically ready to play but I wasn't worried; if I hadn't been getting in the team in the second year either I would have been more concerned. That 1992 team was brilliant and obviously I wanted to be a part of it but it was no surprise that I wasn't.

Chris Casper: Ben was just an absolute shoo-in during that Youth Cup and there isn't any doubt that he would have gone on to play many, many times for the first team. I'm convinced of that.

Phil Neville: You know what, there are only certain players you'd say this of but you could hang your hat on the fact that Ben would have become a first-team Man United player. He'd have been talked about as part of the famous Class of 92.

Paul Devine: Even now when you think about everything that everyone's experienced, good and bad, what happened to Ben still feels raw. And I know it does for him.

Gary Neville: He was one of the most outstanding talents that I ever played with.

11

Halifax, Bacup Borough, Salford City & Witton Albion 2003–2008

2003/04 (continued)

At the age of 28 I was starting to think that football had done me as many favours as it was going to. It had got me back from a career-threatening injury and I'd managed to have another ten years, so maybe it was time to quit while I was ahead. But when you've had a life of doing something that you really, really love, it's tough to work out what you're going to do next. I started doing my coaching badges at The Cliff. I passed level one, moved on to level two but didn't take it any further. I never really had any aspirations to be a coach, it just felt like something I should be doing.

In January 2004 my former Aberdeen captain, Derek Whyte, got in touch to ask whether I fancied a trial at Partick Thistle, where he'd become co-manager. Because the offer came out of the blue and because I'd kind of given up the ghost, I was out of shape. It wasn't a good time to be trying to impress anybody. Still, I went, we trained for a day and then I played in a trial game. I was completely, and noticeably, unfit, so it was no surprise when Derek rang to tell me they weren't going to offer anything. I was a bag of shit.

In the same month I had David Miller, the manager of Stalybridge Celtic, mithering me to death to go and train with them. Eventually I gave in but I didn't like it: it was a long way from where I lived, it was an awkward place to get to and for a club that had a good reputation in the Greater Manchester region, I found it a bit shambolic. I played in a game against Prescot Cables that we lost 2-1 but after that I phoned David to say I wouldn't be going back.

The next opportunity arose in March and saw me joining Halifax, of the Nationwide Conference, on non-contract terms. I can't remember how it came about but it was probably via the assistant manager Sean McAuley, who'd been a couple of years ahead of me at United (the one who used to get his tackle out, which thankfully he'd stopped doing by this point). The manager was Chris Wilder, who's at Sheffield United now, and I got on well with him. There was a good bunch of lads there too. A few of us took it in turns to drive into training, including Colin Little, who went on to play with my brother at Altrincham and is an under-18s coach at United now.

I was due to make my debut on 2 March but the game was postponed. And I wouldn't have been able to play anyway because I was at hospital with Claire, who was giving birth to Lucas. The following day, because of the weather, Halifax hired the Soccerdome at the Trafford Centre for training, which was ideal for me, and I can remember everyone congratulating me when I arrived. No paternity leave, you'll notice – straight back in. That's dedication for you.

Halifax play their home games at The Shay, which – in 2004 anyway – was very open and had a massive pitch. I made my debut there against Forest Green Rovers on a Tuesday night, coming on in the second half, but we lost 1-0. The following Saturday I was in the starting line-up when we lost 2-1 away to Telford, who weren't a bad side and had a nice set-up. I was up against a young Sam Ricketts, who's got a very distinctive nose. He went on to play for Swansea and Hull and got 50-odd caps for Wales.

My third appearance was away to Scarborough, where we lost 1-0. Despite arriving in the middle of a ten-game losing streak, and discovering that the Conference was a lot rougher than league football, I was starting to really enjoy it. Then they told me it wasn't happening because of their lack of money and I was out on my ear. It was a club that needed vastly updating everywhere you looked, which obviously didn't happen because they went into liquidation four years after I left.

I was unemployed again, which was a worry. I had enough in the bank to keep us going for a while but I wanted a job and hadn't earned anywhere near enough to be sat on my arse. And, of course, the following year Claire and I were getting married, which wasn't a cheap affair. But that stint at Halifax made me think that I still had plenty to offer if I got back to an appropriate level of fitness. I didn't want to let my career peter out with a whimper.

2004/05

A new season started and I was still clubless. Then my old mate Lee Richardson rang; I played with him at Huddersfield and he's a lovely guy. He's got a degree in psychology and has worked as a consultant with the likes of Hull City and Crystal Palace. At the time he was the assistant manager at Chesterfield, who were in the newly rebranded League One, and he invited me over to train.

Handily their training ground wasn't anywhere near Chesterfield but in Sheffield, so I'd travel in over the tops of the Peak District from Manchester. The manager was Roy McFarland, who was a very good player in his day and had already managed Derby and Bolton, among others. Ricko got me in to let Roy take a look at me, maybe with a view to signing me. But Ricko had jumped the gun: when Roy had told him, 'Of course Ben can come and train with us,' what he'd neglected to add was, 'But there's no chance of me signing him.'

I gave it a month and then told Ricko that I couldn't keep travelling so far without being involved in the team, especially with a newborn at home. I was sad because I'd enjoyed it but I didn't fall out with him over it; he'd just thought there was a chance to help out his mate but got the wrong end of the stick.

Brent Peters was next to call – and call a fair few times. He was the manager of Bacup Borough, who were in Division One of the North West Counties Football League. It was a bit of a distance for me to travel so I wasn't sure but what did it for me was that Brent wanted to sign me from the get-go – there was no talk of a trial. He wasn't getting me there for nothing.

I really liked Brent. More than liked him: I admired him because of what he did for that football club. Still does, in fact, because he's still there, having celebrated his Ferguson-esque 20-year anniversary this year. When I was there he was the chairman, manager and bus driver: he bought an old charabanc, with its back window boarded up, to take us to away games. He was also the barman, pulling pints after all our home games. His enthusiasm was infectious.

I started in the November. Former Welsh international Ian Hughes, who I'd played with at Blackpool, was there, as was David May, who I'd played with at United. Brent had convinced him to come out of retirement but he didn't last long because he started a business importing wine from South Africa. Once it took off, he was justified in not being bothered about playing for Bacup anymore and that was his last club.

Gary Lloyd was also there. He was cousin to George Switzer, the left-back in the Class of 92 team. When I first met Gary he was a postman and he'd get his deliveries done by 11am, which was kick-off time for A and B team games at United. You'd spot him on the sideline in his shorts and sky-blue Royal Mail shirt. Because I'd played with George for Salford Boys, Gary took a bit of a shine to me – and Ryan, for that matter – and was incredibly supportive.

After George left the club I'd still see Gary out and about and at some point he told me he'd started playing at non-league level. Next thing you know, we found ourselves on the pitch together.

Not for long though: he got sent off in one of the very first games I played in and although he came back, I've got a feeling he was sent off again fairly swiftly and then I never saw him at Bacup after that.

However, he was doing his exams to become a football agent and he'd qualified by the time I saw him next. He always had a table in one of the hospitality lounges at Old Trafford and he was at every game with his one glass of what I'd say was prosecco, but he'd tell me was champagne. I'd always stop and have a chat with him at the end of a game and 18 November 2017 was no different. We'd beaten Newcastle 4-1 and he told me he'd just bought a place not far from me: Chelsea Harbour. I told him that it was actually a million miles away from me in more ways than one but he said I'd have to go over for a Christmas drink regardless.

We chewed the fat for a couple more minutes, gave each other a bit of a shoulder hug and I went on my way. The next day I was on the phone to Paul Devine, who was talking to me while stood outside his front door. Suddenly he said, 'Just hang on there a minute, Ben.' There was a faint conversation before he came back on and said, 'Oh my God, I've just been told that Lloydy's died.'

He fell down the stairs at his home in Worsley. He was 47 and had a daughter, Havana. Of all the people who turned out at his funeral, of which there were many, I must have been one of the last to speak to him before he died. People talk about him as though he's still here and it's hard to believe he's not. He had a big smile, he always had time for people and he would do anything for you. A lunatic on the football field but just a great guy.

Our home ground at Bacup was West View and the pitch was terrible. There were rolling hills in the background, which was lovely, but a 1 in 20 slope down to the ground meant that when the heavens opened, all the rain came whooshing down and pooled just in front of the tunnel. It didn't help that the pitch itself was on a slope.

We came up against some good sides at that level, with Skelmersdale United and Cammell Laird the two best. We had a decent side with some decent players ourselves but come the end of the season, we were constantly playing catch-up. That's because we'd have so many matches postponed; it was a struggle to get a game on our pitch between October and February. With it being a semi-professional team, the knock-on effect of games coming thick and fast was that there were times when lads just couldn't get out of going to work. So the results didn't go as we'd have liked but I enjoyed it so much. And to be fair we were ninth that season, which was Bacup's highest finish in that league to date.

When I first arrived at the club, Brent was a little unorthodox in his tactics: he wanted us to play man for man *at all times*. If, for whatever reason, your man got past you, nobody else was to leave their man to go to him. That was Hughes's job, who played as sweeper.

So I said to Brent, 'You mean to tell me that if I slip and their right-back gets past me, you want to allow him to run the length of the pitch before Hughsie engages him?'

He said, 'That is *exactly* what I want.' And I said, 'Well that is fucking nuts.'

He didn't stick with that plan, fortunately, though he made out it was because everybody was moaning about it. However, to be fair to him, he didn't shout people down if they had something constructive to say. And when it was half-time he'd let us all have our rants at each other for a couple of minutes before he'd say, 'Right, now it's my turn.' Steve Bruce was the same actually.

I didn't really have a position in that team and I played some of my best football in years as a result. And while I'm not saying that I ignored what Brent told me to do, the fact that I played well, created chances and scored the odd goal meant I could get away with not doing exactly what he told me to do.

We were only training a couple of evenings a week at Bacup so I needed to do something that would fill my days and bring in the sort of steady income that football couldn't guarantee at that stage. Driving a taxi seemed like a quick fix. My brother was friendly with the son of the guy who owns Lynch Taxis, a Salford firm, so I arranged to go and do the knowledge test. I passed that, got my private-hire licence and paid £1,000 for a Ford Mondeo, which did a great job until it packed up in early 2007, which is when I did the same with my taxi-driving career.

I had to pay a weekly fee of around £100 to hook up to Lynch's radio system. Then, as long as I picked up within the area code I'd been assigned, I could take people anywhere. The furthest I ever took someone was to the other side of Chorley, which is about 30 miles north of Manchester. When Collette, the girl on the switchboard, gave me this job she said, 'Listen, it pays well because it's a return job and he's a millionaire but I warn you: you'll probably need to clean your car afterwards.' As soon as I heard 'pays well' and 'millionaire' I stopped listening but I was a bit confused when his address was a caravan park. It turned out that this guy, despite inheriting a shitload of money, refused to move out of his static home. And I soon understood why most of the other drivers would turn down driving a man of such wealth: as well as being filthy rich, he stank to high heaven.

I usually worked Tuesday, Wednesday and Thursday mornings, then Friday and Saturday nights, leaving Sundays and Mondays free. It could get a bit monotonous so I'd break up my day by popping home to see Lucas or going to the gym. And if I happened to make a lot of money in one day, I wouldn't work the next. I should have done a lot more.

The only time it was really good fun was over Christmas and New Year: if you put the hours in you could easily make about £3,000 in the space of that one week.

One job Colette gave me was to collect some people from what is now Giggsy's restaurant in Worsley and take them about 500 yards up the road to the Marriott Hotel. And who should it be but Mark Hughes and his Blackburn Rovers coaching staff. He didn't clock me because a) it was dark, b) I had a baseball cap on and c) they'd had a few. I was going to turn around and say something but I decided not to because the journey was so short and it would probably have taken the full length of it for him to work out who I was.

Lynch is still going now and I still book cabs with them – and more often than not it's with Collette.

2005/06

In my second season Brent increased my money to £175 per game, which was more than the others would have been on, but it was on the proviso that I took charge of some training sessions. I enjoyed doing it because they were good lads. I did the pre-season with them and based it on what I'd done with Kiddo at United. Though obviously I couldn't just stand and watch because I needed it as much as anybody.

At the start of the season we got a towelling in the FA Cup when Pickering Town battered us 5-0. Though in the FA Vase a month later we were 3-0 up against Horden CW (now known as Darlington Reserves) within about 20 minutes, and I scored two of them. Brent waxed lyrical about my second. The goalkeeper threw the ball out, I intercepted it and beat two players. After I'd beaten the second man I was facing the side of the pitch but without looking, I looped it over the goalkeeper with my left foot.

In the October, Chris Casper became Bury's manager. He asked me to come back but I said no because I didn't see how the situation had changed and I felt like I'd be chasing my tail. It was tricky because I didn't want to let him down. What swayed it for me was the thought that after a couple of months, the board could have turned around and said that they still couldn't keep me. That would have put Casp in an awkward position.

Not long after that, Ian McLellan, the assistant manager at Salford City, rang to say they wanted me. It took them a couple of months to convince me and I was getting a call a week in that time. It was quite flattering even though it was only a small club then. Moving there meant taking a big hit on my money but they were on my doorstep and it was where I'd grown up. Plus, I could see they were a decent team.

I was a non-contract player so Salford had to give Bacup notification of seven days, which they did once I agreed to go in January of 2006. Brent was pissed off. He thought he'd done right by me by upping my wages and getting me involved on the coaching side, yet now here I was going to a rival team. Plus, there was an element of prestige for him in having an ex-Man United player at Bacup, which I get. He thought I'd let him down but I didn't think I had, so things ended frostily.

So frostily in fact that when we played Bacup in the April, he barracked me from the touchline throughout. He was quite vocal about it: he made sure I heard him saying to his players, 'Go and fucking hit him!' But my manager, Gary Fellows, who's so Salford that he makes me sound like I've had elocution lessons, was being as vocal in return.

Gary had friends in rough places. In March 2006 there was a notorious incident in Salford when two guys walked into a pub called the Brass Handles to shoot another guy to death, but ended up being shot and killed themselves. That was Gary's local. He did well by me though. He was a great guy but he was very serious when he got into the dressing room; there was no banter. Which didn't really suit our left-back George Switzer, my old mate from the Class of 92, who was still very loud. Gary also wasn't one to waste time shouting instructions from the sideline, though he would happily stand there and shout on that we were rubbish. And most people elected to stand on the sidelines at Moor Lane, our home ground: the bench was literally one long stone bench. It wasn't a particularly cosy place.

When Gary got me on board he told the *Manchester Evening News* that he hoped my arrival would spark an increase in gate receipts. Well that didn't happen (if anything I'd guess that they decreased) but we finished fifth in the league that season and got to the final of the Moore and Company Constructions Solicitors

North West Counties League Challenge Trophy. It was played on a hot night at Skelmersdale United's ground, which was packed, and we beat that season's league champions Cammell Laird 3-2 to win the thing. All the goals came in the last 20 minutes and it was Salford City's first-ever trophy.

After that I left Salford and I didn't go looking for another club. Instead I carried on with 2006 as I'd started it: going off the rails.

2006/07

After I split up with my wife Claire in the January I had a year of boozing, womanising and annihilating myself. There would always be different people going out but it got to the stage where it wouldn't even matter if they were.

The way I justified my behaviour to myself was by working out in the gym all week because I'd drunk and eaten so much over the weekend. And when I say 'weekend', I'm not talking about going out for a few drinks on Saturday night: I'd start on Thursday evening and go right the way through to last knockings on Sunday. Come Monday morning I'd very often be finding my way home from some random bird's house.

I went on Paul Devine's stag do and stayed awake for three days and nights solid, just drinking and drinking and drinking. I was poleaxed before we even got on the plane to Portugal, so when we got to Faro airport I was having running races with the luggage trolleys and generally being a complete dick. Inevitably I pulled the brake by mistake, went careering over the top and landed in the middle of the arrivals hall. Everyone stopped and stared; you can imagine how busy it was in the middle of summer. I'd split my head open and worst of all, I didn't even realise.

My mate played Florence Nightingale and patched me up. He gave me some tissue to press on the wound and said, 'Just hold that there while I go and get more.' By the time he got back my hand had strayed to the other side of my head and my arm was covered in blood. He's since told me that he wishes he'd taken a photograph but at the time he was genuinely concerned because my head was split wide open.

When I got back from that trip and the effects of the alcohol wore off, it was like I had Parkinson's because of all the shaking I was doing from the withdrawal. It lasted two days, to the extent that my mum printed off something from the internet for me to read, trying to show me what I was doing to myself. Because while it wasn't the first time, it was the worst time.

And then I met a girl called Lex, who in short order became my girlfriend and let me move in with her. It was perfect because it got me out of my mum and dad's house, which meant I was isolated from the areas where I was engaging in these antics – and the mates I most often engaged in them with.

But I treated Lex's house as a stopgap and I treated Lex like shit. She thought I was marvellous until she picked up on the fact that I was a layabout. Fortunately I realised that I couldn't keep living like that so I enrolled to do a sports-management course at Macclesfield College; around the same time I started coaching school kids at Wilmslow Academy. Ultimately I didn't complete the course because it was tedious and nor did I do the coaching for long, but they both made me feel better. A lot better. Because that year had been a nightmare.

2007/08

After Salford City I did keep my hand in to an extent by playing for a Sunday team called Wilmslow Albion. Meanwhile, my brother was playing for a non-league side called Witton Albion in the Northern Premier League Premier Division. The manager, Jim Vince, was the cousin of Rod's then wife, so Rod said to him, 'Get my brother down, he's not doing anything.' I'd always wanted to play in a team with my brother and I think the same went for him, so once the opportunity arose for us to give it a whirl I was up for it.

I trained with them but for some reason, Jim was reluctant to include me in the team. He did manage to play me in the last game of that season at North Ferriby, where I came on as a second-half substitute beneath the shadow of the Humber Bridge. But then he left in acrimonious circumstances and poached a load of Witton players when he took over at a newly reformed Halifax. Only the captain, Brian Pritchard, and my brother were left at Witton. The nucleus of the team, which had missed out on promotion via the play-offs two seasons in a row before I arrived, had gone.

That summer I went to Portugal and met a certain someone. She's going to help with this next bit:

Lesley Tanner: I was one of three on a girly weekend in Vilamoura and Ben was there on a stag do. When us girls got to the hotel the rooms weren't available and, as my friend put it, there was this 'lairy northerner' moaning at reception because he couldn't get into his. You can guess who the lairy northerner turned out to be.

Ben: That same holiday I fell through a patio window trying to take my jeans off; it was like Del Boy falling through the bar in *Only Fools and Horses*. I was pissed, obviously.

Lesley Tanner: The first time I spoke to Ben was on our last night. I'd seen him by the pool in pink shorts before that, but that was about it. When I saw him that last night he was dancing on a table in a place called the Irish Pub, and I thought he had a nice bum. One of the guys on the stag do had told me that someone in the group used to play for United but I didn't know it was Ben until we were coming home. Then when I got back I couldn't remember his surname so I was googling Ben Thornton. I'm a Spurs fan anyway so I wasn't really bothered.

Ben: There was nothing majorly exciting about the way we met – the excitement came afterwards when she told me she had a husband.

Lesley Tanner: I'd had years and years of upset; he'd dented my confidence and I thought that was just how life was. As much as I didn't want to be the one to end my marriage, Ben was the lifeline I needed to get out of that situation.

Ben: What Les didn't know was that I had a girlfriend.

Lesley Tanner: Well, Ben told me he didn't but then his friend told my friend that he was with someone.

Ben: I'd already decided to knock it on the head with Lex, Les or no Les, come what may.

Lesley Tanner: Either way it meant that we were both still in relationships when we got back to the UK, plus I was in Essex and Ben was in Manchester. So all we did a lot of the time was speak on the phone.

Ben: Once Lex went to work I'd phone Les at 9.25am every morning.

Lesley Tanner: Then I'd forget that she only did a half-day on Fridays and ring Ben at home.

Ben: She rang once and Lex was stood right next to me. So I went outside, had a conversation, came back in and told Lex it was an energy company. I'd been on the phone for 20 minutes and that was the best I could come up with.

Lesley Tanner: The first day back at work after New Year, it all changed.

Ben: Her husband rang me up and said, 'Do you know someone called Lesley?' I said, 'No, I don't know who you're talking about.'

He just said, 'Right, OK.' I knew exactly who it was so I rang Les straight away and told her.

Lesley Tanner: He probably found out by looking at my phone bill because they were on paper then.

Ben: Anyway, that was the catalyst for me making the breakaway from Lex and Lesley splitting up with Mark. Ten years later, here we are.

2008/09

In between developments in my personal life I was very much back into playing football again, so my brother said I should come and do the pre-season with Witton Albion, which I did. And the more involved I got with football, the less inclined I was to go out drinking. Win-win.

I put in a real effort. The new manager, who was promoted from assistant manager, was a lovely guy called Nigel Deeley. He brought in a couple of people from outside to oversee the running and what have you, while he did the stuff with the ball. I knew that Nigel wanted me at the club even while Jim was there so I had a good feeling about the fact that he was going to play me – and he did. What also worked in my favour is that they didn't have any players left.

We played at Wincham Park and I think I was on £180 per match. I also got a goal bonus of £10 that, in general, was perfectly fucking safe.

Though I did score one goal for Witton, against Prescot Cables, and it was a beauty; a bit like Benjamin Pavard's for France against Argentina at the 2018 World Cup. As the ball was cut back to me on the edge of the area I had to angle my body, because it looked like it was going behind me. I managed to lean back, swing my foot at it and admire it going in off the underside of the bar (which always looks good).

It wasn't fun playing with Rod in the end but that was nothing to do with either of us: it was because we didn't win any games. The pair of us would have had a lot more happy memories if I'd been crossing them in and he'd been volleying them home on a regular basis, but it never happened. Nigel was sacked after nine defeats in a row and the ninth game in that run was also my last for the club, because I didn't fancy it if Nigel wasn't in charge. I came off after 67 minutes of a 2-1 loss to Eastwood. Witton went on to get relegated that season.

Next came something I never could have predicted: an opportunity to go into management.

12

Youth Cup Final
1992

Ben: We had a good three weeks to prepare for the first leg of the Youth Cup Final against Crystal Palace. We didn't watch any videos or anything – all we went off was what Eric told us. He went through each individual and said George Ndah was their best player and would play centre-forward or on the left wing. Good news: I didn't have to worry about him because he was on the opposite side to me. All Eric said to me was, 'You play as you've been playing this year and you won't have a problem with the full-back. He's a Steady Eddy: no-frills, no left foot and not particularly quick.'

So we listened to what Eric had to say – and I imagine none of us took it on board. It was because we'd beaten Spurs and there wasn't going to be anybody better than Spurs. We knew if we were focused and listened to Eric five minutes before kick-off, we'd be fine. And Eric didn't have any doubts so that filtered through to us. He had this incredible belief that once we'd beaten Spurs, there wasn't anyone to touch us. I wouldn't mind betting that he realised that long before we did, but it was his job to make sure we didn't get carried away.

Gary Neville: We were confident. I wouldn't say arrogant, but we believed in ourselves. And Ben was at the elite end of our group. He was the first name on the team sheet.

Ben: The first leg was at Selhurst Park. The day before the game we travelled down to London in a Jones Executive coach. We had a training session after we arrived to loosen up our legs and then we headed up to our rooms. To start with I used to room with Keith on away trips but then I roomed with Becks. They tried to put people together who were going to be starting in the team and Becks had dislodged Keith in the semi-final.

Gaz hated rooming with Becks or me because we're night owls and he's not. Great fun while he's awake but then that's it: 9.30pm, bang, lights out.

Gary Neville: Those two were a disaster for me in terms of professionalism. There's a difference between being great friends with somebody and wanting to share a room with them. I loved him but the last thing you'd want is to room with Ben Thornley.

Ben: Gaz would normally room with Casp because they're on a similar wavelength: a boring pair of fuckers. Becks would be relaxed the night before. Where Gaz and Casp would have had the tactics board out, Becks and I would say, 'Leave it to us, you'll be alright. Just head the ball away and we'll do the rest.'

David Beckham: They were a little bit more sensible than us.

Gary Neville: When I was in the first team, around the age of 24, we all started being given our own rooms. That was a godsend.

Ben: The night before the final we had chicken and pasta or something like that. Nutrition wasn't a massive thing back then. I'm not saying they'd nip out to get us doner kebabs but not a lot of thought was given to what we should be eating. All of that came in about two years later when there was a massive overhaul, with chips not being served in the canteen anymore and that sort of thing. If you have the privilege of walking into Carrington now it's like a five-star hotel, with three sides of the canteen serving as much food as you could possibly want – all healthy of course. You can dine like a king in there.

On the morning of the first leg we had our breakfast at about 10am and then all met in the foyer afterwards to go for a walk and stretch our legs. Then we went back up to our rooms for an hour before coming down for lunch at about 12.30pm. After that we were expected to shut our curtains and sleep; it's how the first team did it as well. I was never a great afternoon sleeper and if I actually did manage it, I didn't want to wake up. I'm not one of these people who can get their head down and tell themselves they're going to bed for two hours.

In fact, Becks and me were the worst. We may as well have gone for a game of snooker. Very often we'd just lie there chatting with the TV on. For someone like Gaz it wasn't a problem because he could just sleep. It wasn't a problem for Casp either, as long as he'd had a conversation with Gaz beforehand. But for me and Becks it was murder. We were night owls but I think we might have been day owls as well.

All Eric cared about was that we weren't exerting ourselves. If he wanted us in bed by 2pm and then saw any of us in or around the hotel after that we'd risk being dropped, even for the final.

It was a 7.30pm kick-off so we were downstairs again at about 4.30pm for our pre-match meal. Then we went back upstairs to change into our suits – jackets and grey flannels – and set off on the coach at 5.45pm to get to Selhurst Park about an hour and a quarter before kick-off.

Once at the stadium, everyone did whatever they needed to do to prepare for the game. I'd always go straight to the dressing room, put my bag down on my spot, then go out and have five or ten minutes on the pitch. There was a meeting exactly an hour before kick-off. Eric told us the team and then went through the tactics, which were basically: 'If you all do your jobs, you'll win.'

John O'Kane: There was never a lot of tactical jargon because Eric knew he could trust us to do our jobs.

Ben: Then we were told what time we were going out to warm up and it was up to you if you wanted to get changed 35 minutes before that or five minutes before that. And I wasn't one for superstitions about putting my socks on in a particular order, tying my bootlaces at a certain time or anything. My brain didn't work like that.

Nicky Butt: It was intimidating at Palace because the stadium's really small.

Ben: It was also, and still is, a shithole. But the pitch was immaculate. It was wet because it had been raining heavily in the lead-up and that suited me down to the ground. With the way I used to play, it was an advantage for me to have a slick surface and be able to move the ball quickly. I remember us playing some really good stuff and not even worrying how waterlogged the pitch might be.

We played in our blue away kit. My first touch of the ball was a good one, which always helps. I can remember puffing my chest out and thinking, 'You know what, you haven't got anything to worry about.' Tim Clark, the full-back Eric had mentioned, really struggled and I was amazed that he was in the team again for the second leg. I could have played against him every day of the week and he still wouldn't have got close to me (he would now, mind you).

We scored after 17 minutes when I crossed for Nicky Butt to score with a header. Our second goal came 11 minutes later when I intercepted the ball from Andrew McPherson, a ginger-haired lad from Scotland, and pulled it back to Becks, who took aim and bent it into the top corner with a left-foot volley. Though the weird thing is that I intercepted it going out towards their left-back and I have no idea what I was doing there.

Palace got a goal back with five minutes to go through a guy called Stuart McCall but then right at the end, Becks crossed for

Butty to score again and make it 3-1 on the night. To be honest they were lucky to finish with only a two-goal deficit because the way we played, we probably should have scored four or five.

Nicky Butt: Beforehand they must have thought us Man United lot were all fan-dabby boys who couldn't dig in. But we all played really well that night and went home with the result we wanted.

Ben: Eric was over the moon. He was thrilled that we had a two-goal lead to take back to Old Trafford and he could not see how they were going to score three goals. I couldn't either. It was a great coach journey back, knowing that we were in a position whereby all we had to do was not lose one more game and Manchester United were going to win the FA Youth Cup.

I drove home from Old Trafford and was back by 2am. Mum and dad, who'd been in the stadium, had got back before me and were in bed, but I went in to see them and they were thrilled to bits.

Elizabeth Thornley: I thought we didn't go to Selhurst Park?

Philip Thornley: Yes, we did.

Ben: During the next few days at the training ground I remember first-team players like Mark Hughes saying 'Well done, boys.' They were very supportive, whether that was on the manager's say-so or not. We looked up to those lads. Number one because we'd been watching them for years and number two because we wanted to be them. In fact, ultimately we wanted to dislodge them and move them on, but in the interim they were people we admired.

I'm not sure why but there was a whole month between the first and second legs of the final. In training we worked on defending set pieces; they had a tall team and Eric reiterated that we shouldn't give away needless free kicks, throw-ins or corners. George Ndah was 6ft 1in even back when he was 16. It meant that training was a boring time for me because I wasn't involved in defending set pieces. That was owing to the fact that, shall we say, I don't have a distinct height advantage. It was more a case of, 'Oh, you go and stand over there somewhere.'

Finally, 15 May arrived. It was a warm evening.

Chris Casper: It was hot. The match was tough going.

Ben: The game kicked off and within five minutes, Palace had scored through Andrew McPherson. And after all that work in training on defending set pieces? It came from a corner. They'd pulled it back to 3-2 on aggregate. Eric went mental; fortunately I was on the other side of the pitch so I couldn't hear what he was saying. And anyway, it wasn't anything to do with the guy who had to 'go and stand over there somewhere'.

Nicky Butt: We started off rubbish but then Ben scored.

Ben: It was ten minutes before half-time. I came in from my flank, Simon Davies passed the ball to me as I ran into the box and I planted it in the bottom corner with my right foot. We had a two-goal cushion again.

John O'Kane: He used to score that type of goal a lot.

Ben: I remember the noise when it went in being deafening. I turned and ran back towards the left-hand side of the pitch and one of the first people to congratulate me was Gaz, having run the full length of the pitch from centre-half. If you're a defender who's conceded after five minutes of the game, there's great relief when someone gets you out of the shit.

Meanwhile Giggsy, stood right next to me, was the last to congratulate me.

Ryan Giggs: I was probably playing it cool because I was in the first team.

Chris Casper: We were under a bit of pressure so it was an important goal for us.

Colin McKee: It was a peach as well.

Ben: It was a decent finish and a great feeling but I hadn't been remotely nervous when we'd gone behind because we weren't being outplayed. They were aware that they had a chance because we were worried about them from set pieces, and they seized upon that. But what *I* was aware of was that we had such good players. Forget me: we had Becks, Giggsy, Butty, Colin McKee; we had Gaz and Casp at the back. We had players who, despite their age, weren't that far off the peak of their game.

That said, at half-time someone – I think it might have been Keith – said to me, 'Thank God you scored because Eric was snapping.' Apparently a never-seen-before nervousness and uncertainty had set in with him. He was probably thinking, 'Can these boys handle it? Are they going to crumble or are they going to grow a little bit and make sure it doesn't happen?' Once he had us in the dressing room he said, 'Good job Ben scored because you're all over the fucking place. But don't worry about it, you'll be fine.'

Kevin Pilkington: Eric had a proper go at me at half-time. I didn't come for a couple of crosses and he tore into me, saying, 'Is there any chance you might come out and collect one?' So I thought I'd better help out my defenders in the second half.

Ben: Five minutes after half-time we scored a second. I passed the ball inside to George, who ran half the length of the pitch and had a shot that Simon Davies followed in and scored on the rebound. That restored a three-goal lead: 5-2.

Palace managed to pull another one back through Niall Thompson but then Colin McKee scored the third in the 68th minute. He stooped to head home a cross from Giggs, who I'd passed to as I was running in from the left. At 6-3 it was game over. It might have been more if an outrageous overhead effort from Butty had gone in.

Nicky Butt: Becks put the cross in for that. It's just something you try and if it comes off, it comes off. It did come off but I didn't score so I might as well not have done it.

Ben: I was subbed off in something like the 75th minute with a touch of cramp. I read afterwards that I got a standing ovation as I came off but if I did, I think I must have started it. The truth is that I didn't have a great game in the second leg. I did OK but had I not scored – and if the goal hadn't had the significance of restoring a two-goal advantage – then I would have been pretty much anonymous. But other people stepped up: Simon Davies had a good game, Colin McKee had much more of an impact than in the first leg and Butty played well again.

Nicky Butt: I remember Ben playing really well in that game.

Colin McKee: Ben was the best winger there. For me as a striker, his deliveries were phenomenal; a lot of my goals over the course of the season came from them.

Robbie Savage: We were unstoppable that season. Every game we just knew we were going to win. And you think how Becks only came in for the later rounds and Scholesy didn't even get a game. It just goes to show what a team it was. Never did we think, when we stepped out at Roker Park, that this was going to be the greatest youth team of all time. What that group of lads achieved is amazing.

Nicky Butt: All the talk beforehand was Tottenham, Tottenham, Tottenham – but we won it. And it was like, 'Right, we've actually won something now, time to move on to the next level.' That was a massive thing for us at that age.

Ryan Giggs: Not a lot of people know this but I'd played in two previous Youth Cup campaigns and we got beat in the semi-final in both: in 1990 we were beaten by Tottenham and the next year by Sheffield Wednesday. So I'd missed out twice and that meant I was desperate to win.

Ben: Jimmy Glass was Palace's goalkeeper and a bloody good one at that; he's the guy who famously went on to score for Carlisle United to keep them in the football league in 1999. He has since talked about all the stars he played against who went on to be huge and said that the problem that Palace had when they played against us was not Butt or Beckham but Giggs and me.

However, I think my main input in that second leg was moaning at people doing things they shouldn't have, like giving the ball away. I was having a pop at people, whereas Gaz, Chris Casper and Simon Davies were all being positive. I really was a gobshite when I was on the pitch.

Robbie Savage: God almighty. He had an answer for everything. Oh, he was a nightmare.

David Beckham: He could talk a lot and to be honest, it wasn't all great.

Rod Thornley: That was his biggest problem and his biggest let-down. A referee's decision or a linesman's decision was always wrong in his eyes, he just couldn't get his head around it. I was the opposite on the pitch: I'd try to butter them up and be nice to them. He'd just lambast them and then wonder why he never got any decisions his way.

Paul Scholes: All mouth, whether it was to his own players, the opposition or the referee. He never shut up: always chirping, always squeaking and always having something to say. He still has now.

Andy Scott: Even at Salford Boys he gave it loads.

George Switzer: He certainly had a bit of a gob on him sometimes. If he didn't get the pass he wanted off one of the lads he'd throw his hands in the air and vent his anger in his little squeaky voice.

Michael Appleton: He had a right temper on him when I played with him the following season too. He just did not stop moaning at people and that's when the squeakiness would come out: when he was screaming and shouting at someone, it was really high-pitched. I must admit, I thought it was hilarious but I know it pissed a few people off. I suppose I forgave him because he was a Salford lad.

John O'Kane: He was a bastard towards refs, the opposition and even his own team-mates but that's what made him a winner and that's what I liked best about him. You knew he'd deliver so you let him get on with it. It brought the best out of him.

Robbie Savage: Yeah, he was that good that he could get away with it.

Ben: Believe it or not, I didn't do it so much once I got to Old Trafford because I was playing with better players. Suddenly it wasn't just me moaning at everybody else, it was a cacophony of people saying, 'Well, *you've* not done that and *you've* not done that.'

Robbie Savage: The reason we could be like that with each other was that we all got on so well. At times it was like talking to your brothers because you could get away with stuff. We knew we'd all be great mates again after the game.

Paul Devine: He really was an absolute gobshite. He'd go after every referee regardless of the game. A few years ago I got him to play in what was essentially a charity game for a firm that was a client of mine – and all night he hammered the referee and linesmen, who'd given up their time on a Friday night to be there. At one point he shouted at one of the linesmen, 'Just put that fucking flag away!' I said, 'Ben, he's the linesman, what do you want him to do?'

Phil Neville: He was a moaning sod in training as well but that was part of his character. Everything you think of in a Class of 92 member – the drive, the determination – Ben had those qualities. It's why he's still working for Man United now, because you've got to have a special personality.

Ben: Once we'd received the trophy we did a lap of honour, with 'Simply the Best' playing over the tannoy, and somebody in the crowd put a scarf around my neck. It was the last game at Old Trafford before they ripped down the standing terraces at the Stretford End to make it all-seater but to be fair, everybody in the stadium was on their feet. Though do you want to know the bonus we got for winning the Youth Cup? £40. Fucking hell. For all that.

Colin McKee: If you watch the video of the celebrations in the dressing room afterwards, we're all drinking cans of lemonade. They were probably just for show, right enough.

Ben: Alex Ferguson came in so we were absolutely buzzing. He was going around patting everyone on the back and having a chat, and you had George Switzer saying, 'Gaffer, I was brilliant wasn't I?' 'Yes George, you were great.' It was perfect psychology on the manager's part: he made sure he was there but he was in the wings. He wasn't at the forefront because this wasn't his team, it was Eric Harrison's.

Eric – fucking hell, he was brilliant. I'm a better footballer, or was, and a better person for having known him. No question. He was tough but I wouldn't have changed him for the world.

Gary Neville: There were ups and downs, unpleasant times, times when it wasn't easy. It is tough to play for Manchester United. You have to be excellent at everything and you have to have a good attitude every day, not just once a week.

Ben: When I speak to Chris Casper, as well as reciting *Blackadder* over the phone to each other (all the time) we still speak about Eric. He could be really cutting and sometimes it was difficult not to laugh – but you just daren't. For example, one of his favourite phrases, which I still don't fully understand to this day, was to tell us we were running around like a 'mad man's shit'. Giggsy could keep a deadpan face with things like that but me and Gaz, less so. It meant that when Eric was on one you looked at the floor, unless he called out your name: then he expected you to look him in the eye.

If Eric had a favourite in that first year, I'd hope I was close but Butty was right up there.

Nicky Butt: I didn't pick up on that. Maybe he saw a bit of himself in me because I played aggressively and he was like that as a player as well. But he loved Ben, Ryan, Chris Casper and Gary Neville too. And he secretly loved Becks but he always had a go at him for passing the ball long – 'Hollywood passes' he called them.

David Beckham: I liked to knock nice long balls to people's feet but they didn't always come off, which is when Eric would have something to say. Ben also used to get a lot of stick for sometimes taking on that one extra player that he probably shouldn't have taken on. But that's the way he played: he was a flair player, all about the last third of the pitch.

Nicky Butt: I think Eric just loved us as a group and had moments with everyone in terms of who was his favourite.

Ben: Nicky was the epitome of what Eric wanted in a footballer: he was down to earth, he would give you everything, he was talented and for someone who wasn't particularly tall, he was exceptionally good in the air. His timing was impeccable. When I played in central midfield with him at county level I just used to move to one side. Think Tim Cahill, Shane Long and Les Ferdinand. Even my dad used to say, 'Nicky's timing is incredible.' I used to think, 'Dad, *I'm* your son – is there any danger that we could talk about me?'

Philip Thornley: He *was* good in the air, was Nicky.

Gary Neville: He was *unbelievable* in the air.

Ben: And he was a dream to play with. When he got the ball, first thing he did was give it to me and then bang: a Bryan Robson-esque run straight into the box. He passed me the ball and he knew that it was coming in … at some stage. If I messed about with it too much I'd hear, 'Ben! Get it in!'

Nicky Butt: Ben was really two-footed so he was always checking in and checking back, checking in and checking back, making the full-back dizzy. I think he got a bit bored sometimes because it was too easy for him. But I just wanted him to get the ball in so I could score.

Robbie Savage: Everyone had different attributes but for me the three standouts that season were Ben, Nicky Butt and Keith Gillespie. Imagine: as a centre-forward I had Ben on one side and Keith on the other. The problem was keeping up with them.

Keith Gillespie: In terms of consistency throughout that whole Youth Cup run, Ben was our best player.

Cliff Butler: I was the club photographer that year. I was on the pitch afterwards talking to Eric and I said, 'Do you know what happened the following year after we won the Youth Cup in 1964? The first team won the league.' And that's just what happened in 93.

They were just ordinary lads, they loved playing football and they complemented each other. It was almost a perfect team. They just clicked. And Ben was one of the highlights, without question.

Gary Neville: At the time you don't know you're the 'Class of 92'. But from the moment of the Youth Cup win we almost became unstoppable. You had lads who lived near the club, supported the club and would die for the club. We were driven by each other, who were driven by the greatest manager of all time, and we had the two most demanding coaches you could ever wish to meet in your life in Nobby Stiles and Eric Harrison. One was an angry Manc, the other was an angry Yorkshireman and they basically hated anything that went near a Manchester United player. The idea of giving less than 100 per cent for them was intolerable.

So we had everything. And we had a first-team manager who believed in opportunities for young players, who believed in what Sir Matt Busby had created. It was the perfect storm. When you were playing in that youth team it was like, 'Jeez, how good is this?' Sometimes I was at the back watching them and it would be 5, 6, 7-0.

Phil Neville: And do you know what? Ben was probably the most popular member of the Class of 92; he was liked and respected by everyone. And in that year he was the best player.

Chris Casper: I'm the sporting director at Salford City now. We have an academy and I'm not saying we're going to recreate the

Class of 92 but it's a case of giving these lads the opportunities that we had. Playing for the A team back then, it would be Liverpool one week and Marine Youth the next. And with all due respect, Marine not only wanted to beat us but wanted to beat us up because we were Manchester United. So we're creating the same sort of experiences at Salford and we've already had a couple of lads make their debut in the first team.

They do what we used to do: they clean up, they tidy up and they're respectful of the environment. And actually, we've got a lad who's very similar to Ben. He's from Salford, two-footed, quick and brave. He's probably not as funny as Ben, but then not many people are.

Rod Thornley: It was a *joke* how good Ben was. He was so quick, he knew where the goal was, he was clever and he was strong. He was a freak at 14. Do you know how good he was? He was absolutely brilliant. The best in the country at his age by a mile. He really was. But he got done by that injury.

13

Semi-retirement
2008–13

It was Gaz who got me the job as manager. He knew an owner who was looking for someone and told him he had the ideal person: a good communicator who could start straight away. So I went to meet this guy, we spoke for ten minutes and he said, 'Yep, you look alright and you seem alright so I'll see you next week.'

He owned a restaurant called the Buddha Lounge, which was in Ramsbottom and served Thai and Cantonese food. It's not there anymore but it was very popular at the time; it was one of Gaz's favourites and Sam Allardyce came in a lot. The chicken pad Thai was out of this world.

It meant I had to knock Witton Albion on the head because I was needed at the restaurant in the evenings (which clashed with training) and from early afternoon on Saturdays (which clashed with playing). And the bottom line was that I could earn more at the restaurant than I could playing football.

The owner was called Kin Lau and he had a business partner called Scott Murray (coincidentally, Scott's younger sister Dina was Becks's first proper girlfriend when he lived in digs). Scott was a bit more intense than Kin, who if anything was a bit of a wide boy; I think there might have been a few shady business dealings going on.

I had to greet and seat everyone as they came through the door and find tables for all the phone bookings and walk-ins, which wasn't easy when we got really busy. The phone would ring constantly and I had to divert the answering machine to my mobile on Fridays and Saturdays (I forgot once and Kin went mad). I got quite good – so much so that one day Kin gave me a bit of a bung. He said it was because the numbers had shot through the roof in the time I'd been there. I don't think it was anything to do with me but I wasn't going to say no.

There were a few other perks too. Alan Lee, the guy who ran the bar, lost his driving licence and was having to catch multiple buses to work, so I offered to give him a lift. He liked to nip to the bookies round the corner and every so often he'd come back and give me anything from £20 to £100. It's a Chinese tradition to share your good fortune but I think it was also his way of thanking me for ferrying him around. He also knew what was kept in the cellar so sometimes, when no one else from the management team was there and the CCTV wasn't on, he'd pull out a couple of really nice bottles of wine and send me out the back through the kitchen to put them in my car.

Mr Fu was the psychotic head chef and a massive United fan, as well as being one of the very few people in the kitchen who could speak English; the rest of them were Thai and couldn't. I'd started to enjoy the odd cigarette so I'd go out the back with a couple of the Thai lads for a fag. We used to stand outside for 20 minutes and have a right laugh, even though we couldn't say a word to each other.

I'd been there about 18 months when I got a call from my old Huddersfield boss, Lou Macari. He asked if I wanted to go on a Man United football trip to Dubai to play in a Masters tournament involving Celtic, AC Milan, Arsenal and Everton. I did want to so I quit the restaurant job, which felt like it had run its course anyway.

It was March 2010 when we headed out to Dubai. We beat Everton, lost to Arsenal, got a towelling off Celtic and then faced a final, meaningless group game against AC Milan. It almost goes without saying that we chose the day before that game to get paralytic. We were staying at a huge complex and I managed to get hold of about 500 Strongbow tokens for this VIP tent. David May took a picture of our table – or, rather, he didn't because you couldn't see it for Strongbow cans and my full-to-the-brim ashtray. Me, Maysie and Lee Martin were mangled.

That episode tipped Lou over the edge. It was already obvious that he was disgusted by how much we were drinking on that tour but when we woke up the next morning, he'd gone. He'd got an early flight home because he was so appalled.

That tournament wasn't actually my first experience of exhibition games: my initial trip came about two years earlier thanks to a car crash.

It was 2008 and I was still with Lex. I was staying the night at her place in Wilmslow and Lucas was with us too. At 2am we were awoken by one of the loudest noises I've ever heard in my life: somebody driving their car straight into the front room. Lucas was screaming but fortunately no one was hurt. We got out via the back of the house, came round to the front and saw the carnage that this very powerful Mercedes had caused. The smell of burning rubber was horrific. The guy driving only lived up the road and how he got away with it I'll never know.

So, unsurprisingly, the house was off-limits while they put it back together. Until they got us sorted with a static caravan to live in on site (nice) they relocated us to Mottram Hall, previously the scene of two memorable events: my wedding and smacking George Donis in the face with a football (separate occasions). And it was in the gym at Mottram Hall that, by chance, I met Arthur Albiston in the sauna. I think he vaguely knew who I was but I recognised him straight away because he was one of my favourite United players when I was growing up (which I've never told him for fear of sounding like a knob, but chances are he'll find out now).

Arthur asked me how old I was, I told him I was 33 and he said we could get around that (you're supposed to be over 35 for these things) if I was interested in getting involved in a tour he was going on. I gave him my number and a few weeks later I was invited on a trip to Belfast.

We played Liverpool and they brought a good side: John Barnes, John Aldridge, Rob Jones, Mark Walters, Michael Thomas, Ronnie Whelan, Ray Houghton, Jason McAteer and Mike Marsh all played. Playing for us were the likes of Frank Stapleton, Lee Martin and Russell Beardsmore.

Soon after that we went to the Republic of Ireland. Both trips were organised by John Aldridge and Colin Telford (who was part of the Class of 92 squad but only played one game that season because of a back injury). They saw a niche in the market to get all these former United and Liverpool players together and go around the country playing exhibition games. It was brilliant but I think it cost them a hell of a lot more than they thought it would.

By the time I said hello to Jason McAteer in Dublin at the start of that second trip, I'd been to Jeff Kerfoot's wedding in Cyprus prior to the Belfast tour, followed by the stag do in Portugal where I met Les. Which is why he was moved to say, 'Fuck me Ben, every time I see you you've got a tan.'

Also on that trip was Jimmy Case, who played in midfield for Liverpool in the 70s and 80s. He booted me in one of the games – honestly, he didn't half give me a whack – and was delighted about how I'd taken it, so when he saw me in the bar afterwards he bought me a pint. He was a fascinating fella and I ended up drinking with him all night.

Once the dust had settled on all of the above, I hadn't played any football, league or non-league, since leaving Witton Albion. So, strictly speaking, you'd have to say that I retired in November 2008 – I just didn't notice. I was 33, which in hindsight was about three years shy of what I should have been capable of. But it had been on the cards for a while, probably since I'd left Bury in 2003. Once I'd dropped out of the football league I pretty much said to myself that I'd never play for a full-time club again.

I don't know why that was my mindset, particularly bearing in mind that I was still only 28 when I left Bury. It might have been the snowball effect of not enjoying football anywhere near as much. If I had been more successful at Huddersfield, Aberdeen and Blackpool – made more appearances and scored more goals, basically – maybe my outlook on non-league football would have been a lot brighter.

I wouldn't want anyone to think that I went into non-league because I wanted an easy life. Not a bit of it, because I trained and played as hard as I had when I was playing league football. And I'd have loved somebody to come in and tell me that they wanted to give me a chance at league level, I just didn't have the motivation or confidence to go looking for it.

Plus, it was difficult to make the transition from going straight out of the professional game into the semi-pro game. I went from having my days filled with football to only training on Tuesday and Thursday evenings for a game on the Saturday. The knock-on effect is that managers at that level don't have the time to spend with you on the training pitch, which means you don't have the chance to impress them. I've been at many a league club where somebody has trained well all week and worked their way into the side on the Saturday; in non-league it's difficult to get in on merit once the manager has made his mind up.

And I'll tell you what, there's nothing worse than being a professional athlete who's relied on their pace, only to find that you haven't fucking got it anymore. Obviously it happens to every footballer who plays into their mid- to late-thirties, but that doesn't stop it being incredibly disconcerting when it happens to *you*.

Having said all that, in the summer of 2010 I did find myself back in Reading for a trial. But this time Alan Pardew was nowhere to be seen because I wasn't playing football: I was tiling. My brother-in-law Trent, Hannah's husband, had approached me because he knew that I wanted a job and there was nothing happening for me. He's a tiler by trade and managed to get in with River Island, who wanted their stores kitted out with reclaimed brick tiles. He found a supplier, got his bricks cut and palletted, and started transporting them to wherever they needed to be.

They needed to be in a lot of places. That first job was in Reading and we also went to the likes of Swansea, Manchester, Liverpool, Leeds, Bournemouth, Fareham, High Wycombe, Uxbridge and all over London. More often than not we were working in shops that had been temporarily shut for refurbishment or brand-new ones that weren't open yet. But when it came to the flagship stores on Oxford Street in London we had to go in at night, because they took too much money to be closed during the day. They were always a ball-ache because you had to make sure all the floors and racks of clothes were covered so they didn't get stained.

When it was a new River Island store we tended to come across the same contractors doing the same sort of jobs, including a team of painters from Scotland who were gobby as shit but good fun. One chippy was a Celtic fan and come what may, if his team were playing he was off – train, plane, whatever. Nobody was there all the time to oversee what was going on; as long as the job was done by the deadline it didn't really matter if you had a day off here or there. And the majority of the guys would head to the pub at the end of the day, not least because some of them were away from home for five or six weeks at a time. Our part in proceedings usually took about a week.

One day, on site in High Wycombe, this random old guy with a cane walked on to the building site. Fortunately, before I had chance to bluntly question his presence, somebody quickly pointed out that he happened to be Sir Bernard Lewis, the billionaire owner of River Island. I decided not to question his lack of a helmet and hi-vis jacket.

Another time we were in a huge store on Oxford Street where, in order to start putting our tiles up, we first had to smash all the existing marble ones off the wall. The wall had to be smooth so we were also having to drill off the cement that had been used to stick them up. And make no mistake, massive marble tiles need a hell of a lot of cement to stay attached to a wall.

Three of us started at 10pm and we had till 6am to get it finished, at which point the skip lorry was booked to arrive. We were putting everything in these cages that were usually used to transport clothes, which we then wheeled out the back to where they'd positioned the skip: at the near end of an alley below a little balcony, so we could just tip everything in from on high and not have to navigate the steps.

Come 6am it was backslaps all round: job done. As we dusted ourselves off and had a stretch, the skip lorry appeared right on time at the top of the alley – but it was too big to reverse down the fucking thing, wasn't it?

The shop was opening at 9am, so now we had three hours to shift the ten tonne of marble tiles and cement that we'd just moved in eight hours. And this time we had to do it all by hand. Fortunately some shop staff were sent out to help us and we just about managed to get it finished in time. When the lorry finally lifted the skip it reared up on its back wheels and looked like it was going to tip over. I also thought I was going to keel over from exhaustion but, fortunately, neither happened.

While I was working for Trent he also got some work for a restaurant chain; I was pleased to hear it wasn't Pizza Hut as I wasn't sure they'd let me back in after the Huddersfield incident. Instead it was Pizza Express, who wanted their interiors decked out in white plaster brick. Trent started off using a place in Dunstable that made dummies and models for film sets, as it had the facilities to make these plaster panels. But then he quickly learnt how to make his own and acquired a warehouse in Manchester for that purpose.

Very often I was in that warehouse preparing the panels. They weren't easy because there was a lot of mixing to be done and a lot of buckets to be cleaned; it was a messy job but quite rewarding when you saw them all lined up in the racks we put them in to dry. If you could make 40 panels in the space of ten hours you were doing well. As for putting them up, you could smash out a Pizza Express in eight hours if there was a decent team of you.

That said, the whole process had the potential to take a lot longer. One morning Trent and I set off at 5am to get to a Pizza Express down in Worcester, right in the west of the West Midlands. It took about three hours to get there but when we arrived, something wasn't quite right. I said, 'Trent, this restaurant is not shut for refurbishment, nor is it a new one about to open.' He said, 'It must be!' He got his phone out to show me the email. 'Look!'

I took a deep breath. 'Trent, that says Worcester *Park*. That's in fucking Surrey.'

So we had to set off in rush hour for Worcester *Park* and didn't get there till 1pm because the traffic was that horrendous. It then took us till 2am the next morning to finish; they actually left us there with the place still open. It was right in the middle of the high street, we had music blaring out and the door was wide open because it was a really nice summer's evening. Anyone walking past must have been thinking, 'What are those two barmy fuckers doing?' This particular barmy fucker didn't get to bed until about 4am, nearly 24 hours after the whole charade began.

Because I was working on building sites, I was in an environment where everyone was stopping for cigarette breaks. It's like, 'Go on then, I'll have one,' and before long you start bringing your own in. My captain at Aberdeen, Derek Whyte, started smoking menthols and fed me the line that they were nowhere near as strong as filter cigarettes. I gave it a whirl when I was socialising and didn't feel like I was harming anyone but myself. To be fair, I've never got close to 20 a day or anything like that and after we got knocked out by Iceland in Euro 2016 I decided that was me done. Almost – I have lapsed a couple of times since. Shisha pipes in Dubai spring to mind.

One thing I quit more convincingly was tiling. It came in 2015, when I had three football trips lined up in the space of three months. I was away in Stockholm in the September, then Hong Kong and China in the October, followed by some United vs Liverpool games in Singapore and Bangkok in the November. So I was with Trent till the end of the September but never worked for him again after that. It was time to go back to where it all began.

14

Class of 93
1992–93

Ben: After the Youth Cup win, all we got in the way of any instructions before we broke for the summer were two words from Eric: be sensible. Well, it might have been three with an expletive thrown in the middle for good measure.

Anthony Rouse: We'd just turned 17 and our parents allowed us to go to Tenerife for two weeks. Jeff Kerfoot, who was still 16, came with us. Ben was up most mornings running up and down this hill in Las Americas and he didn't drink; neither did Jeff. I did, even though we weren't old enough to, and Ben looked after me on numerous occasions. But you couldn't get him off the football pitch, even in the heat of the day – unless he wanted to sunbathe.

Elizabeth Thornley: I was absolutely fine with him going to Tenerife.

Hannah Scott (née Thornley): They weren't bothered about any of us doing anything.

Rod Thornley: I went missing for five or six days on the trot and they weren't bothered.

Elizabeth Thornley: You did not! Don't be so horrible.

Rod Thornley: I'd get home at 5pm every night and there'd be no sign of them; I'd have to make a bowl of Frosties for my tea.

Hannah Scott: They were very liberal parents.

Elizabeth Thornley: I don't think I like the sound of that.

Rod Thornley: No, all my mates were scared shitless of mum.

Hannah Scott: Only when they disturbed her when she was watching *EastEnders*: 'Get out!' But generally we could go anywhere and do anything we wanted. Within reason. But we didn't want to do anything other than normal stuff.

Philip Thornley: Apart from emptying the drinks cabinet.

Rod Thornley: I don't remember anything about that.

Philip Thornley: I'm sure you don't.

Ben: When we came back in for the 1992/93 season our wages went up from £29.50 a week to £39.50 a week. One of the main changes to the team was that I now had Steve Riley – otherwise known as Riser – playing behind me rather than George Switzer, who had got a year's pro contract and moved into the reserve-team dressing room. I loved Riser to bits, even though he was a City fan; we got on like a house on fire. On the field he knew he wasn't the most talented person in the world and he was very right-footed – but if he was going to play in the youth team, he was getting in at left-back. Whenever I think about him I just laugh because he was a real character in the dressing room; it's such a shame we haven't been able to track him down for the book.

Come the morning of the first day of pre-season, I'd been feeling funny for a while. I'd been getting intense pain in my stomach and I had no idea what it was (and Giggsy, before you ask, no it wasn't me craving a burger before pre-season). When it was bad it was excruciating; I'd never felt anything like it.

We were walking round to the training ground because the minibus had packed up and gone in for a service. It was a red-hot day and Eric Harrison and his fellow coaches were coming up and down the line asking where we'd been on holiday. My mind went blank and, bearing in mind that I take a good tan when I'm away, I went white and fell to the floor. They took me to the medical room and asked if it was something I'd experienced before. I said yes, for the best part of six months, but it would come and go – and go more often than it came. So they took me for an X-ray and discovered I had appendicitis. They sent me home again but in the middle of the night I was in absolute agony, so my parents called an ambulance.

Hannah Scott: I could hear him in his bedroom from the bottom of the stairs and I was in a panic because he was screaming so much. He was literally screaming because he was in that much pain. Horrific.

Lucas Thornley: He's told me since that it's the worst pain he's ever been through.

Ben: It was worse, by a long shot, than my knee.

Rod Thornley: He had appendicitis, did he?

Ben: In the space of 36 hours it had grown to such a size that it could have caused me immense problems – well, peritonitis.

Philip Thornley: We phoned the club, who said to take him down to Whalley Range Hospital. So we shot down the M602 with Ben on the floor in the back of the car. I was trying to drive faster and faster but I couldn't go any faster.

Elizabeth Thornley: Ah you see, you should have let me drive.

Rod Thornley: What did he have done? Did he have his appendix removed?

Elizabeth Thornley: Yes. If it had burst he could have died.

Rod Thornley: Could he? I didn't know that. When were you going to tell me this?

Ben: So that wasn't a great start, not least because it meant that I missed pre-season. After that the team were playing in a tournament in Sunderland and Eric wanted me to go as part of the group, so I didn't want to turn around and say no. Inter Milan beat us in our first game – and after playing in it, I soon knew the value of a full pre-season. We stayed in the same hotel as Inter and I remember being on the second floor, looking out the window to the next floor down, and there were all these 16-year-old players drinking little cups of coffee and smoking cigarettes.

Phil Neville: The first game I ever played with Ben was against Crewe at the start of the season. I remember it well because I was only 15 and it was my first match for the A team, so it was one of the biggest games I'd ever played in. We beat them 5-1 and Ben was in front of me. Because we were both right-footed, either he used to come inside and I used to go on the overlap, or he'd be on the outside and my right-foot pass out to his right foot was always easy. I loved playing with him because he worked up and down, and he was always there to show for the ball. He was fantastic.

You look back at those games in the youth team as the defining moments of your career. More than the Champions League Final, because it was when you didn't know whether you could handle playing for Man United.

Ben: Obviously we went into the Youth Cup that season as defending champions. However, my recollection of the first three games against Blackburn Rovers (who my co-writer tells me we beat 4-1), Notts County (3-1) and Wimbledon (3-0) is ... even 'sketchy' doesn't come close. That's really bad, isn't it? I've forgotten three ties there.

Nicky Butt: I haven't got a clue who we played.

David Beckham: I can just about remember who I played in the last game of my career.

Mark Rawlinson: I can't really remember a lot of the Youth Cup games from that year either.

Paul Scholes: No chance. Gary will remember.

Gary Neville: I can't!

Phil Neville: I can remember the Notts County game. My mum and dad got a call off Eric Harrison in the morning, they picked me up from school and that night I made my debut at Old Trafford. Gary scored in that game.

Ryan Giggs: Fucking hell, he should remember that then.

Ben: To be fair I didn't play against Notts County. During training one day we were playing 11 vs 11 in the usual manner: the team that was going to start the game against the rest. I was crossing the ball from a really acute angle but as I wrapped my left foot around it, my right foot gave way in the turf. Straight away my knee was in agony because I'd strained my medial ligament, but after about ten days I was allowed to run around The Cliff. And that was brilliant; I thought, 'I can't feel this.'

The lads were out doing shooting practice and behind one of the goals was the wall of the gymnasium, so any ball that missed bounced straight back on to the pitch. So somebody had this shot, the ball came right into my path and I just wellied it – and collapsed. The physio, Jim McGregor, went nuts. He shouted, 'I haven't told you to kick a ball!' Before adding, intuitively, 'And now you fucking know why!' So that set me back by another week – and my God it didn't half hurt. And that's why I missed the game against Notts County.

In between the Blackburn and Notts County games, on 23 January 1993, we signed professional four-year contracts, 18 months into our original apprentice contracts.

Gary Neville: You don't get four-year contracts at Man United at the age of 18 unless something's happening.

Ben: We all moved up to £210 per week, which was decent in those days. In addition to that I got a signing-on fee of £24,000 in four instalments over four years. And I think David's was the same, whereas others were getting £20,000. But obviously after a while those contracts were ripped up and more lucrative ones were offered – just not to me.

The next game in our cup run was the quarter-final against York City and I can remember this one. Kind of. The lad I was up against was a little Chinese lad called Sammy ... something. He was a really good player – but York were crap. We battered them 5-0 and I think we were 3-0 up at half-time. Coming into the dressing room we all said, 'How the fuck have this lot got this far?' Either they'd been very lucky up to that point, they were having an extreme off day or they'd played *nobody* to get there. They just didn't look like a team of footballers.

So we were breezing through the competition up to that point. That all changed when we got to the semi-final, where we had a tough time of it against Millwall. While we didn't feel that the football club was representative of its supporters, for the first leg at Old Trafford they certainly looked like thugs: the entire team came out with shaved heads.

Nicky Butt: I enjoyed that.

Paul Scholes: It was supposed to scare us – and given the result of that game, it probably worked.

Ben: The tie started well enough: we were 1-0 up at half-time thanks to my goal. I picked the ball up, roughly on the halfway line, then rather than going down the wing I found myself running down the centre of the pitch, which felt really weird. I went on a little bit of a mazy, beat three – maybe even four – players and got to the edge of the box, with at least one more player to beat. Everything seemed to slow down, the goal opened up and I slotted it home.

Nicky Butt: It wasn't a shock because I trained with the lad every day. I'd seen what he was capable of and I'd seen him do that a few times.

Hannah Scott: Scoring goals from the halfway line was just the norm for Ben.

Paul Scholes: Yeah, he did it quite often.

Phil Neville: He was a brilliant finisher, which was probably one of his greatest qualities. But he also had unbelievable balance. Because of his low centre of gravity and thick-set frame he could wriggle in between players without getting knocked over.

Philip Thornley: He'd get the ball and you'd see lads coming in to get him from both sides. And the number of times we watched him move at the last minute – and they'd hit one another. Bang! We used to laugh.

Ben: Back then the tunnel at Old Trafford was still on the halfway line and when I got to it at half-time, Giggsy was stood at the top; he was too old to play in the youth team by that point. The first person he spoke to was me: 'Good goal, Ben.' He was chuffed that a Salford lad he'd grown up with had scored a cracker. We'd known each other for ages and there was a mutual respect.

I appreciated it because he didn't have to say anything, not least because he could have been thinking, 'Bloody hell, this lad is after my position.' Though I genuinely don't think that concerned him.

Ryan Giggs: It never ever occurred to me. And that's not me being big-headed, it's just that I always believed that if I played well, it didn't really matter. But Ben was ahead of the lads who went on to make it. It was between him and Butty, because physically Butty developed a bit quicker. Ben wasn't huge but he was robust and he could look after himself. I expected him to be in the first team pretty soon.

Ben: Hopefully, with an occasion like a semi-final and the fact that you're playing for Manchester United, you feel as though you're untouchable when the game kicks off. Yes, you have to have nerves but the adrenalin rush should shoot you out of a cannon and straight into the sky, as though there's no limit to what you can do. The majority of the time, before I got injured, I felt like I could do anything – or at least try anything.

Thanks to the team-mates I had on the pitch with me, the coaching staff I had behind me and my own ability, nine times out of ten it worked.

Mark Rawlinson: He was explosive. He had this ability to go past people without really looking like he was trying, even though it's one of the hardest things in the game to do.

Ben: Unfortunately that goal against Millwall isn't as fondly remembered by everyone else as it is by me because we lost the game 2-1. For the first time as a team, we'd lost in the Youth Cup. It was at that point we realised that we weren't invincible. And Eric hammered it home with his assessment of Leeds, who were in the other semi-final: 'I've seen them, I've fucking seen them, and they'll batter you if you play like that.'

But first we needed to get past Millwall at the New Den. Now, that is a place; they wanted to kill us.

Paul Scholes: Ooh, scary place. It was a shithole, wasn't it? We came out of that tunnel behind the goal and all the meatheads were in one of the stands. That was an experience. But it did us good.

Nicky Butt: It was weird because we'd never had that before. Normally at youth-team games the crowd was pretty much made up of parents, family members and one or two fans who were football purists; they'd clap you if you did well, even if you were playing for the opposition. That game taught us the right way to silence a crowd though.

Ben: Their fans were unforgiving, just as hateful towards kids of 18 as they were towards senior pros. That stadium was without doubt the scariest place to play as a young lad, both in terms of the atmosphere and what the fans looked like: tattoos, skinheads and all that. I was copping it when I was taking corners, and that was at both ends because they fair on filled the ground. Intimidating.

And actually, my then girlfriend Lucy was at that game and it was a real eye-opener for her, coming from a beautiful 50-odd-bedroom house in the middle of the Kent countryside. She was surrounded by a load of hairy-arsed blokes effing and blinding. When I met her and her parents afterwards she said, 'I'm not sure what I just witnessed but I really don't want to witness it again.'

We were about 15 minutes into that game when Gaz dropped an absolute howler; he was trying to be clever and he got caught out. A Millwall lad nicked the ball off him and was clean through, but either our goalkeeper, Darren Whitmarsh, saved it or it went just wide. I marched towards Gaz shouting, 'Are you fucking lucky enough, you?' I had such a go at him because he'd done something so uncharacteristic. If we'd gone 3-1 down in the tie we would have struggled.

Gary Neville: Ben was competitive. He wouldn't let you drop your standards and he would scream at you as defenders if you conceded a goal, in a way that would sometimes make me laugh: 'What you up to you fucking pricks?' But if you have someone who's willing to take criticism and give it out, nowadays you'd call that being a leader. And our team had Nicky in it, it had Casp, it had me – there were some strong characters in there.

Ben: We managed to score to pull it back to 2-2 on aggregate, 1-0 up on the night, thanks to Butty. As the game wore on, Gaz and Nicky were the only two players who didn't go down with cramp. We were all dead on our feet, stretching each other's toes out; we had nothing left to give at all. With the occasion and the fact that we were up against it, it was tough. I couldn't run. I crossed the ball for the winner, which was scored by our American striker Jovan Kirovski in the 81st minute. I don't know where I mustered the energy from but I managed to get it in the box and he finished it.

Then I was just thinking, 'Please let this be the end of it because I've got nothing left.' It's not a nice feeling. The thing is with cramp, it doesn't go away either; you know that in another three minutes it's going to reappear.

I couldn't move at full time. Eric came into the dressing room and said, 'Don't worry, I'm not in any rush.' It was quite late when we set off back to Manchester but they made sure we had food and plenty of liquid on the coach. We didn't get in until the early hours.

We had Leeds United in the final, who'd beaten Norwich City 4-3 in the semi. Me and Nicky Butt had played for England Schoolboys with Leeds players Mark Tinkler, Kevin Sharp and Jamie Forrester, so we knew they were good. Noel Whelan was another one in their ranks. They had improved dramatically from the previous season because now they were strong and powerful, and had also simply become better players. They were such a good side.

Something similar happened with Paul Scholes: the transformation from when we finished our first season as apprentices to when we came back for our second was unbelievable. He was brilliant. I'd missed seeing him in pre-season because I was having my appendix out, but everyone was making noises about him: 'You should see Scholesy this year' kind of thing. This was somebody who used to mark me in practice matches having been made to play at full-back.

Paul Scholes: I didn't have the greatest of lifestyles growing up as a kid; I was actually quite fat when I was 16 (I am now as well but that's another story). I had no clue about diet or anything. I was never the most cleanest-living of kids and I had parents who just dragged me to the pub all the time. That was the life I was brought up with: being around drink and getting chippies for my tea.

When I came to the end of that first year as an apprentice I realised I needed to change: I needed to be fitter. I was always the one at the back because I just couldn't keep up. I also had a mild form of asthma but my lifestyle was the biggest problem. Seeing people like Ben – at 15 he was already like a professional footballer. And Gary and Phil obviously looked after themselves. It was something I needed to do too if I was going to get anywhere near the level I needed to be at.

Ben: I'd argue that Paul ended up being more influential at United than Eric Cantona – and over a much longer period. When someone asks me the best player I ever played with, I always pick Scholesy. People sometimes react like Tory backbenchers when I say that but it's true.

He was funny in the dressing room too. Whereas when Gaz and Phil talk they get very excited, Scholes doesn't get excitable about anything. But every now and again he'd drop a hand grenade and wait for it go off – and very often it was aimed at people he knew would get wound up, such as Nicky.

Paul Scholes: Yeah, fair description. I might have said the odd thing here or there. Nicky had a bit of a short fuse so it didn't take much. As for Ben, you could always hear him laughing, either at his own or someone else's expense.

Michael Appleton: He was always messing about and being daft. There were times when you'd think he was bloody annoying but then other times he'd have you in absolute stitches.

Paul Scholes: He was always a really genuine and happy lad. I don't think there's a nasty bone in his body.

Hannah Scott: He is lovely. And he's got the best sense of humour.

Rod Thornley: I will say this about him: I never come across anyone in the game – and a lot of people know him – who has got a bad word to say about him. So I hear, 'What a great bloke your kid is,' and most of the time I just agree. But when I'm in a bad mood and I can't be arsed I say, 'You know what, come and spend an hour at home with him.' Bellend.

Hannah Scott: He knows everybody and treats them all exactly the same. We used to go into town together and he'd know the dodgiest people. He's happy in a room full of toffs and he's happy in a room full of gangsters. He makes people feel like they're important.

Rod Thornley: He gives everyone time. He entertains them. He's just got this way about him. I haven't got it.

Phil Neville: I see him when I'm working for television or radio covering United and he's someone I go to straight away because he's always got a smile on his face. And the fact that he has remained a United fan, without one ounce of bitterness or jealousy, tells you a lot about his character. He's like me and my brother: he's got Man United blood.

Ben: Leeds were one step too far. They beat us 2-0 at Old Trafford in front of 30,000 people, with Jamie Forrester scoring in the 16th minute and Noel Whelan in the 62nd.

Gary Neville: I made a big mistake for their second goal. I did what Loris Karius did in the Champions League Final: I went to clear the ball, kicked it against Noel Whelan, it fell into his path and he scored.

Ben: Even at 2-0 we felt like we had the players and the wherewithal to turn it around, especially if we got an early goal in the second leg. But we didn't. They did though.

Gary Neville: Nicky Butt was injured for the second leg. You take him out, particularly in a game that physical, and we were half a team.

Ben: There were 30,000 in at Elland Road.

Gary Neville: The atmosphere in that game was something else. They battered Robbie Savage with a song about him being a gypsy.

Ben: They scored in the 12th minute through Jamie Forrester's overhead kick. Scholesy equalised, just, with a penalty in the 29th minute.

Paul Scholes: It was a bad penalty. It was a terrible penalty. I just didn't connect with it properly at all. And I remember seeing my celebration after the game and thinking, 'What was I doing?' I got my tongue out in the direction of the Leeds fans. Not a wise thing to do.

Ben: That made it 3-1 on aggregate but then a minute later it was back to 4-1: they scored again through a lad called Matthew Smithard.

Philip Thornley: It was a beast of a game.

Gary Neville: It was our slap.

Nicky Butt: We weren't all together that season: Ryan couldn't play for us anymore because he was too old, while others were up and down to the first team and reserves. In that first season we were a really solid unit, training together every day, playing every game. It's not an excuse because we still should have won but it was a factor.

Robbie Savage: I don't know what it was, we just didn't perform that season. But Leeds were good.

Paul Scholes: It was probably the right result in the end. I mean, you want to win it but I think Leeds were probably a bit better than us at that stage.

Ben: They fully deserved to win. They weren't better technically but they were bigger than we were and, dare I say it, probably fitter.

Phil Neville: They were like men. They were like animals.

Ben: We weren't at the races in either game and that left a sour taste because while we didn't expect to win it in our first season, we did in our second. We were another year under a really good coach and we just thought, 'This is ours again.' We didn't think we could have a final as hard as that semi against Millwall. How wrong we were.

To make matters worse, the way our parents were treated on that day was horrendous: the stewards spoke to them abysmally and herded them around like cattle. I think the big man, Neville Neville, gave a few of them a piece of his mind. You could always rely on him to come to the fore and stick up for everybody, sort everything out. A bit like what Gaz does now.

Paul Scholes: My parents rarely went to those games, to be honest. They rarely even went to first-team games. My dad came to the odd few and my mum came to a couple but I don't remember either of them being at this one.

Ben: Alex Ferguson came into the dressing room afterwards and while he didn't go over the top, he did have a few words. He said we'd let ourselves down as a group.

Gary Neville: It was what we needed. He said, 'You're nothing unless you carry on at the level you've achieved. You don't just win it one year, you win it the second year. If you can't handle playing in front of big crowds, if you can't handle physicality, you'll never play for the first team.'

Ben: Eric was a bit more philosophical, saying that he couldn't thank us enough for all the good football we'd allowed him to watch. And that was our last game for him in the Youth Cup because we were too old from the following season.

To top it all off, that was the first season that the final was shown live on Sky Sports, with Martin Tyler and Andy Gray on commentary. And it was only because of our success in the competition the previous season that Sky made sure they were involved when we got to the final again – and got beaten. Bastards.

Phil Neville: Even though we lost, you probably knew we were going to have the better careers because we were better footballers. But it was a hammer blow for us.

Gary Neville: When I look back now it's a big disappointment that we didn't win double Youth Cups. We should have done.

Ben: We did at least manage to win the Lancashire League that season with the A team; I scored 12 goals in 22 appearances. We won the Lancashire Youth Cup too, beating Blackburn 3-0 in the final. What I most remember from that game though is the guy marking me, Ian Berry, committing two horrendous fouls on me in the first 20 minutes and being sent off. To make matters worse, afterwards his dad gave me a right load of verbal when we were on our way out through what is now the Munich Tunnel, calling me a 'cheating fucker'. My dad told me to just walk away and that was that.

At the start of that summer I got a call from Becks to say, 'My mum and dad have invited me to Malta again; do you want to come?' That's not as random as it sounds: Malta has the oldest Manchester United supporters club in the world, having started in 1959, and they've had a huge affiliation with the club over the years, going back before Sir Alex Ferguson to Ron Atkinson. Ferguson always made sure that they had at least one player out there every single season and that a fair old chunk of their members had tickets for every game.

Unfortunately, since Ferguson retired, they've found it more and more difficult to get that level of access. David Moyes and Louis van Gaal, for example: not arsed. The Malta guys have been relying on my brother to help with tickets.

Becks first went out to Malta in 1992 because his parents always used to bump into Joe Glanville (who was then president of the Malta supporters club) at Old Trafford, and he invited them over. In 1993, Gary Neville and Chris Casper joined us, and Ryan Giggs and Paul Ince came with the Premier League trophy.

On my holiday to Tenerife I'd met Lucy, who by now I'd been with for about a year. I was supposed to go and spend some of the summer with her but then I got this invitation to Malta. So I sacked her off but she was younger than me and she was heartbroken. I just kept ignoring her calls, ignoring her calls, ignoring her calls. Eventually my mum phoned and said, 'Listen, you're going to have to speak to Lucy's mum; she's going absolutely ballistic here.' I was at the Beckhams' house in Chingford at the time so with Becks listening in I rang Lucy's mum, she gave me a load of verbal down the phone, I listened, told her I was sorry and that was that.

David Beckham: My mum remembers that.

Gary Neville: Ben's personal life: fucking hell. He was a disaster with girls for five or six years really. He was all over the place.

Ben: The following day we met Gaz and Casp at Euston ready to go to the airport and fly out to Malta. Once there we were put in a double bedsit-type thing. It had a great view but there was no air-conditioning, which was horrendous. Incey and Giggsy, meanwhile, got to stay at the Hilton at the bottom of the hill.

David Beckham: It was ridiculously hot.

Ben: If the Malta guys were to look back on the fact that they put David Beckham and Gary Neville in a sweaty bedsit they would be horrified. But we weren't paying for it and we were 17 years old so it was still brilliant.

David Beckham: It was actually one of the best holidays I've ever had.

Ben: We got a helicopter across to the supporters club on Gozo and Eric Harrison was invited over for that too; it was a function for about 350 people. There was a debate between the four of us lads about who should get up and speak so Gaz said (and this is coming from Gaz, when there's no way anyone else would get a look-in now), 'Ben, I reckon you should say something because you're the one who can talk.' So I went on stage and one of the things I said was that we couldn't have done it without 'that man there', pointing at Eric. Everyone turned around and gave him a round of applause. He came up to me afterwards and said – and I'll never forget this – 'That's one of the nicest things that anybody has ever said about me.'

Another memorable moment on that trip came when we were kicking a ball around outside in a courtyard. All of a sudden these lads appeared and joined in; one of them had dreadlocks and I was thinking to myself, 'Fucking hell, he's good, him.' I mean *really* good. That night John Buttigieg, who was one of the main guys at the supporters club, picked us up and Gaz mentioned this lad with dreadlocks. We pulled up at one of the very few sets of traffic lights in Malta (it's basically a free-for-all), and John pointed at a billboard: 'Is that him?' Ziggy Marley in concert. We'd played football with Bob Marley's son. What a footballer.

David Beckham: He was very good. His dad could play a bit as well.

Ben: Talking of Malta's traffic, this was in the days when there were basically no drink-driving laws at all on the island – and that suited Gary Neville on this trip. He must have had about ten pints of Woodpecker when the lad who we were with, in his wisdom, let him drive his car. From my seat in the back I had a great view when we subsequently went down a ramp and crashed.

The police were like, 'Has anyone been hurt? No? Right, see you later.' Then when Gaz got out of the car he made one of the best comments I've ever heard: 'Ben, there must have been ten fucking pedals in that car and every one of them was the accelerator.' I was absolutely pissing myself. Gaz was devastated and he gave the lad the money for the repairs, because he in turn was devastated about his car – it was a new Renault 19 or something like that.

Gary Neville: It was my first lads holiday. It was the first time I'd ever had a drink. It was the first time I'd ever got drunk. I had the most incredible time and it opened my eyes to life.

Ben: So that was the first year I went to Malta and then I went pretty much every year after that for the next ten years. I haven't been since Gaz had his testimonial year in 2012 but as we put this book together I'm organising a match in Malta to commemorate Valletta's status as 2018's Capital of Culture.

By the summer of 1993 we'd turned 18 and we knew, if we were sensible with it, that there was now no reason why we couldn't go out; we were old enough and we didn't have to be in training the next day. The local lads met up on numerous occasions, though some of the vainer ones among us might have said something like, 'Can we meet up when I've come back off my holiday so I'm nice and tanned to go to nightclubs?'

Gary Neville: We started to go out in Manchester, to Ronnie's, to Cheerleaders, to JW Johnson's. We had some of the best nights out I've ever had.

Ben: Gaz would only ever have a proper binge if he knew it wasn't going to affect his training regime: if he didn't have a game for a week or, preferably, it was post-season. Because he knew he'd still feel it for a good two, three or even four days afterwards.

Gary Neville: To be fair, you never had a bad night out when you were with Ben Thornley; he's one of the best people to be in the company of. He was really funny and he wasn't aggressive when he was drunk – he was always pleasant, always good fun.

Ryan Giggs: He's got a friendly face and one of those laughs that's infectious. He's just a funny lad.

Ben: And yes, the female attention was nice; we were teenage boys, after all. Some of us were already used to the fact that we were quite popular at school – the likes of Becks, Mark Rawlinson, John O'Kane and me were lads who people of the female variety took a little bit of interest in. John O'Kane reminded everyone of Des Walker, both the way he played and the way he looked – just more attractive than Des. Sav, bless him, did his best with that hairstyle.

Elizabeth Thornley: If they went on a night out they'd all end up back at ours.

David Beckham: Ben always used to bring out the Pringles.

Elizabeth Thornley: It was a three-storey house and Ben had one of the attic bedrooms. They used to go up there to play snooker and darts.

Philip Thornley: And watch videos.

Elizabeth Thornley: Sssh.

Gary Neville: Ben had two cricket bags filled with porn videos. Jeff Kerfoot used to bring them round and they'd do swapsies.

Philip Thornley: I'd go up to bed and think, 'What's going on? I can hear some strange noises.' I'd go into Ben's room and they'd have all fallen asleep with a porno still on. I'd just turn it off and carry on to bed.

Ben: Yeah, after 20 minutes.

Mark Rawlinson: I'm a PC working in Lancashire nowadays, though back then Ben was more a case for the fashion police. You opened his wardrobe and it was like fancy dress.

Paul Scholes: I've seen him lately and he likes his flared jeans and small shoes. He definitely dresses to his own taste.

Paul Devine: He turned up at Giggsy's 21st in this top with zips all over it. I just said, 'Ben, seriously, what have you come as?' I think it was very expensive but it was appalling.

Ryan Giggs: You look back at photos and think, 'What am I wearing?' But then you look at Ben and think, 'Fucking hell, at least I didn't look as bad as that.' And it seemed like he didn't care. 'Ben, what have you got on?' And he'd just start laughing. No comeback, he'd just laugh. And then next week he'd come out wearing something else ridiculous.

Phil Neville: He certainly wasn't a fashion icon like David. He was the sort of guy who would put on a £1,000 suit and it would still look cheap. He was a tracksuit-and-jumper man really.

David Beckham: He loved wearing clothes with big brands all over them: he'd have a gold Dolce & Gabbana T-shirt or a big pair of Gucci loafers. Expensive clothes but not always in the best taste.

George Switzer: We were Salford lads so we dressed like rag arses: Rockport, Levi jeans, that sort of stuff. I wasn't far behind him.

Andy Scott: One time we went on holiday to Ayia Napa and he had a few quid, so he had all this designer gear: Versace, Valentino, Armani, the lot. But none of it went together. And because he was quite short, the jeans had to be turned up.

Gary Neville: Basically, he's 5ft 4in but he wore three-quarter-length jackets. Sheepskin things. Weird fucking gear.

Rod Thornley: He was well known in the dressing room for his long coats. He used to get hammered for those.

Hannah Scott: It would be the most expensive coat you could buy but it would be ...

Rod Thornley: ... Horrendous.

Paul Devine: Some of his coats were to die for. He turned up at our house one day looking like Dick Dastardly – this thing had fur everywhere. And even my dad, who had a lot of affection for Ben but didn't say a great deal, said, 'Oh my God, Ben, what the fuck have you got on?'

Gary Neville: If Moschino or Versace brought out the most awkward, ridiculous-looking thing, Ben Thornley would buy that. The thing that's in the window when you go into a shop – they don't buy multiple stock because they know no fucking idiot is going to buy it. Ben would buy that one. Even if it didn't fit him.

Ryan Giggs: *Especially* if it didn't fit him. Even better.

Hannah Scott: All money, no taste, lots of flannel.

Elizabeth Thornley: And it was always in the sale.

Philip Thornley: There was a £1,200 jacket he brought home that he'd paid £700 for so as far as he was concerned, *what* a saving that was.

Elizabeth Thornley: Bargain.

Philip Thornley: It was probably worth about £60.

Hannah Scott: It is disgusting the amount he's paid out on clothes and cars.

Elizabeth Thornley: There was a series of about six expensive cars that he bought every six months and spent an absolute fortune on.

Rod Thornley: He did buy some stupid cars. Mercedes, BMW M3, Jaguar …

Philip Thornley: He borrowed Becks's Jaguar once. It stood outside our house for about three weeks before we said to Ben, 'Don't you think you'd better give that back?' So he asked Becks if he wanted it back and he said, 'I didn't even know you'd got it.'

Rod Thornley: He borrowed Giggsy's Subaru as well but then left it outside someone's house and couldn't remember what he'd done with it.

Hannah Scott: And everyone would come and nick the gold wheels off his Clio Williams.

Philip Thornley: They were worth more than the car.

Hannah Scott: Rod would be woken up in the middle of the night having heard something, because his room was at the back overlooking where the car was parked. He'd look out the window and say, 'Ben, they're nicking your wheels again.' But we'd got so used to it that we'd all just go straight back to sleep.

Philip Thornley: We'd find it on bricks in the morning.

Hannah Scott: I learnt to drive in that car. With Ben. Which was not a pleasant experience.

Ben: It was the summer of 93 that I passed my test. Slowly but surely, all the lads were doing the same and trying to outdo each other with the cars they were buying. I had mine lined up: a little D-registered Fiesta, brilliant. I could get to training on my own now, couldn't wait; first day after passing my test – *bang*.

I went into the back of Steve Kelly, my old Salford Boys coach, just as we were heading into The Cliff; he braked and I didn't. And he'd just bought himself a Jaguar. My first day of driving and I've got to tell my insurance company that I've crashed into a fucking Jag.

To make matters worse, at the same time that I went into the back of Steve, someone else went into the back of me.

Robbie Savage: It was an absolute disaster. I had a Fiesta too; Ben had a maroon one and I had a white one. I just remember Ben and me getting out and there were our two little cars, wrecked. Shocking.

Steve Kelly: To be honest, I'd forgotten that Ben was involved so he must have been totally exonerated in my mind. I only got the XJ6 because my brother was working with a big publishing company and they were basically giving these cars away, though afterwards everyone thought I must be a multimillionaire. I hadn't had it too long so that's when I found out that it costs a fortune to get them fixed.

Tell Ben he owes me a few quid.

Ben: Around the same sort of time, Gaz and my sister started dating. Gaz spent a lot of time at our house because he was friends with me and they got to know each other as a result.

Rod Thornley: She was still at school.

Hannah Scott: I was nearly 16. But yeah, I was still at school. Every Wednesday they used to go out – Chris Casper, Becks, Gaz, Rawler, Ben – and then come back to ours. And I'd come home every day for lunch because my school was just around the corner and those guys had always finished for the day because it's not a normal job.

Elizabeth Thornley: Not a *proper* job.

Hannah Scott: So they'd be there at lunchtime and we'd play Scattergories.

Ben: Gaz used to pick her up from school when he first got his car.

Hannah Scott: He used to *try* to pick me up. Then Ben would arrive and say, 'It's alright mate, you go, I've got her.' And Gaz would be like, 'Oh, alright then.' I'd say to Gaz, 'I thought you were coming to get me?' And he'd say, 'Yeah, but your brother said he was doing it.'

Ben: He wanted to keep the whole thing very quiet until she left school. He didn't want it going into the dressing room because of the banter that used to fly around in there. I wasn't renowned for being Nicky Butt in the boxing ring but I would have given out some beatings if anyone had started on my little sister.

Hannah Scott: Ben was alright about it. He knew I was in good hands because Gaz is a nice guy.

Rod Thornley: He's a bellend.

Hannah Scott: He was gorgeous, shut up.

Rod Thornley: Hannah wasn't your typical wag. She was the opposite.

Hannah Scott: I was with Gaz when he was on £29.50 a week so when the money started coming in, I felt awkward with it. Whenever we went to do's I'd ask him to drop me at the back door because I couldn't do anything like that.

Elizabeth Thornley: Dressing up was not her forte.

Hannah Scott: Thanks, mum.

Elizabeth Thornley: You're too natural for that.

Hannah Scott: Whatever. No, I couldn't keep up with the Joneses. I was much younger than most of them as well. Though Nicky's Shelly was lovely, Claire Scholes was lovely, Becks was going through a fair few different ones initially but they were all lovely. And I got on with Victoria; we had a good craic. But when Gaz was starting out you had people like Paul Ince's wife Claire, who was so much older than me – she was the boss and she used to intimidate me a bit. I just kept a low profile and didn't say much. I could tell you a load of sordid stuff about a lot of people but I'm not going to do that.

Rod Thornley: That's going in *my* book.

Ben: Hannah wasn't arsed about what car she drove or what size house she lived in; she was just very normal and everybody loved her for that. She used to worry about nothing but, when she was moving in those sorts of circles, you can understand why – there is potential for bitchiness and bloodshed.

They were really good together and good fun together. They moved in, they were engaged and do you know what, he would have been alright as a brother-in-law. But I think it all became a bit much for my sister.

Gary Neville: I was almost living at Ben's house when I was in a relationship with Hannah, which gave me a closeness to him during his evolving football career that not many people had.

Hannah Scott: We were together until 2002. It didn't work out because, in a roundabout way, I was looking for a way out, I suppose. I just wasn't comfortable. We'd been together a long time and maybe I just thought it had run its course. I don't know. And that was it.

Ben: At United, as that summer break drew to a close, we were still positive about the team we had going into the new season. Even though we'd lost the final to Leeds, we all knew that we could kick on. We would be treating the Lancashire League – the reserves league – like a stepping stone to the first team. We weren't apprentices anymore and this was a new challenge. We were going to be playing with or against seasoned professionals, lads who had played over 300 games, names that most of us had only ever seen on TV. That was exciting.

15

Present day
2013–18

At half-time when I'm sat in the press box, I'll often get a message from Lee Martin: 'Can you go and get me a pie from downstairs?' He's keen because the ones in the press room are bigger than the ones laid on for the hospitality boxes upstairs where he works. But sometimes Lee has to go without if my commentary partner is hungry. They get the pies from downstairs all the time so, for the sake of variety, I might offer to go upstairs and get them one from the hospitality section.

I'm very fortunate in my role at Old Trafford – and not just because having two different security passes gives me access to a wider range of pies. On matchdays I combine working in hospitality with working for United's in-house TV and radio station, MUTV. It's exactly what I hope to do for the rest of my days and as long as you have remained a friend of Man United, gave your best while you were there and haven't given Sir Alex a reason to turn you away, you're in with a shout of being looked after by them. Look at Alex Stepney and Paddy Crerand: they're employed by the club to this day and were playing for United 50 years ago. It just shows the longevity that you can have at United.

MUTV radio came calling first, in 2009. To begin with they'd ring me five or six times a season to ask if I'd go and do a commentary gig for them and I'd say yes when it didn't clash with my hours at the restaurant. There was no training, they just threw me in. That didn't faze me in the slightest though because I was never worried that I might make a mess of it or wouldn't know what to say.

If there had been training there would have been two main points. Firstly, don't just tell people what's happening because they can see that for themselves, though obviously that only applies on TV, not radio. But either way, the reason I'm there is to try and explain why or how things have happened – the sort of stuff Gary Neville does on Sky Sports. Though Gaz is on a different level because he sees things that others don't (even ex-players like me).

Secondly, don't speak when the lead commentator is speaking. If I'm at home watching or listening to a game, there's nothing more frustrating than two people speaking at the same time so I'm always wary of doing it myself. Every commentator is different so you have to learn their different styles; I've done a lot of games with Dave Stowell, for example, and I always know it's my turn to speak from the tone of his voice.

Of course, sometimes you get an absolutely dire game and it becomes difficult to muster anything to say at all. When a game is that dull you do find yourself drifting off but you can't because very quickly something might happen – even if it's just a substitution – and you need to be on the ball. You don't want to be known as somebody who makes even one glaring error, let alone a succession of them (unless you're Chris Kamara).

I don't do any specific research before a game, though I do like to be able to lob in the occasional weird historical fact. And if there's a player whose name is particularly difficult to pronounce I'll ask for a phonetic breakdown. Apart from that I ask the lead commentator whatever else I need to know: 'Where did Zenit St Petersburg finish in the league last year and who was their top scorer?' Stuff like that. Sometimes I feel like a charlatan because I don't know any of that stuff, whereas somebody like Jamie Carragher – or my son, for that matter – could just rattle it off. Then again, even Gaz wouldn't know who Zenit St Petersburg's top scorer is.

My seat in the press box is a tight squeeze, not helped by all the wires we've got hanging down everywhere (big winter coats don't help either). To make things worse, directly behind us there are benches that have loads of space; they go from the row behind us all the way to the top of the stand. Sometimes, when three of us get squeezed into this one little row of seats, I look behind me and there can be four benches not being used. We have asked if we can commandeer one in the future – it is our stadium, after all.

Depending on the magnitude of the game, the press box can be half empty or absolutely packed. There are a few faces I see in there fairly regularly: Robbie Savage, Kevin Kilbane, Graeme Le Saux, Jan Molby, Lee Dixon, Phil Neville and Jan Åage Fjørtoft. Plus journalists I've got to know, like Steve Bates from the *Sunday People* and Henry Winter from *The Times*. Stewart Gardner and Paddy Crerand too of course, the regular MUTV commentary team for United home games. I can't count the number of times a message has been sent down from Stewart as the second half starts saying, 'Is there any chance that somebody can get Paddy back to his seat? We've kicked off.' Paddy does have a tendency to be a bit lax with his timekeeping – not to mention being a cantankerous old so-and-so – but I do love him.

Sometimes the tone of my commentary has to change. For example, United's under-23s got relegated in 2017/18. Yet for the times I commentated on them for MUTV there was actually a protocol sent around by the in-house media team that said under no circumstances were we to mention what a poor season they were having. The idea was to stay positive. No such problems for the under-18s, for whom nothing was set in stone because they were winning – and ultimately won – their league.

You find yourself in all manner of places commentating on away games. For example, at Leicester for the under-23s in 2017 we were put on to a purposefully erected scaffold; we weren't in a stand because they didn't have one for their training pitch. Huish Park, where United's first team played Yeovil in the FA Cup last season, wasn't exactly high on grandeur either, but they were unbelievably hospitable. At the opposite end of the scale, I commentated in Brighton's stadium for the first time last season and it was brilliant.

I have to bite my tongue sometimes when I'm behind the mic and it's so much easier for me to get annoyed when it's a member of the opposition doing something, so I have to be really careful. Diving, rolling around on the floor, trying to get people booked, time-wasting: it all adds up to cheating. As far as I'm concerned, diving is just as bad as smacking somebody in the mouth. The result is the same – alright, apart from the fact that getting smacked in the mouth hurts – because you are trying to gain an unfair advantage.

I'd like to think that I'm getting better at commentating all the time. Especially now that I've started doing a few bits and bobs for BBC Manchester, where I've again had to learn to change my tone, this time to be that little bit more subjective. That said, the worst part of my job is MUTV being accused of being biased, of being pro-United. The truth is that if the game you've just seen is absolute dross, it would be embarrassing for you to turn around and say, 'Well, I thought everybody played brilliantly.' That would lose viewers. You have to make sure everyone knows you've been watching the same game they have.

I actually did a bit of TV work for Sky Sports in 2012 and I have Martin Tyler to thank for that: he'd heard me on MUTV radio and was sufficiently impressed to give Sky Sports my number. I was a bit nervous because they expected a little bit more of me and I was working with people I didn't know (including one producer who, while I was commentating live on Norwich vs QPR, said in my earpiece: 'Jesus Christ, this is fucking boring'). But I did a few games with Joe Speight, who I enjoyed working with and listening to, and was starting to enjoy myself – until they had a reshuffle and I was pushed out of the equation (or maybe they just thought I was shit).

I do some front-of-camera work for MUTV too, including the preview show on matchdays and a post-game analysis show called *Box to Box*. I'm always talking directly to a presenter, which I'm happy about. When we first started as apprentices at United we did some media training covering all different scenarios and by far the most difficult one was talking into a camera. It's very disconcerting.

I heard that Jose Mourinho put in a good word for me at MUTV towards the end of the 2017/18 season. My commentary on our game at Crystal Palace that season, when Matic scored a last-minute winner to make it 3-2, was played at United's player of the year event because Matic won goal of the season. I don't know if anything will come of it but it was nice to hear.

Meanwhile, my hospitality work started in 2013 – on 5 March to be precise. I was on the train back from a River Island job in Swansea when I got a call from my brother to say that someone had been over at the training ground asking if I'd be interested in doing some matchday hospitality. He gave me her number, I gave her a ring, she explained the role, I said I was up for it and she said, 'We're playing Real Madrid in the Champions League quarter-final on Tuesday night – get yourself into a suit, get yourself to Old Trafford and we'll sort out the rest.'

The evening's entertainment saw Nani sent off for a dubious high tackle and United knocked out; I thought they might never ask me back as a result but fortunately I've been doing it ever since. I've only missed one game since I started: we beat Burnley 3-1 in a midweek kick-off in February 2015 when I was in Singapore for Gaz's 40th birthday. We couldn't go at the weekend because he was working.

That first night in 2013 I knew what was required of me but because it had been so long since I'd played for the club, I didn't know how I was going to be taken. For that game and the next one I went round with Sammy McIlroy and Russell Beardsmore but after that I was on my own. I was in rooms I'd never been in before (I didn't even know where to find some of them), meeting emcees and room managers I'd never come across in my life. It was a bit strange and daunting but I think my experience of working in the restaurant helped.

I've since found that some days can be more difficult than others. There will be times when you'll go into a box, tell them who you are and they'll look at you as if to say, 'That's nice. Can we help you?' It can feel like you're juggling sand when you sense that you're there because you have to be there, not because they want you to be. Yet in other boxes there are people who I've ended up becoming friends with outside of Old Trafford, so the tricky moments are in the minority.

Then again, it's not for everyone. Normally speaking, if you need someone to break the ice, former United defender David May is your man – yet he tried the hospitality gig and hated it. He's larger than life and likes to swear and crack jokes, so he found making small talk with people a bit alien. It just wasn't him.

There are four parts of the ground where you can be put in hospitality boxes (we work on rotation from game to game, coordinated by Anna who's brilliant) and the rest of the time you could be in the Red Café or the museum. They're great because it's completely different clientele for every game and we do Q&As up on stage, which is one of the highlights for me. People still have fond memories of the Class of 92 and I'm the only member of that team who is part of matchday hospitality. People enjoy that because it gives them the opportunity to ask about it.

As well as Russell and Sammy, the other ex-United players who do the hospitality are Clayton Blackmore, Alan Gowling, Jimmy Greenhoff, Ashley Grimes, Lee Martin, Sammy McIlroy, Stuart Pearson, Frank Stapleton, Alex Stepney and Norman Whiteside. Also involved but working under a slightly different banner are Arthur Albiston, Andrew Cole, Quinton Fortune, Denis Irwin, Lou Macari, Albert Morgan (our former kit man), Gary Pallister, Andy Ritchie, Bryan Robson and Mickey Thomas.

I've met a few famous types over the years. Will Ferrell was a nice man, as was Errol Brown from Hot Chocolate, but Tyson Fury didn't speak so I didn't stay long in his box. Duran Duran were in for one match but Simon Le Bon was just odd and withdrawn, whereas I was expecting him to be outgoing; I was a bit gutted because I grew up listening to Duran Duran and would have liked more of a chat. John Taylor was great though and Yasmin was there too: she was as attractive as you'd expect and lovely with it. I actually sent some of the other guys in there to say hello to John – and Yasmin, obviously.

Olly Murs has got a box but stipulates that under no circumstances does he want ex-players, Fred the Red or the Manchester United Foundation going in it. When you get to each door it has a little slit of a window; Olly is the only one who has his frosted out. I did go and see him once before he came to his decision and I think it was probably just afterwards that he decided he didn't want people in. (Blame me, lads.)

One day a guy grabbed me and said, 'You don't remember me, do you? Eddie Hilditch.' And I said, 'Bloody hell – St Helens.' He marked Ryan Giggs in the final of the National Schools Trophy in 1989 and is now a season-ticket holder at United.

I love being at Old Trafford, I love doing what I'm doing on matchdays and I love being part of MUTV. Not only that but I'm getting to know the club again because I've been covering all the youth games, so I'm seeing who might be coming up into the first team. And obviously I get paid for doing it but if I didn't need the money, I'd do it for nothing. I enjoy it that much and I love the club that much.

Sunday kick-offs are great because I can spend the whole of the weekend leading up to them with Lucas. It's great that my line of work means I get to see him so regularly and, so far, I don't think Claire and I have done a bad job with him. She's done the lion's share because he lives with her but I'd like to think that in the condensed time we have together, I show him just as much love. He means the world to me. He's starting to show that he's quite a clever guy too. I want him to always have a go at things, always try things (without breaking the law) and generally do as much as he possibly can. I'm certainly not going to push him down the road of being a professional footballer and it isn't my decision anyway.

I just want him to be happy. You have to be happy in what you're doing to be successful because if you're not, why would you want to make a success of it? And I want him to be respectful of other people. If he does that and he's polite, he'll be fine. He's a good kid.

As for Les, it is sometimes a nuisance that we spend so much time apart because I'm forever commuting between Manchester and Essex. But I think we both agree that if it was any other way, we might have ended up killing each other by now. What we have together, and the way that our lives work, works. We're not trying to fix something that isn't broken. So we're not getting married, we're not having children and we've not yet got a dog (although I don't think that will tip us over the edge).

We're both very fortunate to have close families and both our parents still alive. I am grateful every single day when I look at Casp losing his mum, or Gaz and Phil losing their father. It's all very relevant when it's lads you've grown up with. Paul Devine and his brother Phil too, whose father passed away in 2012. Like my dad, he was there for every game at Salford Boys. He used to run up and down the touchline, zipping his coat up and down because he was getting frantic with Paul on the right wing. He was a gentleman.

In addition to my Old Trafford duties, I'm still involved in various games and tournaments with fellow ex-pros. Arthur Albiston now takes it upon himself to organise matches that, to be fair, are usually quite good. Though there have been times when he's been asked to take a team to go and play somewhere like Spain and ended up not being paid, so now he always tries to get the money up front.

Clayton Blackmore and David May are often on Arthur's trips too, and Maysie is a nightmare for giving Clayton a tremendous amount of grief. I don't feel sorry for him though, do I heck, because he can give as good as he gets – and when someone else is bearing the brunt of it, it means it's diverted from me. But it's all done in the right spirit and Clayton is a really lovely guy. Unless you get him started on golf, as then you can't shut the fucker up. In fact, even if you avoid the subject like the plague, he'll still find a way to bring it up.

Another fairly regular gig is Masters Football, which David May first got me involved with. The CEO is called Steve Black and he organises tournaments around the world, particularly in Asia; we've been to Malaysia, Brunei, Indonesia and Thailand, among others. Brunei was an odd one because it's dry, which defeats the point of the trip for some players. They did manage to get some alcohol in for us but we had to have it in the hotel in one special room upstairs – we couldn't go out and drink, which made a few of the players antsy.

Over the years I've occasionally helped Steve to get players in and put teams together; I got Scholesy to come out to China and Hong Kong in 2015, for example (and he scored an absolute wonder goal, by the way). I'm under no illusion that there are players other than me who people would rather see in these games but you always need the shitkickers. You're never going to be able to fill a team with big names because it's not as important for the lads who earned millions while they were playing. Whereas if someone is willing to pay us lesser names a few quid to play a game of football in Asia, have a few drinks and see a few lads, of course we're going to accept.

Invariably the marquee players are the ones who have to earn the money anyway; we just sit there to make up the numbers. We realise that Scholes and the rest get more than we do but as long as we're not made to feel like second-class citizens, we go because we're happy with the amount we're getting. People would be prepared to pay up to £500,000 for the likes of Giggsy and Beckham. And I'd love to know how much Eric Cantona got for turning out at Soccer Aid.

For the 2015 trip, Steve put together a team containing Des Walker, Emmanuel Petit, Darren Anderton and Robert Pires – players who played at the top of the game when I never fucking got anywhere near it. But because I was instrumental in getting Scholesy to come, I got to go on the trip and be paid to be part of it.

Fortunately I'm happy to make conversation with anybody – and so I got on with everybody. Des Walker was my best mate by the end because he didn't care how many England caps I had or hadn't got. He made the point that when your football career is over but you're still getting to go on trips like the one we were on, you soon find out who's alright and who isn't. He said he'd shared a pitch with some brilliant players but now he wouldn't piss on some of them if they were on fire. After that conversation I didn't worry about the esteemed company I was in. At this stage of our lives it's how we are as people that's going to get us through life, not how we were as footballers.

My former Class of 92 team-mate Keith Gillespie has played in a few Masters games and he's in magnificent shape. He can run and run and run, though for the life of me I don't know how he has maintained his physique and pace because he drinks like a fish and smokes like a chimney.

Just as he did, in fact, when we went on a Masters trip to Kuala Lumpur. I was rooming with him and had come back early from a night out. A few hours later he came in half-cut (which you don't often see because he's such a big drinker) and he had company. When he saw me he said, 'Oh, I didn't know you were here! That's fine though.' His companion seemed less sure – probably because she was a lady (though this was Kuala Lumpur so who knows) of the night.

I told them I'd order room service and go in the bathroom to eat it while they got better acquainted. It was a nice hotel, a Hilton, and the bathroom was one of those with a glass wall and an electric shutter. So once I was in there I could still just about make them out. However, our guest spotted my silhouette and realised that I was spectating, so she gave Keith the remote control to roll the blind down (as I bent down lower and lower to peek underneath it). He tried to leave a little gap at the bottom for me but she snatched the remote off him and put paid to that.

After about five minutes I'd had enough so I came out of the bathroom and announced that I'd wait downstairs in the bar until they'd finished. In the midst of his vinegar strokes Keith said, 'What about your room service?' I told him it was probably best if he concentrated on his own.

The PFA is another to have hosted a couple of six-a-side tournaments, in Barbados and Tobago respectively, but for some reason they were discontinued. In Barbados I was joined by Maysie, former Liverpool winger David Thompson, ex-Newcastle defender Steve Watson and former Forest and Celtic striker Pierre van Hooijdonk. As for the Tobago trip, we managed to drink the plane dry on the flight over.

A one-off game I was involved in was a 2014 friendly between Salford City and a Class of 92 XI, to mark the fact the lads had bought the club. I didn't particularly enjoy that experience: I hadn't played much football for a while so I wasn't in great nick, whereas Salford were a group of kids who had just done a full pre-season and were flying. They spanked us 5-1. The less said about the entire affair, the better.

Then there are the games organised by the Manchester United Foundation, which is the club's charity arm. Since 2013 we've played Bayern Munich, Barcelona and Real Madrid, coming up against the likes of Mark van Bommel, Patrick Kluivert, Ronaldinho, Luis Figo and Zinedine Zidane. We've also played a Liverpool XI in Stockholm's Friends Arena and an Aussie Legends team in Perth. It's a nice opportunity for us to all get together, earn a few quid and make money for a decent cause.

I always look forward to these trips but I don't know how long they're going to last because it's not like I'm on any sort of contract.

I'm only 43 so if I can continue to look after myself, I've got a bit of a shelf life left. And because I'm never going to be someone who people are falling over themselves to see in action, I'm only ever going to play half a game (at the outside), which means I don't need to be 90-minutes match-fit.

I'm hoping that I can do it for at least another ten years. The pool of players to choose from is not as huge as you might think because the generation of players who are turning 35 now have probably earned their money already. Unless it's really lucrative, they won't be arsed.

I will miss it when I'm not asked along anymore or I'm not in any physical condition to keep doing it (and I'll have to be honest with myself there). Maybe it will feel more like my retirement than my actual retirement did, though I haven't been walking into dressing rooms for years so it won't come as a massive shock. As long as I can keep the other stuff going – commentating on and talking about football – then that's fine because the playing side is already secondary to me.

That's not to say I don't still enjoy getting on the pitch. When I'm at Les's house of a weekend I turn out for the Paringdon Vets, who are in the premier division of the Essex Veterans Football League. It's a Saturday afternoon league that's sponsored by Greene King brewery; for the most part no one is there to kick lumps out of you and the pitches are good. Teddy Sheringham graced them for a while and then there are the brothers Michael and Tommy Black; Michael started his career at Arsenal and Tommy played for Crystal Palace. These days they both turn out for Hutton Old Boys, who beat us 3-2 in the final of the Essex Saturday Veterans Cup at the end of 2017/18.

My involvement is negligible because of my weekend commitments at United. But they are a really chirpy set of lads, some of whom are very good footballers who could quite easily have played at a higher level – semi-pro certainly. But a lot of them are now reaching their forties so it's about time the manager, Nathan, had a shake-up and recruited some 35-year-olds if he wants to win the league.

I think that pretty much brings us up to date. I've enjoyed putting the book together (for the most part) because it's been an adventure, it's been a focus and it's been exciting. And I feel humble that so many different people, many who I haven't spoken to for a long time, have all agreed to help me. I can't ask for any more. It makes me feel proud.

Looking back (which is the point of an autobiography, isn't it?), I don't have too many regrets. But in my personal life I should have had a lot more respect for the women I was in relationships with. It wasn't that I treated them like they didn't matter, just that I mattered more. I did what I did because I wanted to and because I could, and that's out of character for me because it's not the type of person I am. I was young but that's a reason, not an excuse – because I have no excuse for some of the things I did.

To the people who were involved, I apologise.

In terms of my career, after my injury I wish I'd done extra work in my own time in addition to what I was doing in training. I should have been well on top of my fitness and, because of the position I played in, my short, sharp stuff. Little and often would have been fine and I had control over that – but I didn't do it.

Though perhaps I was too fucked after all the work I did to get back to full fitness after surgery. There was many a time when I'd look at my knee and think, 'This is just not happening.' But that's where the determination kicked in; it's a cliché but I had it in the back of my mind that where there's a will, there's a way.

However, I couldn't have done it without all the good people, exceptional people, who gave me their support and loyalty. It meant that I could fulfil my dream: to play professional football again.

16

First-team debut
1993–94

Ben: When we reported back to play for the reserves in the first week of July it was a case of, 'Alright, I'm here now.' I was a man playing open-age football; I wasn't an apprentice anymore. And we all wanted to make sure that the result against Leeds United was just a blip. We were desperate to get back on track and we wanted our first-team debuts.

Mike Phelan: It was a massive step up for them but it helped that they came through as a group. They were well schooled because they were in an environment that pushed and pushed and pushed, and made sure they developed. And Ben was strong-minded anyway; he was always keen, he was always willing to do more.

Andrei Kanchelskis: There was excitement within the squad when those lads started training with us because we'd heard that they were quality. Ben was no exception.

Dion Dublin: He raised a few eyebrows in the first-team dressing room. He was known as the little left-winger with ridiculous amounts of pace who delivered a cross with quality. Once I heard that I thought, 'He sounds right up my street.' It's very rarely you get a winger who, more often than not, gives you an end product.

Gary Walsh: He was brave. No matter how big his opponent was he'd put his foot in and he'd never duck out of a tackle. Not that you could duck out of a tackle when you were coached by Eric Harrison.

Ben: During the first few weeks of pre-season we were in every morning and afternoon, Monday to Saturday. Jim Ryan – who played for United in the era of Best, Charlton and Law – managed the reserves. He was nowhere near as fierce as Eric Harrison. He had a different coaching method, a different way of speaking. Arguably he was more lenient but he still expected the lads to work.

Paul Scholes: Jim was tough when he wanted to be and he could fly off the handle. Before he came to United he was manager at Luton and I think they had a bit of a thing with Derby County. So whenever we played Derby County it was like his big cup final and if we got beat, he'd go ballistic.

Ben: While training was very structured under Jim, it was always different in terms of numbers and personnel. There were all these different permutations so come Monday morning, you never knew where you were going to end up.

Jim Ryan: I had to think on my feet sometimes. We could be getting close to going out to train but I'd still be waiting to hear what Brian Kidd wanted to do. And often he didn't know himself, because he hadn't had chance to speak to the manager. Then eventually he'd come over and he might tell me he needed three players and a goalkeeper, so suddenly the session I had planned would be up in the air.

Ben: And then it would be: who's involved in the first team, who didn't play in the reserves in midweek, who was on the bench, who's going to be playing in the A and B teams? The previous Saturday you might have been drafted in to play for the A team in Carlisle or you could have been in the first-team squad reporting to Old Trafford. So it was a case of who needs a game, who wants a game and who doesn't want a game but is going to get one anyway because they've not played?

We also had all manner of characters on that field, from players who were there to be in the shop window for scouts because they wanted to get away to those who were desperate to get themselves back into the first team. And then you had us youngsters, of course.

Jim Ryan: For a reserve-team coach the thing is, can you get the young players through to the first team? Can you help them if they suddenly hit a wall and aren't doing well? But with those boys, everyone at the club was already sure that they would make the grade. That meant my thing was to make them ready to play against men rather than boys.

Paul Parker: Ben wasn't just a normal winger; he had a lot more to his game. He was one of those you came up against in training who straight away, as an older pro, you wanted to kick. He was a wide player with pace who was willing to run beyond you *all the time*. Players in the Premier League didn't want to do it: their mindset was to not attack Manchester United too often because we might hit them on the counter attack. So when you had a young lad in training who wanted to, it was a bit of a rarity.

He had a desire to prove himself and wasn't going to be held back, which is the difference between the good players and the ones who are just OK. He was very respectful of us senior pros but on the pitch, he didn't care who you were.

Ben: When I first came into reserve-team football, which was sporadically in my first two seasons as an apprentice, the first thing I'd do when the team sheets appeared was work out who I was going to be up against. My main concern was that I didn't want to see names I'd heard of. But it wasn't long before I *wanted* to see established names; it was important for my development and to gauge where I was. And yes, there were a couple who I played where I thought, 'Wow, tough.' But I wanted to come up against these players who had a taste of having been there and done it – and I needed to make sure I was better than them. I had faith in my ability. Eric Harrison, Brian Kidd and the manager had given me that.

Dion Dublin: Ben's body language on the pitch was easy for me to read. It was very much: 'I'm in this position, Dion, and I'm going to put the ball there.' That was great for a big centre-forward with not too much finesse. Ben was so important to me.

Gary Walsh: He was very direct and quick. He played in a similar vein to Andrei Kanchelskis: get the ball and attack people. He never scored any past me in training though, obviously. To be fair I was quite good when I was young so it would have been difficult.

Jeff Kerfoot: I'd go and watch reserves matches and it was a hell of a team when he broke through, what with the lads dropping down from the first team and the youngsters coming through. There was some wonderful football played. And Ben was more than holding his own; he was outstanding most weeks to be honest. And just phenomenally quick.

Bryan Robson: That season was the first time the reserves had won the league for I don't know how many years. So even for me as an experienced player, it was a joy to play in that team because we always won.

Ben: Bryan Robson was immense. He's one of the only footballers I've ever known to have broken a femur and that takes some doing.

Bryan Robson: I broke both.

Ben: He's such a lovely fella as well. The first day that I walked into The Cliff, he asked me what shoe size I was and he had all these boxes of New Balance football boots. We happened to be the same size so he said, 'Will you do me a favour and wear these in for me for a couple of weeks?' I wore them for a few training sessions and played a game in them, then cleaned them up, put them back in the box and found him to give them back. He said I could keep them. I wore them for the whole season and treasured them.

Bryan Robson: I was trying to get rid of them.

Ben: In October 1993 we played a reserve game against Wolves in front of about 20,000 at Molineux. Steve Bull was playing for them and it was a really good game; we won 3-2 and I scored the winner. Up against me, playing on the right wing, was Kevin Keen, who they'd just paid £600,000 for. He never got near me. I thought to myself, 'If they've paid that for him, what must I be on my way to being worth now?'

That said, going back a bit further, I remember one Saturday morning when I was still an apprentice being given an absolutely torrid time by Pat Nevin. What a tricky little fucker. He was playing for one of the junior sides at Everton; he must have been coming back from injury or something. But I tell you what, he was tremendous.

In the November of 1993 I was included in the first-team squad for our away game against Galatasary in the Champions League. When we arrived at the airport we were greeted by fans sweating with hatred, only separated from us by Perspex screens. When we got to the stadium I didn't get changed because I wasn't a sub, so me and a couple of other players in the same boat went up into what was loosely called the 'directors box'. It was like a cattle market. And you couldn't see anything because of the smoke from the flares.

The crowd really were incredible: three sides of the stadium would chant and the main stand would answer them back. They had it off to a tee.

Group stages didn't exist in the Champions League then so this was the second round and we needed a goal because they'd drawn 3-3 at Old Trafford. Instead we drew 0-0 and that's when it all kicked off between the entire Turkish police force and Eric Cantona. Then, when we were coming away from the ground on the coach, I was at a table of four with Steve Bruce sitting diagonally opposite me, next to the window. Someone lobbed a brick at it and he just went white. Being on a coach that's under siege from fans is quite something.

A week later we played a reserve game at Old Trafford against Liverpool and drew 0-0. Jim Ryan came into the dressing room and said something but then Darren Ferguson, the manager's son, started laying into Gaz. Big time.

Gary Neville: I thought I'd played quite well, to be honest.

Ben: And then Darren's dad walked in. 'Don't you fucking *dare* have a go at these lads, who are trying to learn their trade, when you play for the first team and have just put in a performance like that.' And for the whole of the remaining 15 minutes of that match post-mortem, it was just Sir Alex Ferguson ripping his son to pieces. Fuck me, it was immense.

Gary Neville: He probably did it to make a point rather than because what Darren was saying was wrong. You know what the boss was like – he'd do something like that. In fact that sort of thing happened a lot in the youth team and even when we broke into the first team. The manager would catch you out sometimes by praising you – or battering you – when you didn't expect it. Or he'd praise your team-mate, who you thought you'd outplayed. It was a case of making a young player tougher.

Ryan Giggs: Butty got told he'd never play for United again in his first youth-team game.

Gary Neville: You wouldn't call it bullying but you might feel like you were being targeted – yet everything was in your best interests. You had to come through those moments.

Ben: Now that we were no longer apprentices we were training more regularly with the seniors, either when they joined us in the reserves or when we got involved in first-team sessions. In the case of the latter, the senior lads always made us feel part of it. The likes of Gary Pallister, Bryan Robson, Paul Parker and Brian McClair were all seasoned professionals who knew what it was like to come into a set-up where you're a rabbit in the headlights. They settled us down in order to get the best out of us. That's not to say you wouldn't get a bollocking.

Steve Bruce, Peter Schmeichel and Roy Keane didn't care who you were – if you were training with the first team you needed to be at the right level.

Dion Dublin: Around the first team, when he was on the fringes, Ben was pretty quiet. Which is how you have to be – you can't come in and give it stacks because you'll be shot down sharpish.

Denis Irwin: When you're a young lad – and I was the same when I was at Leeds – you're just weighing up the situation. But listen, you can tell from Ben's demeanour now that he's a bubbly lad and you could tell back then too.

Mike Phelan: Ben was respectful towards senior players. But there was a different vibe then – it's not like the youth of today, who will tell you they're the next Pele when they're 15. He was just quietly confident in his ability.

Bryan Robson: We always liked it when the boss brought one or two of the young lads across to train with us because when you're playing with people you can gauge how good they are – or not.

Ben: He didn't just bundle us all in at once. John O'Kane and Becks were the first players to go on tour with the first team, to South Africa at the start of that season, and we were all like, 'What's the matter with us?' But then again, we could see his mentality.

Gary Neville: He'd make us all feel good at certain points and then he'd bring us back down a peg.

Bryan Robson: The boss always did that. He'd talk to Eric Harrison and say, 'Right Eric, who's done well, who's improved and who deserves to step up and play with the first team for a couple of weeks?' And if I'd played in the reserves that week he'd have a cup of tea with me on Friday morning to find out what I thought of Ben and the others.

Ben: Talking of tea: Mike Phelan. He would always be one of the last people to get changed and then he'd sit in the dressing room, legs crossed (something I could only do up until 1994), with a cuppa in his hand.

Mike Phelan: I still like a cup of tea, ideally with a bacon sandwich. I also used to have a nip of brandy every time I played. The kit man, Norman Davies, was a good bloke and he used to hand me a miniature. It would just get me buzzing a bit before I went out. I'm not sure I'd get away with that now.

Ben: During that 1993/94 season, every time I saw a reserves team sheet go up I took great heart from the fact that I was on it and, invariably, in the starting line-up. I was scoring goals and really enjoying my football. I knew that whatever it was I'd been doing up to that point, I'd been doing it right. I'd had the thrill of winning the Youth Cup, then here I was with the same group of players and we were hardly losing a game. I was allowing myself to think that I had a chance.

Then come February, a Thursday morning, I was in reception at The Cliff on my way into training. I spotted Brian Kidd, the assistant manager; he was always up and down the stairs, in and out of the dressing rooms, making sure the kit was ready and what have you.

He grabbed me and said, 'Listen, you'll be, you'll be ...' – he can never finish a sentence, Kiddo – '... you'll be travelling tomorrow. Train with Jimmy today but tomorrow morning you're with, you're with the first team. Make sure you've got all your gear and bring your suit because we'll be going straight on, straight on the coach to Upton Park after training.'

I just said, 'OK.' It was as simple as that. I didn't read anything into it. It's not as if I thought, 'I'm going to be making my debut for Manchester United.' For all I knew I was going to be sat in the stands. In fact the first thing that came to mind was: where will I leave my car when we get on the coach?

I was able to ring my parents straight away because I'd just bought my first mobile phone; I asked my mum to dig out my blazer, tie and grey flannels. When I told the lads – the likes of Becks and Gary – that I was going, they all said that I'd be making my debut, otherwise why was the manager taking me? I didn't want to assume that but they were adamant.

Neither Giggsy nor Sharpey were in that squad (they must have had a night out planned). I'm sure their absence had something to do with why I played but I'd also hope that I'd earned it. As well as it being tactical I'd like to think that it was a reward, a merit thing.

On the Friday morning before we travelled we did a warm-up and a box (when two people go in the middle and you have to keep the ball off them) before playing a game of seven-a-side. There was no chat about how the team was going to play because that had already been covered during the course of the week. And anyway, for the amount of time the manager was intending to put me on for, all he cared about was me doing what I'd done all season. Kiddo gave me a couple of pointers but it wasn't anything that was going to mash my head. Sir Alex didn't want to frighten and bamboozle me with too much information when I was an 18-year-old kid set to make my debut at a notoriously difficult place to play.

After the training session we got changed into our tracksuits. I drove my car over to Old Trafford from The Cliff (as Kiddo had helpfully suggested) and got on the coach there. Once on it, I needed to be sure of which seats *not* to sit in. I asked Norman Davies, the kit man, to help me – and not wind me up by telling me it was alright to sit somewhere only for it to turn out to be Keaney's spot.

Denis Irwin: Players tended to sit in the same place when they were on the coach; I think it was superstition. The card school would have been top for being territorial: Brucey, Robbo, Pally and me.

Ben: We arrived in London late afternoon and dinner was at the hotel at 7pm. There were two tables for the players and a table for the management, though sometimes Sir Alex decided to come and sit at one of the players' tables or requested someone like Bryan Robson or Brian McClair to go and sit at his. My strategy was to make sure I was down there first, not help myself to any food and just sit there with a cup of tea. I was confident I wasn't sitting at the manager's table because it was smaller than the other two.

After dinner, most lads were back in their rooms no later than 9pm. It was then up to you when you went to sleep. I roomed with Dion Dublin and fortunately he didn't mind having the telly on.

Dion Dublin: Ben made rubbish hot chocolate though and I gave him stick about that. 'You're stirring it the wrong way Benji, what's wrong with you? Come on.'

Ben: The next morning, breakfast wasn't compulsory; management allowed players to have their own routines. Everyone had to be downstairs for a walk around the hotel grounds though, which was around 10am.

Then everybody had to be down for the pre-match meal, whether they ate or not. That was at midday, then at 1pm the manager gave a team talk, complete with flipchart. The length of said talk would vary. I remember one later on where he came in, said not three sentences and walked straight back out again. Kiddo said, 'He's lost it! He's lost it!'

But more often than not the manager would have the opposition's team from their previous game written out. If there were suspensions, or injuries we knew about, he'd cross them out and put in who he thought was going to play, then dissect their team. He'd then leave and Kiddo would have his flipchart out, covering corners and free kicks, for and against. Who was marking who, who was staying up the field, who was taking them from which side and all that. Even as a substitute you needed to study it because you might not have half-time to look at it again – you could be on after ten minutes. And then you'd think, 'Shit, what was the guy I've just come on for doing again?'

At roughly 1.15pm we were on the coach. To get to the ground you had to go past the notorious Boleyn pub on the corner, where they hung the effigy of Becks after the 1998 World Cup. So that was lively. All the United fans used to try to take it over and I think, more often than not, they succeeded. But that day it was packed with West Ham fans. And a big thing for all clubs' supporters, not just Hammers fans, was to wait for the Man United coach to turn up. It's not like it was difficult to spot either: it was nicer than theirs and it had a bloody great police escort in front of it.

Alex Ferguson wanted us in the dressing room about 90 minutes before kick-off. All the talking was done so it was our preparation time. The changing rooms at Upton Park were really small and you had to go upstairs to reach them. When we got there, Norman had already been in to lay everything out. I looked around and I didn't need to wait to be told I was involved because there, right at the end, was a shirt with my surname on the back of it.

I was number 29. It was my favourite kit as well – the black one. That was the first I knew I was part of the matchday squad; nobody had pulled me aside and said anything before that. It was their way of not making a big thing of the fact that in my previous game I'd been playing for the junior side and now here I was hoping to make my full league debut, all within the space of a week.

We dumped our bags, went for a wander around the pitch then ambled back in. Then it was just a case of getting ready in your own time, though I needed to be ready a bit earlier because it was my job to warm up the goalkeeper. That was the first time I'd done it and on my way out Kiddo said, 'Good luck, all the best.' Fortunately I didn't kick a ball straight at Peter's face on this occasion. Though it wasn't easy concentrating in front of thousands of people piling into Upton Park, all saying, 'Who are you, you little shit?'

Paul Ince, meanwhile, was even getting abuse during the warm-up.

Denis Irwin: Incey used to get the bulk of the stick having moved from them to United but it was a tough place for us to go anyway, particularly in the early 90s. I don't think we ever did particularly well down there.

Dion Dublin: Every time Incey got the ball he was getting dog's abuse. Early on in the game the ball went out of play and he was closest, but in retrieving it he got stuff thrown at him – pies or coins, I can't remember. He didn't take any more throw-ins after that. I'm surprised he got out of the stadium actually.

Ben: We were back in the dressing room for 2.45pm and the manager was ready to give out last-minute instructions. There weren't many; he'd normally be having a cup of tea and not saying much, though there might be the odd person he'd approach to give them some extra information.

Among the players, Incey was the most vocal before we headed out. Eric Cantona always went off into the shower area to go through rigorous stretches. Then it was time for us to head out, starting line-up first and then the subs walking with the manager, Kiddo, Norman and the physio, Rob Swire. Me being the youngest, I was carrying the water bottles.

Again, Norman was the man for telling me where to sit on the bench. I wanted to make sure because I was on it with Dion Dublin and Les Sealey (there were only three subs in those days), and Les was one of these fernickety goalkeepers you didn't want to upset. I liked Les, don't get me wrong, but I would have been on the end of a proper East End, 'Gerrout my facking seat you little cant!'

At 3pm on Saturday, 26 February 1994, the game kicked off. Kiddo was up and down to the touchline while the manager stayed seated, though after a while he joined in. He only ever spent prolonged periods up there if he wasn't happy. We scored after six minutes through Mark Hughes, which was good, and it stayed 1-0 until half-time.

We got back in the dressing room and I sat in the corner, keeping an eye on Norman in case he wanted me to grab anything. He was walking around making sure everyone was happy with what they were wearing; if someone had wanted to change their boots, for example, he would have asked me to go and fetch some. I also needed to listen to what the manager was saying but he was fine – we were 1-0 up. In the second half, Lee Chapman equalised for West Ham in the 69th minute. When that went in I was thinking, 'Stick me on now.' But the manager might have been protecting me because they'd just equalised, they were in the ascendancy and they had a vociferous group of supporters. And if that was the case he was proven right: Trevor Morley put them in front three minutes later.

Because I was one of only three subs, and only two of us were outfield players, deep down I was starting to think, 'He's going to try me out. Even though we're losing, he's going to give me a whirl. What's he dragged me down here for if he doesn't want to see what I can do?'

While Les Sealey was warming up he was also winding up the West Ham fans like you wouldn't believe. He was giving them some real grief. I wanted to say, 'Is there any chance you could stop that, Les? I'm hoping to make my debut here.' But he didn't care.

And whenever he got in between those goalposts he was like a man possessed; Peter Schmeichel was bad but Les Sealey was dreadful. If you tried to chip him in a training session he'd chase after you. God knows what he'd have done. But he was a great bloke and a really wonderful character to have in the dressing room; even if you couldn't see him at The Cliff you could always hear him. But the poor guy died of a heart attack in 2001. He was only 43 – that's my age now.

Dion Dublin: Les Sealey, God rest his soul. He was a big talker, proper cockney like. 'Alwight, Dizz, 'ow's it goin'? Alwight, Ben? Get warmed up Ben, go on, go on!' He was keeping us entertained the whole time we were on that bench, having bants with the fans, suggesting they'd only paid their money to come and see him play.

Ben: Upton Park is about the worst place I could have made my debut in terms of how vociferous the fans were. I had to try and drown it out but they were so close to the pitch that it was hard to miss things like: 'Who's this fucking arsehole? Another wonderkid who's going to turn out to be wank.' I'll have to try and get hold of that guy and tell him he was bang on.

I knew I was going to make my debut when Kiddo sent me out to warm up with the words, 'Go and have a run, you're going on.' Before I had chance to really do anything I saw him waving for me to come back to the dugout and get my tracksuit off.

I was nervous and my stomach was doing somersaults but I was buzzing, absolutely buzzing. This was what I had dedicated my life so far to doing. It was all for this particular moment: to actually play for Manchester United's first team. And it was happening when I was still 18. I never thought it would come so soon.

Philip Thornley: I was listening to the radio because we knew he was in the squad.

Ben: I came on in the 78th minute. Sir Alex and Kiddo said to go and enjoy it. That's what everyone was saying, anyone who was on the bench: go and enjoy it, son. And I did. I really did. That was the contrast between me pre-injury and me post-injury: it wasn't just a difference in my physical attributes but my mindset. When I came on against West Ham I thought, 'Yeah, this is me.' The idea of skipping past players, who three or four years ago I'd been watching on TV, didn't faze me one bit.

Denis Irwin: Ben came on for me. And this wasn't a comfortable home match with the team winning by three goals; the manager's taken him down to the Boleyn Ground in a really tough atmosphere, in a tough game, with the team 2-1 down. That shows you how much he trusted Ben.

Andrei Kanchelskis: It was a very tight game and it was time to freshen things up. It's always a surprise for the opposition when a player makes his debut as there is an element of the unknown. From what I remember, Ben did well.

Ben: I played on the left wing where I was up against Tim Breacker, a steady full-back, but I didn't really get much chance to have a pop at him. Dion came on in the 85th minute but neither did I get the opportunity to stick a cross in for him. That would have been nice because it would have been familiar territory – if in front of far more unaccepting people than usual.

Andrei Kanchelskis: I came off a few minutes after Ben came on.

Dion Dublin: They must have put me on for Andrei to inject a bit of pace. I can't remember exactly what happened when I got on but I can only assume that I made a massive difference.

Ben: In the 87th minute, Ince stabbed the ball in when it was pinballing around in the box to make it 2-2. If you watch the footage you see me appear in the bottom left corner of the screen and put my hands on my head as it goes in. I don't know why I did that – maybe I thought it was going to be disallowed for some reason. But it was great to be on the pitch when he scored, even though I had absolutely nothing whatsoever to do with the goal.

Right at the end Ian Bishop tackled me as I went past him. The ref blew his whistle and Incey thought it was for a foul but he was actually blowing for the end of the game – so Incey went nuts. But that was that and it was great: I wouldn't have to forever remember my league debut as a game that we lost. I didn't set the world alight while I was on the pitch but nor did I miscontrol it, watch my first pass go out of play or anything like that. I didn't touch the ball that often but what I did do was alright. I came off thinking I hadn't done myself any harm and Kiddo said the same when I spoke to him.

Jim Ryan: The general consensus was that another player had stepped up and survived it.

Ben: I went and applauded the United fans with the other players because it was a decent result, that. And of course, when you score that late on and you've been 2-1 down, it feels more like a victory. Afterwards virtually all of the players, including Parks, Denis and Brian McClair (who has always been complimentary towards me, though I've never known why), came up to say well done.

Brian McClair: The thing was that Ben had made it into the first team, which meant he had to be good – and he was right at the top of that group of players. He had everything you need to be a first-team player: he had the mental strength to cope with it, he was determined and he was single-minded, in the sense that he knew what he wanted. He was there on merit – but then it was taken away from him.

Ben: On the way back to Manchester, as the youngest member of the squad I had to help kit man Norman 'prepare' a load of ready-meals for the other lads, using the microwave we had down the back of the coach.

Dion Dublin: Ben was fucking rubbish at that as well, by the way.

Ben: Somebody loud – it must have been Incey or Roy Keane – shouted down, 'I want another one!' Me and Norman had just sat down to eat ours by that point so Norman said, 'Do you know what, me and Ben have been up there for an hour and a half sorting all this out, so you can fuck off. If there's any left, you can wait until we've finished.' And whoever it was said, 'Oh, alright then.'

I got on really well with Norman. Salt of the earth he was; didn't give a fuck about telling anybody what he thought of them. I didn't give him any trouble so he was alright with me. Sadly he died of cancer in 2010. He was great.

When we got back to Manchester, everyone else got off to pick up their cars at the Four Seasons because they lived on that side of the city in Wilmslow, Altrincham – the Cheshire belt, essentially. But I lived in Eccles, which was why my car was at Old Trafford. Club secretary Ken Merritt was still on board too and he said, 'Will you be getting a bonus?'

I said I hoped so because at the time it was £100 per point and £200 for an appearance. So add that to the one-off £6,000 bonus for making my first-team debut and I made £525 per minute against West Ham. And that was on top of my wages, which weren't wonderful at the time. So that was nice.

I drove home from Old Trafford and was eager to get back in time for *Match of the Day*.

Jim Ryan: I can remember running in to watch it on the telly so I knew he'd done well and not let anybody down. Though I wasn't prepared to judge him, or anybody, on the basis of one performance for the first team. You kind of get that one for free.

Ben: I was ready for my dad to say, 'Well, you didn't do much.' To be fair that's not his style but certainly if my son Lucas had been around then he would have said something along those lines. I think it was John Motson, or possibly Tony Gubba, doing the commentary who said something like, 'What a moment this is for young Ben Thornley.'

I couldn't sleep that night. I was really, really wired. The next day I went and bought a few newspapers to see what my mark was, to see what *The People* and the *News of the World* were giving me. And just to see if anyone had written anything that mentioned my name – which they all had, even if it was only a sentence to say that I'd made my debut. A few family and close friends got in touch to congratulate me, including Gaz.

I was back training with the reserves come Monday morning. If I'd have come on in the West Ham game and scored a hat-trick in the space of 12 minutes I would have seen it as a demotion but as it was, it made sense. Our next reserves game was away to York City and it was a 0-0. Crap.

Then I played Oldham Athletic for the A team (not sure why I was playing for the A team) and we won 4-0. That was followed by a game against Derby for the reserves where Paul Simpson – who now coaches England's under-19s – ripped Gaz to pieces. Brilliant.

Next it was Notts County reserves away (we won 2-1 and I scored), then Leeds United's reserves, who we absolutely battered that day. It finished 7-0 and that was against largely the same team who had beaten us in the Youth Cup Final ten months prior. A load of the Maltese contingent were over for that game, as well as our next one against Sheffield Wednesday, where our standards slipped a bit: only 6-0 this time. The Malta lot all knew me, Becks, Casp and Gaz from our trip the year before and they were buzzing that they'd come over to see us win flaming 7-0 and 6-0. They were all there at the top of the stand at Hillsborough celebrating and it was great because me and Becks were the last two scorers.

And I have a feeling, because he was very close to some of those Maltesers, that the manager was at that Sheffield Wednesday game. If he was that might have been the catalyst for what happened next.

He called me into his office on Tuesday, 5 April, after we'd trained. I don't think he was particularly planning it that way but I just happened to bump into him not far from where his office was at The Cliff. He said, 'Come with me a minute.' We got in there and he said, 'How are you?'

'I'm fine,' I said.

'Well, Ryan's struggling for this weekend so I want you to go and express yourself in the reserves against Blackburn tomorrow night because I might need you on Sunday for the FA Cup semi-final.'

'Right, OK.'

'Fuck off now, that's it.'

I already knew I was going to be playing against Blackburn but I didn't know what was slated to come afterwards: an FA Cup semi-final appearance at Wembley. If Giggsy didn't make it, I was in. That was a definite. The manager had seen that I could handle West Ham in a tough atmosphere and he told me his plan to boost my confidence. It worked.

Ryan Giggs: It was around that time that I was starting to get a few of my hamstring and calf injuries so it could have been one of those.

Chris Casper: If Ben was going to be involved at Wembley he was ahead of everybody else from that youth team.

Ben: My confidence levels were as high as when I was in the youth team in the first year, scoring goals and being pretty much top dog. I'd had a quieter season when we lost the final to Leeds (possibly as a result of my appendectomy depriving me of a pre-season) but I'd come back all guns blazing again. I felt on top of the world.

When I realised I was on the bench for the West Ham game I was excited but I was really nervous. Whereas when the manager told me about Wembley I was like, 'Yeah, bring it on.' I'd had a taste of it at West Ham and held my own. This was an FA Cup semi-final at Wembley, playing alongside great players – I thought, 'I reckon I can do this.' But I never got the chance to find out, did I?

Gary Neville: There's one question that's devastating for an injured player to hear: 'When are you back, mate?' You're asked 100 times a day; it starts like a pinprick, then it becomes a hammer. In the end you feel embarrassed and you don't want to see people. I know, because I got injured when I was 32. When I came back into the first team, nothing felt the same: I'd changed – both mentally and physically – the players I was playing with had changed and it seemed like the game had moved on. I started to feel less sure of myself.

To think of that happening at 18. We were developing so fast as a team – jump, jump, jump. I went from winning the Youth Cup to winning the reserve-team league to winning the Premier League in four years. Ben was stuck. By the time he came back he was below us in terms of confidence, mentality, talent, physicality – every way. And then you can't make up the ground.

David Beckham: That's the sad part because Ben would have outdone all of us. He had everything. Without doubt, and I'm sure he's heard it so many times and is fed up hearing it, but he would have been one of the best for United and England.

Nicky Butt: I'm 100 per cent certain that if Ben hadn't got injured, England wouldn't have had a left-wing problem for so many years. Ben would have been the answer.

Paul Scholes: I wish he had been.

Ben: I know that it's all speculation because what we're talking about is potential. But do you know what, I'd *love* to have been able to give it a go. For one full season I'd love to have played 40 games for Manchester United without having had an injury at 18 years of age. Just to see.

There is, genuinely, no jealousy attached to the fact that so many of the lads I was playing with at the time went on to have glorious careers. It's the fact that I never got the opportunity to try and go along for the ride with them – or, more to the point, that somebody took that opportunity away from me.

Rod Thornley: He wasn't the same person after the injury. He changed. If I'm brutally honest, since that day he's never been as happy as he was before. Simple as that. It's a horrible thing to say but he had the world at his feet, then he realised it had gone. I don't care how strong you are in the head, that's always going to affect you.

Ben: I always tried to put a cheerful face on it. But because they're my family and because they know me better than anybody, they could see that inside I wasn't quite so happy. What I will say is that I am at peace with it now. There were plenty of things I wanted to say to Nicky Marker 24 years ago but not anymore. I wish him no ill will, no harm, no nothing. He was an important part of my life because of what happened but he's not on my radar anymore.

I'll always be grateful for the gift of being able to play football the way I played it. And here I am, aged 43, still playing and having crossed the finish line in the London Marathon this year. It could be worse.

Hannah Scott (née Thornley): He never, ever blamed anything on the injury. And he never said, 'I can't believe this has happened to me, it's so unfair.'

Ben: I never said it but I felt it. But I didn't want anybody to feel sorry for me. And maybe this book is my reward for not walking around with a face like a smacked arse. One thing my co-writer said to me before we started contacting people – it was tongue in cheek but it still rang true – was, 'Now we'll find out how popular you really were.' When we approached people they could have said, 'Do you know what, Ben was alright but I can't really be bothered.' But they didn't. People have been prepared to vouch for me. That's very touching.

Gary Neville: I've never really said this to Ben but he should pat himself on the back and be proud to have still played games for United after his injury, because many wouldn't have. Most wouldn't have been able to.

Lucas Thornley: After he got injured I reckon dad would have been annoyed. Angry. He would have been upset because the way things were going, it looked like he was going to be successful. But it wasn't his fault.

Ben: As the minutes ticked by in that game against Blackburn's reserves, 39 days after my first-team debut, I was just living for the there and then. I was 18 years old, I was having a good game, I was playing with great players, I had my mum and dad in the stands, I had Alex Ferguson up there too and I was just enjoying my football so much that night.

I wasn't thinking about what may or may not be coming up at the weekend; it never even crossed my mind. Most people would say that's a good thing. But if I *had* been thinking about it then maybe when Jim Ryan asked me if I wanted to come off after 65 minutes, five minutes before Nicky Marker struck, I'd have said yes.

Jim must have had a glance up to Alex Ferguson in the stands. And if Sir Alex had decided that enough was enough, he'd have come down and said so and the decision would have been out of my hands. I wish that had happened.

But it didn't. And we all make decisions in our lives that we wish we hadn't. This was one of mine.

'Are you alright to carry on, Ben?'

'Yeah Jim, I'm fine.'

Epilogue

One day Ben got into this taxi and got talking to the driver, who said, 'Are you interested in football?' Ben said, 'Yes, quite interested.' They established that they both followed United and the driver mentioned that he went to watch the youth team a fair bit. Ben said, 'Oh yeah, they're pretty good aren't they?' And the driver said, 'Yes and they've got this fantastic player. My son and I go just to watch him play. Left-winger, he's out of this world – Ben Thornley.' At the end of the journey Ben paid his fare and off he went.

I asked him afterwards, 'Did you not tell him?' Ben said, 'I didn't know how.'

Philip Thornley

Special thanks

Firstly I'd like to thank all my school friends, teachers, managers and coaches, in particular Tony Potter at Clarendon Road Junior School, for playing me in my first ever competitive football match when I was just seven. Harold Bloor too – may he rest in peace.

I'd like to thank all my ex-team mates, who took time out from their busy schedules to share their memories of me; without you this book would have been a non-starter. Where Manchester United are concerned I have been extremely fortunate to be able to call upon globally recognisable players: Bryan Robson, my hero and the best England captain I've ever seen; Paul Scholes, arguably the best midfielder the Premier League has ever seen; David Beckham, one of the most recognised sportsmen in the world; and Ryan Giggs, whose achievements in the game are mesmerising and will never be surpassed.

Special mention goes to Gary Neville, who did such a magnificent job of writing the foreword. Gary has become the most respected football pundit around, not to mention his glittering playing career. I'm incredibly grateful that you took the time to do this for me as I know you're probably busier now than you were when you were playing. Thanks, Gaz!

To Paul and Jane at Pitch Publishing, who took a chance on me and agreed to publish this book. Thank you so much.

To Bury Football Club, who allowed me to visit their stadium to relive some of my earliest memories as a professional, and to Manchester United Football Club, who provided access to Old Trafford for the cover shoot.

Last but definitely not least, to Dan Poole, my co-author. Dan is a great bloke and, once he'd managed to convince me that I had a story to tell, we hit it off straight away! He has travelled up and down the country and worked tirelessly, alongside having a family and a full-time job. Not only has he made it a really pleasurable experience for me but he's also had the chance to speak to ex-players from a team that he, like me, has supported all his life, so there has definitely been an upside to all his hard work! Cheers Dan, you've become a good friend, I've enjoyed every minute – every up and every down – and your dedication has been overwhelming.

Thank you to each and every one of you. I feel incredibly humble and I hope this means that, having met me along the way, you thought I was, at the very least, alright!